The Big Business of Small Enterprises

EVALUATION OF THE WORLD BANK GROUP EXPERIENCE WITH TARGETED
SUPPORT TO SMALL AND MEDIUM-SIZE ENTERPRISES, 2006–12

Library of Congress Cataloging-in-Publication Data

The big business of small enterprises : evaluation of the World Bank Group experience with targeted support to small and medium-size businesses, 2006-12.

  pages cm

 Includes bibliographical references.

 ISBN 978-1-4648-0376-5 — ISBN 978-1-4648-0377-2 (ebk)

 1. Small business—Developing countries. 2. Economic development projects—Developing countries—Evaluation. 3. Economic development—Developing countries. 4. World Bank—Developing countries I. World Bank.

 HD2346.5.B52 2014

 338.6'42091724—dc23

                              2014025856

Contents

Figures

Abbreviations

AAA	analytic and advisory activity
AMS	agribusiness, manufacturing, and services sector (MIGA)
BDS	business development service
DO	development outcome
DOTS	Development Outcome Tracking System (IFC)
E&S	environmental and social
FDI	foreign direct investment
FPD	Financial and Private Sector Development Network (IBRD)
GDP	gross domestic product
GEF	Global Environment Facility
GTFP	Global Trade and Finance Program (IFC)
IBRD	International Bank for Reconstruction and Development
IDA	International Development Association
IEG	Independent Evaluation Group
IFC	International Finance Corporation
M&E	monitoring and evaluation
MAS	manufacturing, agriculture, and services
MIGA	Multilateral Investment Guarantee Agency
MSME	micro, small, and medium-size enterprise
PEF	private equity fund
PEP	Private Enterprise Partnership
PER	Project Evaluation Report (MIGA)
PRI	political risk insurance
SIP	Small Investment Program (MIGA)
SME	small and medium-size enterprise
SMI	small and medium investor
TSME	targeted small and medium-size enterprise

Acknowledgments

This evaluation of the World Bank Group's targeted support for small and medium-size enterprises was prepared by an IEG team led by Andrew Stone. It was carried out under the direction of Marvin Taylor-Dormond (Director) and Stoyan Tenev (Manager), and the overall guidance of Caroline Heider (Director General, Evaluation).

Team members (in alphabetical order) were Jacqueline Andrieu, Maria Baldauf, Amitava Banerjee, Jack Glen, Hiroyuki Hatashima, Sara Mareno, Maria Pinglo, Anqing Shi, Aurora Siy, Stephan Wegner, Robert Wight, Khaliun Yadamsuren, Izlem Yenice, and Hanlei Yun. Professor Thorsten Beck conducted a valuable literature review, providing background for the study.

The peer reviewers were Mary Hallward-Driemeier (World Bank), Eric Oldsman (Nexus Associates), Kris Hallberg (Consultant), Michael Barzelay (London School of Economics), and Leora Klapper (World Bank). Additional guidance was provided by Ade Freeman.

Emelda Cudilla provided administrative support and formatted the report.

Overview | SUMMARY

The World Bank Group promotes small and medium-size enterprise (SME) growth through both systemic and targeted interventions. A critical challenge is to root the many activities now undertaken in this broad space in a clear understanding of the characteristics and dynamics of SMEs' role in the broader economy; and their actual and potential contribution to jobs, growth, and shared prosperity. A closely related challenge is to formulate clear strategies that connect interventions to intended outcomes and are accompanied by solid measurement systems that provide evidence of results and allow learning.

Targeting means focusing benefits on one size-class of firms to the exclusion of others. Targeted support for SMEs is a big business for the World Bank Group, averaging around $3 billion a year in commitments, expenditures, and gross exposure over the 2006–12 period. In the context of broader reforms, targeted small and medium-size enterprise (TSME) support can be a powerful tool and, given the size of the recent program, it is vital for the World Bank Group to use it effectively. Targeting SMEs is not an end in itself, but a means to create economies that can employ more people and create more opportunity for citizens to achieve prosperity. A thriving and growing SME sector is associated with rapidly growing economies.

As the World Bank Group continues to support SMEs, to help them realize their potential contribution to developing economies, the Independent Evaluation Group (IEG) evaluation concludes that, to make TSME support more effective, the Bank Group needs to do several things.

▶ Clarify its approach to targeted support to SMEs. The International Finance Corporation (IFC), the Multilateral Investment Guarantee Agency (MIGA), and the World Bank should harmonize their SME approaches to make clear the objectives and analytic justification for TSME support, how it relates to systemic reform, where it is appropriate, what main forms it will take, and how it will be monitored and evaluated. Targeted support for SMEs needs to be firmly rooted in a clear, evidence-based understanding of how the proposed support will sustainably remove the problems that constrain SMEs' ability to contribute to employment, growth, and economic opportunity.

▶ Enhance relevance and additionality. Relevant World Bank Group management should refine its SME approaches to shift benefits from better-served firms and markets to frontier states (those with underdeveloped financial systems, especially low-income and fragile and conflict-affected countries), frontier regions, and underserved segments.

▶ Institute a tailored research agenda. World Bank Group management should institute a tailored research agenda to support and assist these clarifications and refinements of its SME support approach, utilizing the best qualified researchers.

▶ Strengthen guidance and quality control. World Bank Group management should provide guidance and quality control so that project documents for Bank Group projects targeting SMEs define and justify the specification of the beneficiary group, provide specific targeting mechanisms, and include impact indicators in its results and monitoring and evaluation frameworks.

▶ Reform MIGA's Small Investment Program. MIGA should radically rethink its approach to providing guarantees for investments in SMEs through its Small Investment Program (SIP), considering either a merger with its regular program or a fundamental redesign to improve performance.

The Logic of Targeted SME Support

In this evaluation IEG has found that many targeted projects are weakly justified, are weakly focused on SMEs, and/or have limited potential for additionality. Furthermore, TSME support has been justified by one of two kinds of reasoning:

- SMEs make special contributions to developing economies—to growth, employment, productivity, and investment; they therefore merit special support. Yet the literature does not provide conclusive evidence of a bigger contribution of SMEs than large firms to growth and employment in developing country contexts, and there are considerable gaps in knowledge.

- SMEs face special challenges that do not apply to other sizes of firms. Addressing these challenges "levels the playing field"—contributing to the resolution of systemic economic constraints and hence to better functioning of markets and institutions. This would allow SMEs to realize their full potential for generating jobs and growth in developing economies. This second argument is amply rooted in a number of country and cross-country diagnostics showing size-based differentials in how firms experience the investment climate and business services such as finance.

However, the literature offers surprisingly little guidance on the actual efficacy of the most common forms of TSME support, either for direct beneficiaries or, more broadly, for markets and economies, much less the appropriate sequencing and complementarities of interventions.

Furthermore, enterprise survey data collected by the World Bank suggest that how firms are constrained depends not only on size, but on the interaction of size with country conditions, especially income level. The survey evidence and the literature also suggest that any holistic view of SMEs needs to focus a great deal of attention on systemic (nontargeted) reforms, including a reliable electric power supply, an honest and transparent public sector, moderate taxes, political stability, fair rules of the game, and an adequately educated workforce. Systemic priorities also include establishing the legal, regulatory, and institutional environment supporting a deep, competitive, and stable financial sector, where financial institutions seek SMEs as clients.

A credible theory of change for TSME interventions must be focused on leaving a sustainable supply of the service (such as financing, business development services, or training) by establishing well-functioning markets and institutions, not simply providing a temporary supply of benefits to a small group of firms during a project's lifespan. The scale of gaps identified for SME services, especially finance, dwarfs the direct benefits the World Bank Group can deliver.

Thus, targeted interventions need to be strategic, leveraging resources to produce broader benefits for institutions and markets.

Targeted support for SMEs needs to be firmly rooted in a clear, evidence-based understanding of what distinguishes an SME and how the proposed support will sustainably remove the problems that constrain SMEs' ability to contribute to employment, growth, and economic opportunity. Selectivity is required for both efficacy and efficiency of targeting. The definition of SMEs (both the upper and lower limits) establishes projects' relevance to development objectives and differentiates some firms from others based on criteria of employment, sales, and assets. Selectivity affects both efficacy and efficiency of targeting—directing benefits to those who need it and controlling costs.

Currently, there are problems with each World Bank Group institution's approach to defining SMEs. The definitions of IFC and MIGA, although they bring advantages of standardization, appear ill-tuned to many local contexts, whereas the World Bank's lack of any institutional definition can lead to project-specific definitions that lack solid links to the underlying rationale for the assistance offered.

In addition, currently, only a minority of projects defines SME (what firms are eligible for benefits), and fewer still apply that definition through their provisions. A minority identifies the market or policy failure they are seeking to address, and a smaller minority provides a solid rationale for how the project will ameliorate that failure. Limited relevant information on portfolio performance makes it difficult to learn from experience or even to establish the existence of additionality of World Bank Group interventions. Although each World Bank Group institution operates differently, there are benefits from collaboration, communication, and shared strategic objectives. Inconsistencies and lack of coordination across institutions result in missed opportunities. The lack of institutional consensus on what constitutes an SME, when it is appropriate to support them, and what constitutes success seems especially inappropriate as the World Bank Group moves toward global practices crossing traditional boundaries under a "One World Bank Group" model.

IFC Targeted Support

For IFC, SME support is seen as a strategic objective based on SMEs' job creation potential.

INVESTMENT SERVICES

IFC has had a long-standing commitment to the support of SMEs, starting with its first project development facility more than 30 years ago. Most recently the support is manifested in its Roadmap for FY14–16. IFC sees SME support as a strategic objective based on the job creation potential. Its targeted SME portfolio constitutes 17 percent of total projects and 15 percent of commitments, concentrated in the Financial Market Industry Cluster.

Leading investment services include on-lending, investment funds, and leasing. By contrast, direct investments in SMEs comprise only one percent of IFC's commitments (although 10 percent of projects). IFC's strongest contribution to SMEs is developing markets and institutions that can then operate sustainably on their own. This means that IFC's relevance is greatest where the financial sector (or other service markets) is weakest in serving SMEs. Thus IFC's relevance is greater when it operates at or near the frontier, especially in low-income and fragile and conflict-affected countries or regions where SMEs are not served; in countries where the financial sector has not yet developed to serve SMEs; with intermediaries that lack a firmly established SME practice; and in extending financial services to the underserved.

Many clients value IFC's support, professionalism, and standards, especially when IFC is able to tailor its products to their needs. However, these projects often lack key features that would enhance their relevance to the targeted firms, such as an appropriate SME definition; a clear connection of the intervention to correcting a market, policy, or institutional failure; or language in the project's legal documents that requires benefits to be directed to SMEs.

Targeted SME projects have improved their performance over time, although they generally have been less successful than the overall portfolio and the rest of the financial markets portfolio. Projects that on-lend through financial intermediaries have the highest average development outcome, in part because they are located in relatively higher-income countries than other product lines. IFC's indicators for SME lending raise questions about the relative effectiveness of its targeted SME on-lending projects in expanding the SME portfolio compared to Bank projects in the general nontargeted portfolio. The Global Trade Finance Program, although it benefits SMEs to some extent, has been inaccurately characterized by IFC as an SME program. In general, IFC's targeted SME investments lack sufficient monitoring and baseline information to enable reliable measurement of development impact.

ADVISORY SERVICES

IFC's TSME advisory services overall have performed better than the rest of the advisory portfolio, except in low-income countries. Nearly half of projects were in the form of technical assistance, mostly to financial institutions. In general, advisory dollars were focused on poorer countries, and 40 percent of expenditures took place in Africa.

Many advisory projects were linked with complementary investment projects, most commonly in on-lending, leasing, and other financial markets activities. On average, where TSME investment projects were delivered in tandem with advisory services, IFC achieved superior development outcomes in its investment projects. Advisory services appear to gain particular traction with clients where they are well adapted to the country and sectoral context; they can lose traction through excessive standardization.

MIGA TARGETED SUPPORT

MIGA's support to SMEs takes two approaches: directly (retail) to cross-border investors making small investments in SMEs through its SIP, or indirectly to financial intermediaries for their investments in subsidiaries to on-lend to SMEs (wholesale). MIGA's support for SME projects has been substantial during FY06–12, accounting for 45 percent of projects and 21 percent of MIGA's gross exposure. Of these, 57 percent of projects were underwritten under SIP, but they account for less than 8 percent of gross exposure in support of SMEs and 2 percent of MIGA's overall gross exposure.

SMALL INVESTMENT PROGRAM

MIGA is one of only three political risk insurers offering a special facility for supporting SME investments in developing countries. SIP projects are generally highly relevant to three of MIGA's operational priorities of supporting investments in International Development Association (IDA) countries, in conflict-afflicted or fragile environments, and South-South investments. However, the viability of SIP projects is more challenging due to the location of most SIP projects in high risk countries and the inherently riskier nature of smaller firms. Several projects experienced problems due to weak capacity of management. Despite efforts by MIGA to follow up on SIP projects' environmental and social requirements, in some cases it did not succeed in bringing projects into compliance with its requirements.

SIP's streamlined processing of guarantees has not produced efficiency gains in terms of reduced processing time. Feedback from MIGA staff also indicates little savings in underwriting resources compared to regular guarantees.

REGULAR GUARANTEES

MIGA's regular guarantees also offer a means to channel large amounts of political risk coverage to benefit SMEs. However, as applied currently, there is no mechanism for targeting funds to SMEs, that is, for ensuring the funds will be used for the purpose stated in the Board document.

In addition, wholesale guarantees that target SME finance are highly concentrated on a few clients driven by regulatory provisions in their home countries. Wholesale guarantees that target SMEs underperformed relative to a comparable group of financial sector projects in terms of business performance, economic sustainability, and contribution to private sector development, although this is not necessarily attributable to their SME focus. However, there is no evidence that the long-term tenor of funding was passed on to end borrowers.

Overall, the lack of systematic tracking of project performance with regard to SMEs at the intermediary and borrower levels makes it difficult to determine project results or whether the expected project objectives were achieved.

The World Bank's Targeted Support

LENDING

The World Bank's portfolio of TSME projects represented about 7 percent of projects and 2 percent of commitment value. By product line, lines of credit, matching grants, and business development services projects dominate the lending portfolio. Although the Bank is more substantially engaged in low-income and fragile and conflict-affected countries, the relatively low level of commitments in low-income IDA countries and the high level of commitments in upper-middle-income countries raise questions of relevance regarding reaching the frontier and building markets and market institutions where they are weakest.

World Bank targeted support for SMEs is broader than suggested by its formal strategic focus on access to finance and is likely more driven by country and regional strategy and demand than by any central guidance.

The great majority of closed projects achieved successful development outcomes. However, efforts to judge the efficacy and efficiency of World Bank TSME support are inhibited by the lack of serious quantitative evaluation of the development impact of its lending product lines. Some projects rated as successful in terms of their impact on beneficiaries provide little evidence regarding whether they have addressed underlying systemic obstacles.

Work quality exhibits several strengths, including linkage to prior analytic work, a high rate of successful development outcomes, and a high rate of realism in self-evaluations. Weaknesses lie in overly complex designs, overly optimistic timeframes for implementation, and the frequent need for delays, restructuring and partial cancellation.

ADVISORY

Though TSME analytic and advisory activity (AAA) is only a small fraction of the overall portfolio, AAA work is generally both relevant and important to SME challenges. It is delivered mainly to governments. Self-ratings (which are not validated by IEG) indicate a high and rising level of success for TSME technical assistance. Technical assistance in the context of lines of credit appears effective at strengthening institutional performance and therefore in producing positive outcomes.

Economic and sector work appears effective in some dimensions but had limited traction in influencing government policy.

Recommendations

RECOMMENDATION 1: HARMONIZE AND CLARIFY THE APPROACH TO TARGETED SUPPORT TO SMES

IFC, MIGA and the World Bank should harmonize their SME approaches and make clear the objectives and analytic justification for TSME support, how it relates to systemic reform, where it is appropriate, what main forms it will take, and how it will be monitored and evaluated.

For countries where SME development is a priority, any targeted support should be firmly grounded in the Country Partnership Framework/Strategy, the relevant parts of the Systematic Country Diagnostic based on country analytic work, and other instruments that provide an analytic and strategic framework to identify the sequence and mix of systemic and targeted interventions that will address systemic challenges to SMEs, building markets, and access to services. The specification of the target for TSME projects should relate to country-specific conditions and in some cases address small and medium firms differently, based on how they experience existing country conditions. Despite the different business models across institutions, shared country strategies that leverage and sequence the expertise and comparative advantages of the World Bank Group institutions should ensure complementarity, maximize impact, and reduce the potential for redundancies and inconsistencies. Targeted support for SMEs needs to be firmly rooted in a clear, evidence-based understanding of how the proposed support will sustainably remove the problems that constrain SMEs' ability to contribute to employment, growth, and economic opportunity.

The monitoring and evaluation (M&E) framework should be designed to capture the effect of project interventions in these dimensions—at the beneficiary, client, and broader market level. At both levels, information is needed to understand the counterfactual—what would have happened without the project—that is, where possible, a rigorous, fact-based approach that generates information on the baseline, the post-project period, and control group. A longer-term timeframe may be required to collect data to evaluate sustainability of impact.

RECOMMENDATION 2: ENHANCE RELEVANCE AND ADDITIONALITY

World Bank Group management should refine its SME approaches to shift benefits from better-served firms and markets to frontier states (those with underdeveloped financial systems, especially low income and fragile and conflict-affected countries), frontier regions, and underserved segments.

A key indicator of whether such a shift is occurring would be the evolution of the distribution of the TSME portfolio as well as the composition of beneficiary institutions and firms. This also implies including in the M&E of targeted projects indicators of the impact of the project on the targeted population of firms as well as the impact on financial intermediaries.[1]

RECOMMENDATION 3: INSTITUTE A TAILORED RESEARCH AGENDA

World Bank Group management should institute a tailored research agenda to support and assist these clarifications and refinements of its SME support approach. Utilizing the best qualified researchers (for example, a great deal of qualified expertise focused on this agenda resides in the Development Economics Vice Presidency), this should produce more policy- and contextually relevant distinctions of the definition of SME; a better understanding of the dynamic contributions of SMEs to economic growth, employment, and poverty alleviation; deeper knowledge about how the design of interventions should vary contingent upon country conditions; a project-relevant definition of the "frontier"; a clearer view of the correct sequencing and combinations of systemic and targeted; and more rigorous analysis of the actual performance and impact of key types, combinations and sequences of Bank Group and other donor interventions. Enterprise surveys should be refined to better identify market failures and unmet demand for financial and other services; and to generate more panel data that better account for firm dynamics and allows more confident relating of explanatory factors to firm growth and employment.

RECOMMENDATION 4: STRENGTHEN GUIDANCE AND QUALITY CONTROL

Relevant World Bank Group management should provide guidance and quality control so that any project documents for Bank Group projects that target SMEs will:

a. Define the group of firms to benefit by measurable criteria such as number of employees and annual revenues.

b. Justify the definition of the beneficiary group targeted (which could be a subset of SMEs) based on country-specific evidence that this group suffers from size-specific market failures or constraints.

c. Specify and wherever appropriate embed in legal provisions the mechanism to reach the targeted group.

d. Include in its results framework and M&E framework indicators of the impact of the project on the targeted group and on the constraints or market failures justifying the project.

Projects that describe themselves as targeting benefits to SMEs should reflect this approach. In addition, these projects should be coded accurately with regard to whether or not their benefits are in fact predominantly or exclusively available to SMEs. Coding systems and practices should be reviewed and modified to assure that targeted SME projects are correctly coded, to reduce "false positives" and "false negatives."

RECOMMENDATION 5: REFORM MIGA'S SMALL INVESTMENT PROGRAM

MIGA should radically rethink its approach to providing guarantees for investments in SMEs through the SIP program, considering either a merger with its regular program or a fundamental redesign to improve performance.

If MIGA decides to eliminate SIP as a separate window, it can maintain its relevance to the frontier and continue to guarantee small investments under its regular procedures, processing qualifying projects under its expedited "no objection" procedure where eligible. MIGA could maintain its SIP brand by establishing an SIP trust fund or a MIGA-funded, SIP-branded transparent subsidy mechanism to reduce the cost for the premium and underwriting for high value-added SME projects that reflect highly additional new investments into small companies in frontier regions or markets. If SIP is to be retained as a separate window, then the current weaknesses need to be squarely addressed, including through improved selectivity and screening, greater quality control of the preparation process, better targeting to SMEs rather than small investments, and improved M&E. Cost and revenue accounting should be improved to permit informed management decisions about SIP program resources in the context of overall MIGA strategic priorities.

To strengthen capacity of less experienced SME guarantee holders, MIGA should provide stronger capacity-building and technical assistance to implement and manage environmental and social requirements for small projects.

Note

[1] A program of more rigorous quantitative impact evaluation of a defined sample of projects (to limit cost) would allow a far clearer view of the impact of projects on intended beneficiaries. Evaluation methods should include collection of baseline data and the use of control groups for comparison so that the counterfactual can be understood. To the extent that historical or retrospective information can be collected to understand prior trends, and follow-up monitoring is possible to better understand longer-term effects of interventions, this will add to management's learning from experience. In addition, there is a need to collect sufficient quantitative information on the intermediaries (clients) and on the markets in which the intermediaries operate.

Management Response

Management of the World Bank Group welcomes this evaluation as an opportunity to learn from the systematic and careful review of World Bank Group "targeted small and medium enterprises (SMEs) support," as defined by the Independent Evaluation Group (IEG). As the report points out, targeted SME (TSME) activities can be a "powerful tool . . . [not as] an end in itself but a means to create economies that can employ more people and create more opportunity for citizens to achieve prosperity." Management believes that the array of "targeted SME" products across the World Bank Group, as part of a comprehensive approach including support to enabling environment reforms, has the potential to make a profound contribution to the World Bank Group strategic objectives of ending extreme poverty and promoting shared prosperity. Highlighting the strengths, as well as areas for improvement, in TSME activities helps management further strengthen the World Bank Group approach to these products going forward. The Group-wide perspective—looking across International Finance Corporation (IFC), Multilateral Investment Guarantee Agency (MIGA), and International Bank for Reconstruction and Development/International Development Association (IBRD/IDA) products—is particularly appreciated as management looks for ways to better serve clients as one World Bank Group.

General Comments

The findings of this evaluation have broad relevance across the organization, particularly for the new jobs Cross-Cutting Solution Areas. They also contribute to advancing the knowledge base related to the World Bank Group's support for SMEs, through expansion of access to finance and other services and creation of a conducive business environment. Equally important, they will help us further harmonize the work across the World Bank Group as it moves toward becoming a more integrated "Solutions Bank Group" for our clients.

▶ Broad concurrence with conclusions and recommendations. Management broadly concurs with the conclusions and recommendations of this report, and it welcomes the analysis and recommendations for improved design and greater effectiveness of TSME activities. Management responses to specific recommendations in the IEG report are presented in the Management Action Record.

▶ SMEs as important contributors to development solutions. SMEs play an important role in delivering solutions—for example, in numbers of jobs created, services provided, and economic opportunities created. World Bank Group support goes beyond "TSME support" activities and includes specific initiatives related to jobs, services, or finance, and this term is also not used by the World Bank Group as a portfolio definition or reporting indicator. Bank Group support for SMEs will remain an important area of engagement for at least two of the new Global Practices (Finance and Markets and Trade and Competitiveness). This evaluation provides useful insights into how the effectiveness of these activities can be further strengthened.

▶ Targeted versus systemic interventions in support of SMEs. As indicated in management comments to the Approach Paper for this evaluation, the narrow focus of the report on "targeted SME support" activities resulted in exclusion of the full range of complementary systemic instruments provided by the World Bank Group to its clients. Hence, the more comprehensive and systemic approach that the World Bank Group usually follows in SME-specific projects has not been adequately taken into account to inform the conclusions. A systemic approach comprises targeted interventions as part of a broader set of support activities, which can include analytical and advisory work, development policy financing, and investment lending. The report recognizes this systemic approach as strengthening impact and effectiveness of TSME activities in lower-income or fragile/conflict states. However, because the evaluation did not consider systemic interventions, project-level results were effectively penalized for not addressing regulatory and institutional framework issues, even when specific analytic and advisory activity (AAA) work was in place to address those issues.

▶ Harmonization. The report correctly notes the importance of greater harmonization across the Bank Group and the challenges to date, but understates the full scope of cooperation achieved by IBRD/IDA and IFC. This may be explained in part by multiplicity of links between TSME projects and non-TSME activities beyond the scope of this evaluation. There are also efforts under way to establish more integrated approaches across (and within) the World Bank Group institutions. Any future work on harmonization will need to be rooted in the Global Practices, a shared research agenda, and the Strategic Country Diagnostics/Country Partnership Frameworks, which are discussed further in the recommendations section of the report.

▶ Logic of targeted support and research agenda. The report correctly notes that TSME interventions can be justified based on the special role of SMEs in developing economies, and the constraints faced by SMEs not faced by larger firms. Management agrees with IEG that data and analysis on both fronts are often inadequate. Management is moving forward with a research agenda to better understand both parts of this justification and can revisit the scope and scale of that research agenda once the Global Practices are fully operational and the availability of funds for doing so is established.

Management agrees that there is a need for more research into the link between micro/SMEs (MSME) and job creation. The report notes the need to improve the ability of the Enterprise Survey to explain the difference between SME and large-firm job creation, taking into consideration firm exits, which have been excluded from previous analyses. The Enterprise Survey team agrees with this observation and has undertaken measures to address this gap. An initial analysis of panel data from the Latin America and Caribbean Region shows that although SMEs have a higher exit rate than large firms, large firms tend to compress more through layoffs and/or in difficult times more net job losses than SMEs do. Further analysis of this data and similar panel data for other regions will be helpful to better understand the issue going forward.

▶ Finance as a constraint. Management concurs with the findings of IEG's literature review that indicate that financial development can have both a pro-growth and pro-poor impact by disproportionally alleviating SMEs' financing constraints. Management, however, is not comfortable with IEG's characterization of the Enterprise Survey findings as they relate to the main constraints that SMEs face, showing that SME finance is not a top-five constraint for most groupings of SMEs either by size or by country income level. A major component of the analysis presented in the IEG report concerning access to finance is based on one of the two subjective measures in the Enterprise Survey regarding business environment elements. In its review, IEG analyzed Enterprise Survey data using a rating variable as opposed to a ranking variable. It is important to note that each variable measures different things. In particular, the rating variable is an absolute measure of the degree of obstacle of each element of the business environment; each obstacle is evaluated independently of other obstacles. For the IEG review, the analysis artificially constructed rankings based on the independent "rating" variables. In contrast, the "ranking" variable is the only question where respondents are asked directly to rank the top obstacle, thus compelling the comparison of each element to one another. This question provides a direct ranking of the top obstacle of the business environment for the private sector of a given economy. For the purpose of ranking the top obstacle in an economy, the "ranking" question is methodologically superior, yet is not used in this report. Using the ranking question, access to finance is conclusively identified as the biggest obstacle by firms across the spectrum of firms, with the only exception of those with 300+ employees, presenting a significantly different picture than concluded in the IEG report. More importantly, the report ignores other Enterprise Survey information based on objective data regarding the experience of firms when financing their operations (that is, use of different sources of external financing, as well as their applications and responses to market conditions) that has been used to establish that SMEs are significantly more credit constrained than large firms.

▶ MSME credit gap. The recommendation to develop more rigorous methodologies to estimate the credit gap and support further research efforts within the field of access to finance is welcome. The IEG report discusses the challenges and shortcomings of available data on the SME financing gap, including the data and analysis of the "Two Trillion and Counting" report prepared by IFC and McKinsey. The objectives of the "Two Trillion" report were to estimate the global credit gap, using the data that are available today, and to provide a basis for improved analysis going forward. Given data limitations, "best estimate" analysis was proposed based on conservative fixed ratios for estimating the total potential need for formal financing, static firm size distributions and populations, credit supply assumed to be fixed, and reliable statistical data sources. Despite the constraints, the study has provided an initial estimate of the credit gap at an aggregate global level.

▶ Additionality and relevance. The report recommends that World Bank Group TSME activities increasingly move to reach the "frontiers" of SME finance, whether defined by geography or segment. While management agrees broadly with the sentiment, it is important to note that there is not always a strong rationale for moving into very difficult or less formal markets with TSME activities. The relative size of the formal SME sector (as opposed to micro/informal sector) is larger in more developed economies, and policy makers have a more sophisticated understanding of the issues affecting SME development. The enabling environment for SMEs—in terms of policies, regulations, and institutions—is typically more favorable in middle-income economies than low-income economies and fragile/conflict states. In more challenging environments, as the report itself states, SME finance may not be the key binding constraint, and more systematic interventions may be required before TSME activities can be fully effective. Therefore, standalone TSME support activities may be more appropriate for middle-income countries, rather than less appropriate, as the report seems to suggest. Nevertheless, the World Bank Group is already making an effort to support TSME activities in more challenging areas, where there is also a good rationale. In terms of numbers, over half (40 of 73) of the IBRD/IDA-targeted SME projects are actually already in IDA countries, in most cases complemented by other World Bank Group and partner agency activities. Likewise, IFC is focused on underserved geography and segments. For IFC, 156 of 349 country-specific TSME projects are in IDA countries.

In many frontier countries (IDA countries, including fragile and conflict-affected situations) or regions (frontier regions in middle-income countries), SMEs are underserved. At the same time, in countries that are not IDA or fragile or conflict affected, SME finance may be more prevalent, but gaps remain in certain segments, many of which have broader social impacts including on women, health and education firms, very small enterprises, high-growth SMEs, and informal/new firms. However, tracking the evolution of activities in "underserved geography and segments" is not straightforward, and, for this reason, it is understandable that IFC's efforts in this regard appear to have been underestimated in the report. For example, Banking on Women projects, blended finance projects, certain agribusiness value chains, and gender-informed financial institution interventions are all typically addressing segments that are highly constrained. Going forward, World Bank Group country-level diagnostics of financing gaps and financial sector capabilities will further demonstrate market gaps and failures at the country level.

▶ SME definition. The report uses a definition of TSME activities that distinguishes TSME activities from those non-targeted SME activities that may benefit SMEs primarily while not exclusively targeting them (for example, credit bureaus, secured collateral registries, business entry reform, tax reform, and so forth). As the report points out, this results in a smaller number of TSME projects than IFC itself has flagged and a larger number of projects than flagged under the IBRD/IDA definitions. In both cases, the report may exclude activities that could be considered part of the broader SME solutions being provided.

Management shares IEG's concern that some targeted projects have not defined well the targeted beneficiaries. Each project needs to clearly define the type of SMEs that are targeted (if that is relevant to project design), whether by size (as measured by employees, turnover, or other measure) or other criteria (such as formality, sector, female owner, or growth potential). The finding that the definitions for SMEs in World Bank Group projects may not correspond to the relevant SME group affected calls for more thorough analytical work in preparation of investment operations.

With regard to the report's suggestion that the World Bank Group rethink the approach to defining SMEs, management recognizes that neither existing definition is perfect. However, developed as they were to meet the specific operational needs of each institution, they have important benefits. As the report suggests, there is no consensus on the best way to approach relative definitions, and external researchers have not been able to achieve consensus on common definitions. The report also does not present an operational analysis of the costs and benefits of changing approach in any of the institutions. In this context, management will approach this suggestion cautiously.

World Bank-Specific Comments

▶ Crisis context for lines of credit and other targeted financing mechanisms for SMEs. The report could give more recognition to the specific context of crisis response (Chapter 5), when World Bank Group financing for SMEs can play a valuable role. During financial sector crises, countercyclical financing or risk sharing can help maintain a minimum level of access to finance for SMEs (which tend to bear the brunt of credit crunches), while in the aftermath of natural disasters or conflicts the World Bank Group can play a valuable role in making finance available through targeted projects. The relatively large volume of TSME lending in the Europe and Central Asia Region—hit hard by the financial crisis—suggests that these projects sought to ease the credit crunch experienced in these countries, which mostly affected SMEs.

▶ Effectiveness of AAA work on SMEs. The report asks whether economic and sector work "should influence government policy only a minority of the time" and concludes that "the limited traction at the government policy level suggests that a great deal of economic and sector work may not be achieving its potential impact." The report also observes, however, that "strong AAA work can improve development and strengthen the impact of lending projects." While we agree with these conclusions, management would have appreciated a more in-depth analysis of the available data and insights into the topics of target audience, effectiveness, and outcomes of AAA work on SME-related issues. The report, however, notes that much of the Bank's AAA work of relevance to SMEs is conducted as part of activities that are broader in focus and would not fall within the report's focus on targeted SME activities.

▶ Partial Credit Guarantees (PCGs). The report points out that many PCG schemes do not reach small firms, yet this does not seem to refer to World Bank Group-supported PCG schemes in particular. World Bank Group engagement is often designed so that PCGs can be extended to smaller firms, which recognizes the shortcoming of many PCG schemes.

▶ Impact of SME interventions. The report rightly mentions that World Bank Group interventions in this area historically have rarely been evaluated in terms of impact or the efficiency and efficacy by which the impact is achieved. Management also takes the view that monitoring and evaluation (M&E) should be a key feature of any support that the Bank is providing for the SME development. Newer and pipeline projects typically have more rigorous M&E frameworks.

▶ Turkey country case. Management does not agree with the statement that IBRD contributed to a credit bubble in the country after mid-2009. First, the Financial Intermediary Loan was countercyclical, becoming effective at a time when some financial institutions were cutting credit by as much as 50 percent; the share of SMEs in total bank credit fell from 27 percent in 2007 to 22 percent by 2009. Second, the total volume of IBRD Financial Intermediary Loan lending was just $1.85 billion (2008–12), compared to total loan volume in Turkey of $1,661 billion. Third, IBRD loans were channeled to SMEs through intermediary banks to increase their productive capacity and thus did not contribute to increasing consumer spending. Management would also note that there has always been close coordination between the World Bank and both IFC's investment as well as IFC's advisory side, in SME support areas such as lines of credit, capital market development, and leasing.

International Finance Corporation-Specific Comments

▶ Additionality and relevance/frontier. The report makes observations about the reach of IFC's TSME portfolio relative to its non-TSME portfolio. The "non-TSME" projects are primarily projects with financial institutions that serve SMEs, where there is a general expectation that the IFC investment will help the banks serve SMEs, without an explicit objective for the banks to use the funds to target SMEs. There are many reasons why management may decide to support financial institutions—including equity investments in banks serving SMEs to strengthen financial deepening in the country—without explicitly targeting SMEs. There can also be non-TSME projects where a financial institution is already mature in its SME business and IFC's role is elsewhere, but the institution's SME reach growth continues to be robust; or there are TSME projects where IFC is helping a bank that is struggling to launch an SME business in a volatile market and the SME reach growth can be highly variable. The finding that the SME portfolio numbers of some TSME projects have shrunk over time is relevant, and IFC continues to look to identify partners who are and will remain committed to the SME sector with IFC funding. The related point on documentation of these targets is discussed below. Management would like to note that the report uses a definition of "targeted SMEs" that is not equivalent to IFC's classification of SME projects.

▶ Quality control (Board, legal, coding). The report makes the point that IFC rarely includes an SME definition in papers submitted to the Board of Executive Directors. Because IFC has a very clear definition of SMEs, it can be assumed that if a document does not define SMEs, the standard IFC definition is applicable. However, management will strive to be more transparent in Board documents. In cases where the project does deviate from the established definition (using the local client definition instead, for example), management will strive for greater clarification. The report also notes weaknesses in legal documents with regard to defining and establishing provisions for the SME targets in agreements with the clients. While IFC agrees that it can improve on this practice, it also notes that there are many cases where defining and provisioning may not be feasible or advisable, for example, in the case of equity investments in SME-focused banks.

Regardless of whether definitions are included in documents, banking clients are required to report on their portfolios according to IFC's definitions, and management tracks all SME lending based on IFC's definition. While the report raises some questions about the quality of those data, it also makes clear that it has improved significantly over the evaluation period—coverage has increased from 7 percent to 80 percent.

▶ Global Trade Finance Program. The review states that "IFC has often portrayed the Global Trade Finance Program (GTFP) as primarily aimed at SMEs." In fact, the GTFP has never claimed to be "an SME program." IFC has consistently categorized the program as targeting trade finance availability across multiple countries and sectors, with SMEs being one set of beneficiaries. As with other IFC products that work through financial intermediaries, the GTFP enables SMEs and participants in other critical sectors to access financing they would not otherwise be able to access in a commercially viable manner.

The report also comments on the GTFP's SME reach and approach of classifying SME activities based on loan volume proxies. In doing so, the report refers to GTFP data as reporting on "SME firms," yet in actuality the GTFP SME proxy is explicitly defined to track "SME transactions," not firms. While the report does not assess whether the SME transaction proxy is materially accurate, IFC management appreciates the finding that some GTFP clients have transactions that range in size from "SME classification" to "non-SME classification" based on that proxy. Because the analysis does not look at the underlying firms to determine whether they are SMEs, however, it is not sufficient to conclude that these transactions are not reaching SMEs. In the case of Brazil, which is mentioned in the report, the GTFP's deliberate strategy has been to work with second- and third-tier banks, which serve smaller companies. The majority of clients for most GTFP Brazil banks are in fact SMEs, according to original project assessments and ongoing discussions with client management. Finally, the report assesses the GTFP's level of SME support using dollar volume, while IFC management considers it more appropriate to look at the number of transactions that serve SMEs because transaction sizes for SMEs would, de facto, be significantly smaller than transaction sizes for larger corporations. IFC management appreciates the report's GTFP analysis, noting that this provides important input to future assessments of GTFP's approach, which will ultimately need to balance classification precision and financial/organizational feasibility.

▶ IFC Advisory Services. Management welcomes IEG's recognition that many IFC Advisory Services targeting SME projects are highly relevant to the countries and conditions where they are delivered. To strengthen IFC's impact and effectiveness related to SME development, Advisory Services undertakes programmatic approaches that harness contributions from across business lines, including strengthening the enabling environment, increasing access to infrastructure—both interventions that benefit firms of all sizes, though they may disproportionally benefit SMEs—increasing access to finance, and enhancing SME managerial and operational capacity to strengthen their competitiveness. Advisory Services continually reviews and revises its results measurement tools to incorporate lessons of experience and strengthen alignment with the business and our evolving strategy. Management has recently introduced an Advisory Services post-completion monitoring system to obtain more information on the sustainability and later-stage results of Advisory Services interventions.

▶ Monitoring and Evaluation. In recent years, IFC has focused on successfully scaling up its ability to monitor SME reach across its Financial Markets projects. While there are still improvements that management is making to that process, it agrees with IEG that the time has come to look more closely at the much more complex challenge of understanding how SME reach translates into impact.

There have been cases where IFC has measured the impact of its SME work on jobs, including through targeted evaluations and the micro-case studies undertaken for the jobs study, as well as some Advisory Services evaluations. To this point, IFC management notes that as part of the jobs study, it has developed a number of "micro-case studies" of IFC's clients that have provided insights about loan recipients, the use of funds, and preliminary information about job growth. It is important to note that the micro-case studies had some caveats such as selection bias, different MSME definitions, and lack of counterfactuals, so it is not possible to attribute job creation effects just to loans provided by IFC client banks. Nevertheless, positive signs of job growth by firms receiving loans were observed, and IFC will continue to further such work to advance our understanding of the impact of our work on jobs.

In addition, IFC management foresees an increase in the M&E work that is done on our TSME portfolio going forward. The Global SME Finance Facility will provide a key opportunity to test M&E techniques that will look at beneficiary, client, and market impacts for projects targeting underserved SMEs. For that program, an M&E framework is being developed. While management shares many of the questions that IEG has on impact, it is important to note that management realistically cannot expect every one of them to be answered given time, data, and budget constraints. In particular, management stresses that there are significant costs and challenges associated with establishing control groups and counterfactuals, which means obtaining these on a regular basis will not be possible. IFC management will undertake some rigorous impact evaluations as part of the Global SME Finance Facility.

▶ Harmonization. Considering the important harmonization challenges put forth in the report, IFC management notes that in 2012 IFC established an SME and Jobs Steering Committee to improve coordination and focus around its SME work, strengthening IFC's impact on jobs and growth through SMEs and enhancing IFC's leadership role in the SME space. The committee has done extensive work looking at certain topics that are relevant to IFC's work in SME development, such as informality, value chains, and high-growth SMEs. It has also undertaken a number of country SME deep dives, looking at the composition of SMEs, IFC's SME work in country, and how management can deepen outreach and impact in the SME space. The committee has also recently drafted an internal stocktaking and new directions paper covering all aspects of IFC's work. With the inclusion of some of IFC's SME work in the Global Practices, and in light of the recommendations in this report, IFC management notes that further discussion on the stocktaking and new direction paper with the Global Practices when they are fully operational would be worthwhile.

Multilateral Investment Guarantee Agency-Specific Comments

▶ Internal review. Overall, MIGA finds the evaluation report useful and important. In particular, management agrees with the MIGA-specific recommendation on the need to rethink the Small Investment Program (SIP). MIGA notes that IEG evaluation findings will serve as useful inputs for the ongoing internal MIGA review of SIP, as part of the broader MIGA Strategic Directions exercise for FY14–16.

▶ Limitations. The report states that the SIP evaluation is based on a programmatic approach agreed between IEG and MIGA. MIGA finds this to be an innovative solution, given the limited evidence base of MIGA project evaluations. However, MIGA notes the need to exercise caution regarding findings and conclusions, given the limited, nonrepresentative sample of projects with results reviewed in the report.

▶ Context. The report states that the viability of SIP projects is more challenging because of the location of most SIP projects in high-risk countries and the inherently riskier nature of smaller firms. MIGA agrees with this assessment and underscores the importance of the difficult operating environment facing SIP projects. MIGA also notes from the report that the SIP experience is broadly consistent with the performance of IFC's direct SME investments.

▶ E&S aspects. The report suggests that SIP projects faced numerous environmental and social (E&S) compliance challenges, despite MIGA's efforts to work with the client to resolve them. MIGA notes that among the SIP projects reviewed in the report, only one project remained out of compliance because of financial difficulties rather than client willingness (the project has since been cancelled).

▶ Streamlining. The report states that SIP's streamlined processing of guarantees has not produced efficiency gains in terms of reduced processing time. MIGA agrees with this finding and notes achieving efficiency gains in the internal approval process, but not in underwriting. The lack of efficiency gains in the underwriting process is reflective of the due diligence process, commensurate with the high-risk profile of SIP projects. While the original intent of the SIP streamlined process was to have a short SIP checklist and rely more on representations and warranties from the client, in practice, more extensive analysis of projects—including E&S aspects—often has to be undertaken, given the high-risk nature of SIP projects and the limited capacity of clients.

▶ Targeting SMEs. MIGA agrees with the report's assessment regarding the difficulties associated with targeting SMEs through regular guarantee projects in the financial sector, unless it happens to be a specialized SME/microfinance institution like ProCredit. MIGA also notes from the report that the MIGA experience is broadly similar to that of IFC.

▶ Wholesaling. The report states that wholesale guarantees that target SMEs underperformed relative to a comparable group of financial sector projects, although this is not necessarily attributable to their SME focus. MIGA notes the Development Outcome success rate for the mainstream SME projects is relatively high at 71 percent (five of seven), although lower than the 100 percent (eight of eight) for the comparator group.

▶ Tracking results. MIGA acknowledges the challenges of systematic tracking of results of MIGA projects outlined in the report. However, MIGA notes that the results tracking issue is not unique to SIP projects, but applicable more generally to all MIGA projects. Since FY12, all MIGA projects are being evaluated and validated by MIGA/IEG, as agreed between MIGA and IEG. In addition, MIGA is working towards extending the Development Effectiveness Indicator System to all MIGA projects.

▶ Work quality. The report states that the quality of the SIP Underwriting Checklist points to gaps in compliance with the SIP procedures. MIGA notes that with regard to work quality issues, some of the aspects noted in the report are administrative in nature. MIGA has been undertaking records management initiatives that would address some of the work quality issues identified in the report.

Management Action Record

IEG FINDINGS AND CONCLUSIONS

IEG finds that, at present, many targeted projects as defined in the Approach Paper supporting this evaluation are weakly justified, are weakly focused on small and medium-size enterprises (SMEs), and/or have limited potential for additionality. Contributing to the resolution of systemic economic constraints—leveling the playing field—hence to better functioning of markets and institutions would allow SMEs to realize their full potential for generating jobs and growth in developing economies. Systemic priorities also include establishing the legal, regulatory, and institutional environment supporting a deep, competitive, and stable financial sector, where financial institutions seek SMEs as clients. The scale of gaps identified for SME services, especially finance, dwarfs the direct benefits the World Bank Group can deliver, so targeted interventions need to be strategic, leveraging resources to produce broader, sustained benefits for institutions and markets.

Inconsistencies and limited coordination across World Bank Group institutions result in missed opportunities for the institutions to leverage each other. The lack of institutional consensus on what constitutes an SME, when it is appropriate to support them, and what constitutes success seems especially inappropriate as the World Bank Group moves towards global practices crossing traditional boundaries under a "One World Bank Group" model.

IEG RECOMMENDATIONS

IFC, MIGA, and the World Bank should harmonize their SME approaches and make clear the objectives and analytic justification for targeted small and medium-size enterprise (TSME) support, how it relates to systemic reform, where it is appropriate, what main forms it will take, and how it will be monitored and evaluated.

For countries where SME development is a priority, any targeted support should be firmly grounded in the Country Partnership Framework/Strategy, the relevant parts of the Systematic Country Diagnostic based on country analytic work, and other instruments that provide an analytic and strategic framework that identifies the sequence and mix of systemic and targeted interventions that will address systemic challenges to SMEs, building markets, and access to services. The specification of the target for TSME projects should relate to country-specific conditions and in some cases address small and medium firms differently based on how they experience existing country conditions. While recognizing the different business models across institutions, shared country strategies that leverage and sequence the expertise and comparative advantages of the World Bank Group institutions should ensure complementarity, maximize impact, and reduce the potential for redundancies and inconsistencies. Targeted support for SMEs needs to be firmly rooted in a clear, evidence-based understanding of how the proposed support will sustainably remove the problems that constrain SMEs' ability to contribute to employment, growth and economic opportunity.

The monitoring and evaluation (M&E) framework should be designed to capture the effect of project interventions in these dimensions—at the beneficiary, client, and broader market level. At all levels, information is needed to understand the counterfactual—what would have happened without the project, that is, where possible, a rigorous, fact-based approach that generates information on the baseline, the post-project period, and control group. A longer-term timeframe may be required to collect data to evaluate sustainability of impact.

ACCEPTANCE BY MANAGEMENT

World Bank Group: Agree

MANAGEMENT RESPONSE

The introduction of Global Practices offers an opportunity to improve the harmonization of the SME approach across the World Bank Group. Thus, the detailed actions that management will take to achieve this goal will be determined once the new governance structure is in place.

In countries where SME development is a priority, the introduction of Systematic Country Diagnostic/Country Partnership Framework process will also help identify constraints and opportunities at the country level that could be addressed by TSME support, granting these interventions an evidence-based knowledge of how World Bank Group support could help remove constraints that limit contribution to economic growth and job creation.

IFC's engagement with the Global Practices, as it updates its recent discussion document on SME stocktaking and new directions, can provide a forum for discussion of some of the key issues raised in the report.

With regard to M&E, both IFC and IBRD/IDA are strengthening M&E frameworks for SME and related activities and are also working to harmonize monitoring indicators. Management will explore the potential for further coordination on evaluation of impact from SME support projects, bearing in mind that clients between the two entities can be different in nature.

One important IFC initiative already planned will be the Global SME Finance Facility M&E plan to help test new methodologies and learn about how best to measure outputs and impact. IFC management will explore M&E efforts focused on intermediate outputs, but also reaching to enhanced evaluative approaches and impact evaluations. It must be noted that a counterfactual approach will not be feasible in many cases and management has to be selective on impact evaluations as they are very resource intensive.

MIGA will work with IFC and IBRD/IDA in harmonizing the World Bank Group approach to SMEs and seek clarity in objectives and analytic justification for targeted SME support. With regard to M&E, MIGA will build on and learn from IFC and IBRD/IDA initiatives. MIGA will also examine the M&E framework for SMEs as part of its ongoing internal review of the Small Investment Program (SIP). Together with IEG, MIGA will assess the programmatic evaluation approach used for SIP in the current evaluation and extract lessons of experience.

IEG FINDINGS AND CONCLUSIONS

World Bank Group relevance is greater when it operates at or near the frontier, especially in low-income and fragile/conflict countries or regions where SMEs are not served and in countries where the financial sector has not yet developed to serve SMEs. For example, the current portfolio commitment value is relatively concentrated in upper-middle-income countries, so careful attention is needed to relevance and additionality, to ensure that resources are being used to fully realize their benefit for addressing market failures and making markets and services more equitably available to smaller enterprises, thus maximizing poverty alleviation and shared prosperity. Sequencing can be important to build basic system capacities and legal frameworks in low-capacity countries to ensure a reasonable opportunity for success of targeted investments.

IEG RECOMMENDATIONS

World Bank Group management should refine its SME approaches to enhance relevance and additionality by shifting benefits from better-served firms and markets to frontier states (those with underdeveloped financial systems, especially low-income and fragile/conflict countries), frontier regions, and underserved segments.

A key indicator of whether such a shift is occurring would be the evolution of the distribution of the TSME portfolio as well as the composition of beneficiary institutions and firms.

ACCEPTANCE BY MANAGEMENT

World Bank Group: Agree

MANAGEMENT RESPONSE

Management agrees with the thrust of this recommendation, notably of enhancing the relevance of World Bank Group interventions when it operates in frontier, and especially fragile/conflict markets, but with caveats outlined below.

The World Bank Group is increasing its focus on frontier segments and markets, for example, women-led enterprises, smaller firms, and underserved markets. Over half (40 of 73) of World Bank TSME projects are already in IDA countries, as well as 156 of 349 TSME IFC projects. The report does not appear to have conducted sufficient analysis on these trends to underpin this recommendation. It is important to note that there are also frontier markets and underserved segments in middle-income countries.

For IBRD/IDA, as highlighted in the text, systemic programs of support can be more appropriate than standalone targeted SME activities in some low-income and fragile/conflict state contexts, given the need to first put in place a basic enabling environment (legal, regulatory, institutional, policy) and the relative prominence of micro and informal enterprises. Additionally, as noted in the IEG report, informal and microenterprises employ more workers than SMEs in low-income countries. Thus, approach in lower-income and fragile/conflict countries will continue to comprise targeted interventions as part of a broader set of support activities.

IFC will continue to emphasize frontier geographies and segments in its targeted SME work through, for example, (i) its products targeting women, climate, and agribusiness SMEs; (ii) its blended finance programs; (iii) its increased focus on fragile/conflict states; and (iv) its increased focus on financial technology and innovation. In addition, the Financial Institution Group's new focus on Partners in Development is designed to work more intensely with clients that are aligned with IFC in their interest and ability to have development impact and where IFC can have strong additionality.

MIGA will continue to focus on frontier markets and fragile/conflict states for targeting SMEs as part of its internal review of SIP.

Also in FY13, MIGA launched the multicountry Conflict Affected and Fragile Economies Facility to further expand MIGA operations in fragile/conflict states, which has the potential to increase MIGA support for SMEs in fragile/conflict states. MIGA has developed a business development strategy for fragile/conflict states, which will be rolled out over the next few years with the help of the Conflict Affected and Fragile Economies Facility.

IEG FINDINGS AND CONCLUSIONS

Targeted support for SMEs needs to be firmly rooted in a clear, evidence-based understanding of what distinguishes an SME and how the proposed support will sustainably remove the problems that constrain SME growth. An appropriate and correct definition of SME is important to guide selectivity in projects. The definition of SMEs (both the "ceiling" and the "floor") establishes projects' relevance to development objectives and differentiates some firms from others based on criteria of employment, sales, and assets. Selectivity affects both efficacy and efficiency of targeting—directing benefits to those who need it and controlling costs.

There is surprisingly little guidance from research on the actual efficacy of the most common forms of TSME support, either for direct beneficiaries or, more broadly, for markets and economies, much less the appropriate sequencing and complementarities of interventions.

IEG RECOMMENDATIONS

World Bank Group management should institute a tailored research agenda to support and assist the clarification and refinement of its SME support approach.

Utilizing the best qualified researchers (for example, a great deal of qualified expertise focused on this agenda resides in the Development Economics Vice Presidency), this should produce more policy- and contextually relevant distinctions of the definition of SME; a better understanding of the dynamic contributions of SMEs to economic growth, employment, and poverty alleviation; deeper knowledge about how the design of interventions should vary, contingent on country conditions; a project-relevant definition of the frontier; a clearer view of the correct sequencing and combinations of systemic and targeted; and more rigorous analysis of the actual performance and impact of key types, combinations, and sequences of World Bank Group and other donor interventions. Enterprise surveys should be refined to better identify market failures and unmet demand for financial and other services and to generate more panel data that better account for firm dynamics and allows more confident relating of explanatory factors to firm growth and employment.

ACCEPTANCE BY MANAGEMENT

World Bank Group: Agree

MANAGEMENT RESPONSE

Overall, management agrees with this recommendation, with some caveats described below.

We agree that underpinning World Bank Group support to SMEs with sound research and evidence-based knowledge is imperative. Decisions on how to further improve this area going forward—including availability of resources—will have to be made under the new governance structure of the Global Practices. A research agenda would need to bring different World Bank Group units to work together on deepening the understanding of among other things SMEs' role in growth, job creation, and poverty alleviation, sequencing of interventions, and more rigorous analysis of the actual impact of interventions.

Further analysis of the Enterprise Survey's panel research will be conducted to gain more insights into the link between SMEs and jobs. IFC will also continue to conduct and strengthen its micro-case analysis of the link between IFC financial institution financing and SME reach and impact.

Management acknowledges the suggestion to rethink the approach to defining SMEs within the World Bank Group. The existing definitions were developed to meet the specific operational needs of each institution, having important benefits. As the report suggests, there is no consensus on what the best way to approach relative definitions is, and external researchers have not been able to achieve consensus on common definitions. This complex issue would benefit from further research and should be considered in the research agenda if funds are available for that activity.

There are many attributes that could be relevant in designing a TSME project that a size-specific definition will not address (for example, gender of owner, sector or type of activity, level of formality, and so forth). These can vary from country to country and project to project and can therefore be considered as part of the framework for country diagnostics and in project design.

It should be noted that if changes to the definition are to be considered, implementation may be a multiyear process, as there are significant operational ramifications for both IFC staff and clients.

Selectivity is required for both efficacy of targeting and its efficiency. The definition of SMEs (both the "ceiling" and the "floor") establishes projects' relevance to development objectives and differentiates some firms from others based on criteria of employment, sales, and assets. IFC and MIGA's global definitions appear ill-tuned to many local contexts, whereas the Bank's lack of any institutional definition can lead to project-specific definitions not firmly linked to the underlying rationale for the assistance offered. In addition, currently, only a minority of projects defines SME (who is eligible for benefits) and fewer still apply that definition through their provisions. A minority identifies the market or policy failure they are seeking to address and a smaller minority provides a solid rationale for how the project will ameliorate that failure. Limited relevant information on portfolio performance makes it difficult to learn from experience or even to establish the existence of additionality of World Bank Group interventions.

IEG's review of project coding suggests a high degree of imprecision in coding projects, including a higher percentage of "false positives" in IFC and "false negatives" in the World Bank.

IEG RECOMMENDATIONS

Relevant World Bank Group management should provide guidance and quality control so that every project document for World Bank Group projects targeting SMEs will:

• Define the group of firms to benefit by measurable criteria such as number of employees and annual revenues

• Justify the definition of the beneficiary group targeted (which could be a subset of SMEs) based on country-specific evidence that this group suffers from size-specific market failures or constraints

• Specify and wherever appropriate embed in legal provisions the mechanism to reach the targeted group

• Include in its results framework and M&E framework the indicators of the impact of the project on the targeted group and on the constraints or market failures justifying the project.

Projects that describe themselves as targeting benefits to SMEs should reflect this approach. In addition, these projects should be coded accurately regarding whether their benefits are in fact predominantly or exclusively available to SMEs. Coding systems and practices should be reviewed and modified to ensure that TSME projects are correctly coded, to reduce "false positives" and "false negatives."

ACCEPTANCE BY MANAGEMENT

World Bank Group: Agree

MANAGEMENT RESPONSE

Management agrees with the overall thrust of IEG's recommendations. Most of the detailed recommendations repeat previous recommendations. Thus, management comments provided on the related recommendations are also relevant in this case.

The newly established Global Practices will be accountable for enhancing guidance and quality control for SME work.

Coding for SME support will be reviewed as necessary. The forthcoming Guidance Note for Financial Intermediary Financing will also be useful in improving the design and consistency of TSME activities where they involve such financing arrangements.

IFC will continue to strengthen the quality of Board and legal documents and will provide guidance to staff on (i) confirming in Board papers where the standard definition of SME is being used or an alternative is being used; (ii) strengthening the justification for targeting SMEs in Board papers; and (iii) including, where appropriate, definitions and provisions in legal documents pertaining to the application of funds for SME on-lending. Regarding the justification for targeting SMEs, it should be noted that IFC's ability to provide evidence on market failures and financing gaps is dependent on the quality of data and analysis undertaken elsewhere, something that will only improve over time.

IFC will continue to improve its mechanism for flagging micro or small and medium-size enterprise (MSME) projects to improve data quality and relevance, recognizing, however, that the MSME flag for IFC differs from the IEG definition in purpose and composition.

MIGA will strengthen the quality of Board and legal documents and will provide guidance to staff on whether the standard definition of SME is being used or an alternative is being used; strengthening the justification for targeting SMEs in Board papers; and, where appropriate, including definitions and provisions in legal documents pertaining to the application of funds for SME on-lending.

IEG FINDINGS AND CONCLUSIONS

Although SIP has extended MIGA's engagement in frontier countries, the program has fallen short in meeting its objectives of offering streamlined and efficient underwriting of SME projects, had weak development outcomes, and suffered from inconsistent work quality. The viability of SIP projects has proved challenging because of the location of most SIP projects in high-risk countries and the inherently riskier nature of smaller firms, and many guarantees for SIP projects are cancelled early. Despite increased efforts by MIGA to undertake monitoring visits to follow up with projects on their compliance with environmental and social (E&S) requirements, E&S compliance of most SIP projects is not known, and some are higher-risk Category B projects. A couple of SIP projects did not meet E&S requirements in the course of project implementation. SIP's streamlined processing of guarantees has not produced anticipated efficiency gains and time savings, and an IEG file review showed work quality shortcomings. The limited performance data available from 15 SIP projects suggests a disappointing record in terms of development outcomes and delivering results. Prior to the inception of the SIP, MIGA guaranteed small investments through its mainstream program. MIGA also currently reaches SMEs through guarantees of intermediary financial institutions and, in one case, backward linkages to a larger firm.

IEG RECOMMENDATIONS

MIGA should reform its SIP by radically rethinking its approach to providing guarantees for investments in SMEs through the SIP program, considering either a merger with its regular program or a fundamental redesign to improve performance.

If MIGA decides to eliminate SIP as a separate window, it can maintain its relevance to the frontier and continue to guarantee small investments under its regular procedures, processing qualifying projects under its expedited "no objection" procedure where eligible. MIGA could maintain its SIP brand by establishing a SIP trust fund or a MIGA-funded, SIP-branded transparent subsidy mechanism to reduce the cost for the premium and underwriting for high value-added SME projects that reflect highly additional new investments in small companies in frontier regions or markets.

If SIP is to be retained as a separate window, then the current weaknesses need to be squarely addressed, including through improved selectivity and screening, greater quality control of the preparation process, better targeting to SMEs rather than small investments, and improved M&E. Cost and revenue accounting should be improved to permit informed management decisions about SIP program resources in the context of overall MIGA strategic priorities.

To strengthen capacity of less experienced SME guarantee holders, MIGA should provide stronger capacity-building and technical assistance to implement and manage E&S requirements for small projects.

ACCEPTANCE BY MANAGEMENT

MIGA: Agree

MANAGEMENT RESPONSE

MIGA will use the findings from the SME evaluation for reforming SIP, as part of its ongoing internal review, within the broader context of MIGA Strategic Directions formulation for FY14–16.

Chairperson's Summary:
Committee on Development Effectiveness

The Committee on Development Effectiveness considered the document *The Big Business of Small Enterprises: Evaluation of the World Bank Group Experience with Targeted Support to Small and Medium-Size Enterprises, 2006–12* and draft Management Response.

The Committee welcomed the report, endorsed its findings and recommendations, and appreciated management's draft response. Members recognized the role small and medium-size enterprises (SMEs) play in supporting growth and jobs, eliminating extreme poverty, and boosting shared prosperity. They found that the evaluation highlighted important areas where the institution could improve its support to SMEs and agreed they should be taken into account in the ongoing change process.

Members underscored the need to further strengthen the harmonization of the World Bank Group's approach to SMEs, fortify coordination across the World Bank Group institutions, and foster a more robust results measurement framework with comparable indicators. They welcomed that Global Practices and the Cross-Cutting Solutions Areas will offer the opportunity to address these needs. Members also recognized that the new Country Partnership Framework and the Systemic Country Diagnostic will help forge a common understanding throughout the World Bank Group and will be key in addressing constraints faced by SMEs at the country level.

Members agreed that particularly in low-income countries and states facing fragile and conflict situations, broader systemic interventions may first be needed for targeted SME activities to be effective. They welcomed the World Bank Group's increasing focus on frontier markets and underscored that such interventions should include not only low-income countries and states facing fragile and conflict situations, but also frontier segments and underserved markets in middle-income countries. They encouraged management to continue working in all countries using a lens of additionality and development impact with appropriate attention to systemic reforms. With regard to the future of the Multilateral Investment Guarantee Agency's (MIGA) Small Investment Program, members welcomed MIGA management's indication to reform the program and expressed interest to further discuss it within MIGA's overall strategy.

Although members were cautious about standardizing an SME definition for the World Bank Group, some members stressed the importance of having a common understanding of SMEs among the Bank Group within the specific country context.

Juan José Bravo
CHAIRPERSON

1

The Logic of Targeted SME Support

CHAPTER HIGHLIGHTS

- The literature review suggests that targeted small and medium-size enterprise (SME) support has been justified by one of two kinds of reasoning: first, SMEs make special contributions to developing economies to growth, employment, productivity, and investment and therefore they merit special support; and second, SMEs face special challenges that do not apply to other sizes of firms, so addressing these challenges will "level the playing field." The literature and document reviews found inconclusive evidence on the first claim, but a wealth of support for the second.

- The literature review offers surprisingly little guidance on the actual efficacy of the most common forms of targeted SME (TSME) support, either for direct beneficiaries or, more broadly, for markets and economies, much less the appropriate sequencing and complementarities of interventions.

- Enterprise survey data suggest that how firms are constrained depends not only on size, but on the interaction of size with country conditions. Evidence also suggests that SMEs' needs focus on systemic challenges, including a reliable electric power supply, an honest and transparent public sector, moderate taxes, political stability, fair rules of the game, an educated workforce, and a developed, competitive and stable financial system.

- Targeted support for SMEs (the focus of this evaluation) needs to be firmly grounded in a clear, evidence-based understanding of what distinguishes an SME and how the proposed support will sustainably remove the problems that constrain their ability to contribute to employment, growth, and economic opportunity.

- Selectivity is required for both efficacy of targeting and its efficiency. The definition of SMEs (including both the upper and lower bounds) establishes projects' relevance to development objectives and differentiates some firms from others based on criteria of employment, sales, and assets. Selectivity affects both efficacy and efficiency of targeting—directing benefits to those who most benefit and controlling costs.

- Currently there are problems with each World Bank Group institution's approach to defining SMEs.

- TSME support needs to be firmly rooted in a clear, evidence-based understanding of what distinguishes an SME and how the proposed support will sustainably remove the problems that constrain their ability to contribute to employment, growth, and economic opportunity.

- In addition to problems with each Bank Group institution's approach to defining SMEs, relatively few projects define SME (that is, who is eligible for benefits) and fewer still use that definition in their provisions.

- Limited relevant research evidence and information on portfolio performance make it difficult to learn from experience or to establish the existence of additionality of Bank Group interventions.

- Projects need to be credibly justified—a credible theory of change linking SME interventions to desired outcomes should focus on leaving a viable market or institution, not to simply provide a temporary supply of benefits to a small group of firms during the project's lifespan.

- TSME interventions amounted to around $18 billion of commitments, expenditures, and gross exposure in the FY06–12 review period.

- This evaluation employs a variety of evaluative techniques to shed light on the relevance, efficacy, efficiency, and work quality of TSME support activities of the International Finance Corporation (IFC), the Multilateral Investment Guarantee Agency (MIGA), and the World Bank.

The World Bank Group seeks to promote private sector-led growth to contribute to employment creation, inclusive growth, and poverty alleviation. The Bank Group promotes small and medium enterprise growth through both systemic and targeted interventions. TSME support is a big business for the World Bank Group. TSME support comprises a significant part of the Bank Group's portfolio, averaging around $3 billion a year in commitments, expenditures, and gross exposure and 7 percent of projects over the FY06–12 period. It can be a powerful tool and, given the size of the recent program, it is vital for the Bank Group to use it effectively. Targeting SMEs is not an end in itself, but a means to create economies that can employ more people and create more opportunity for citizens to achieve prosperity. A thriving and growing SME sector is associated with rapidly growing economies.

Recognizing that SMEs constitute a big business for the Bank Group (as well as other donors and many developing country governments), this chapter presents information from the development literature on the relevance of TSME support to the broader development objectives of the World Bank, including answers to these questions:

- Why is TSME support relevant to growth and shared prosperity? Why does the Bank Group target SMEs and offer them support that it does not offer to other size classes of firms?

- What does research suggest might be reasons to target support to SMEs?

- What guidance does the research provide on what SMEs need to develop and create jobs?

- What is the importance of access to finance? How robust is the understanding of this?

- What evidence does the literature offer on the efficacy of alternative types of targeted support to SMEs?

- What is an appropriate definition of SME to distinguish which firms should get targeted assistance and which should not?

In this evaluation the Independent Evaluation Group (IEG) focuses on four types of targeted interventions—those designed to deliver financing to SMEs, those providing advice and technical assistance to governments to improve conditions for SMEs, those delivering business development services and training to SMEs, and those seeking to integrate SMEs into larger networks of producers or "supply chains."

IEG then shows that SMEs are big business for the World Bank Group. Next it discerns the theories of change underpinning the typology of four main forms of TSME support. It finds that a credible theory of change in most contexts must go beyond how the intervention delivers benefits directly to individual SMEs and explains how interventions build markets, address market failures, or sustainably resolve constraints to SME growth. IEG maps the identified Bank Group's portfolio of targeted interventions onto the relevant theories of change.

Finally, IEG presents the methodologies it used in the evaluation to assess the relevance, efficacy, efficiency, and work quality of IFC, Multilateral Investment Guarantee Agency (MIGA), and World Bank in designing, delivering, and monitoring and evaluating their programs of targeted support to SMEs.

Literature Analysis

WHY IS TSME SUPPORT RELEVANT TO GROWTH AND SHARED PROSPERITY?

Inclusive growth[1] in this context is understood to involve a large and healthy SME sector, generating productive employment, opportunity, and competitive dynamism.[2] Research indicates an important role for SMEs in growing economies.[3] As income levels increase, SMEs tend to comprise a larger share of the economy, while the informal sector recedes. Studies of transition economies also emphasize the strong role that new entry of SMEs play in generating employment and growth in economies such as China, Poland, and Vietnam (McMillan and Woodruff 2002).

Economic growth creates opportunities often filled by SMEs entering or sometimes "graduating" from microenterprise status. Where market, policy, and institutional failures thwart this role, reformers often seek to "level the playing field" to ensure that smaller businesses have a fair chance to thrive and contribute to market-led growth, employment, and shared prosperity. This is pursued both by systemic means, such as legal, regulatory, and institutional reform, and direct "targeted" efforts to assist SMEs as a size class of firms or as individual firms. In this evaluation IEG reviews IFC, MIGA, and World Bank targeted support for SMEs during FY06–12 to assess their relevance, efficacy, and efficiency and to provide an overall assessment of their development effectiveness.

WHAT DOES RESEARCH EVIDENCE SUGGEST MIGHT BE REASONS TO TARGET SUPPORT TO SMES?

SME assistance is often justified by the special contributions they make or special challenges they face. Empirically, any role of SMEs as opposed to large firms or microenterprises in employment creation and economic growth remains an unresolved question. A traditional view holds that development policies should be size-blind except where there is a specific

BOX 1.1 Do SMEs Really Create More Jobs?

One unique contribution often attributed to SMEs is job creation. International data make clear that smaller firms create more jobs, but they also destroy more jobs. Ayyagari, Demirgüç-Kunt, and Maksimovic (2011) use cross-sectional survey data from World Bank enterprise surveys to show there is more job creation in smaller and younger firms.

However, it is well known that smaller and younger firms are subject to more job destruction as well, especially through firm exit. IEG's literature review finds that cross-sectional firm-level survey data do not allow controlling for survivor bias and composition effects and distinguishing between net and gross job creation. Studies that use panel data, allowing for firms to exit over time, bring into question any special role in job creation for smaller firms. A recent analysis of U.S. data (Haltiwanger, Jarmin, and Miranda 2010) suggests that "once we control for firm age there is no systematic relationship between firm size and growth. Our findings highlight the important role of business startups and young businesses in U.S. job creation." Biggs and Shah (1998) examine World Bank enterprise survey panel data in five sub-Saharan African countries and find that large firms account for the majority of manufacturing job creation in four of the countries.

Page and Söderbom (2012) find a similar net number of jobs created by both small and large firms. However, wages in small firms were persistently lower. They concluded, "To create more 'good' jobs, aid should target the constraints to the growth of firms of all sizes." More recent work linking firm age to job growth, although not yet conclusive, suggests that age, rather than size, may be the most relevant factor, but also that the patterns of employment growth are highly sensitive to market dynamics, sector and enabling conditions (Ayyagari, Demirgüç-Kunt, and Maksimovic 2013; Hsieh and Klenow 2012; Klapper and Richmond 2011).

IEG's literature review and the analytic review conducted for this evaluation raise some important questions about these justifications.

- The literature review casts doubt on whether there was any empirical evidence that SMEs make a disproportionate contribution to growth, poverty reduction, or employment. As economies grow, the share of SMEs tends to increase, but there is no evidence that having more SMEs—other things being equal—causes more growth.

- Smaller firms often face more severe constraints than larger ones, especially in accessing finance and in dealing with weaknesses in electric power supply. As the financial sector develops and deepens, this helps create jobs and growth in part by disproportionally benefiting SMEs. However, there are severe methodological problems with estimates of a credit gap.

- Although there is substantial evidence that systemic improvements in the business environment and the financial sector can promote growth by improving market dynamics and leveling the playing field, especially for SMEs, there is little rigorous evidence to support the positive (or negative) impact of targeted programs. There is no rigorous evidence on the economic impact of lines of credit, a little evidence to support partial risk guarantees, mixed evidence on private equity schemes in developing country contexts, and limited evidence of the benefits of matching grants and advisory services.

SOURCE: IEG literature review and background research.

social objective to assisting very poor entrepreneurs.[4] An alternative view is that SMEs need special, targeted assistance for one of two reasons:

a. SMEs make special contributions to developing economies' growth, jobs (see Box 1.1), productivity, or investment.[5]

b. SMEs face special challenges that do not apply to other sizes of firms. TSME interventions thus level the playing field and contribute to the resolution of systemic constraints to private sector development and better overall functioning of the economy.

The first point demands evidence of the special contribution of SMEs to economic growth and job creation. SMEs' role in shared prosperity lies in claims that they are more likely to create jobs than other size classes of firms. IEG's literature review for this evaluation yielded mixed results, suggesting first that statistically, in low-income countries, more workers are employed by micro and informal enterprises than by SMEs; and second, that evidence on net job creation, which accounts for SMEs' higher tendency to exit as well as to grow, is inconclusive as to the relative net contribution of new jobs by large and small firms (see Box 1.1).

The second justification for targeted assistance demands evidence of size-based constraints (discussed below) but also evidence that targeting SMEs through a particular intervention or set of interventions will lead to the sustained elimination of those constraints. That is, there is need for proof that systemic problems can be solved by targeted approaches. Such evidence could take the form of country experiences, where interventions to strategically engage several banks in providing credit to SMEs (potentially as part of a broader set of reforms) lead to an enduring market for SME finance. Any of these would seem to demand evidence that the approach adopted has proven effective in the past in similar environments. Unfortunately, the evidence on the impact of targeted interventions is limited.

SMEs exist and operate in the same environment as other firms, although they may experience it differently. An IEG literature review of work broadly addressing SME issues showed that an open and reliable ecosystem of policies and institutions whose interactions determine the ability of SMEs to enter markets, compete, and grow or exit is most successful (Figure 1.1). Policies would include and enable complete and efficiently-regulated markets (land, labor, capital, and technology), competitive product markets, and the framework policies and institutions that underpin macro and political stability and openness to trade. The quality of physical infrastructure as well as the market infrastructure created by the legal and regulatory framework and its enforcing institutions each matter crucially (for example, Batra and Mahmood 2003; Beck, Demirgüç-Kunt, and Levine 2005; OECD 2000, 2004; Dalberg 2011; Storey 2003, 2008; IFC 2010; Reinecke and White 2004; Klein 2010; Levine 2005; Lundström and Stevenson 2005; Stein, Goland, and Schiff 2010).

Responses to enterprise surveys indicate that SMEs report their priority "needs" to be a reliable electric power supply, an honest and transparent public sector, moderate taxes, political stability, fair rules of the game so that informal firms cannot compete unfairly, and an adequately educated workforce.[6] In short, an inclusive ecosystem of policies, institutions and markets is needed to enable private enterprises of all sizes to function more productively.

FIGURE 1.1 What Do SMEs Need?

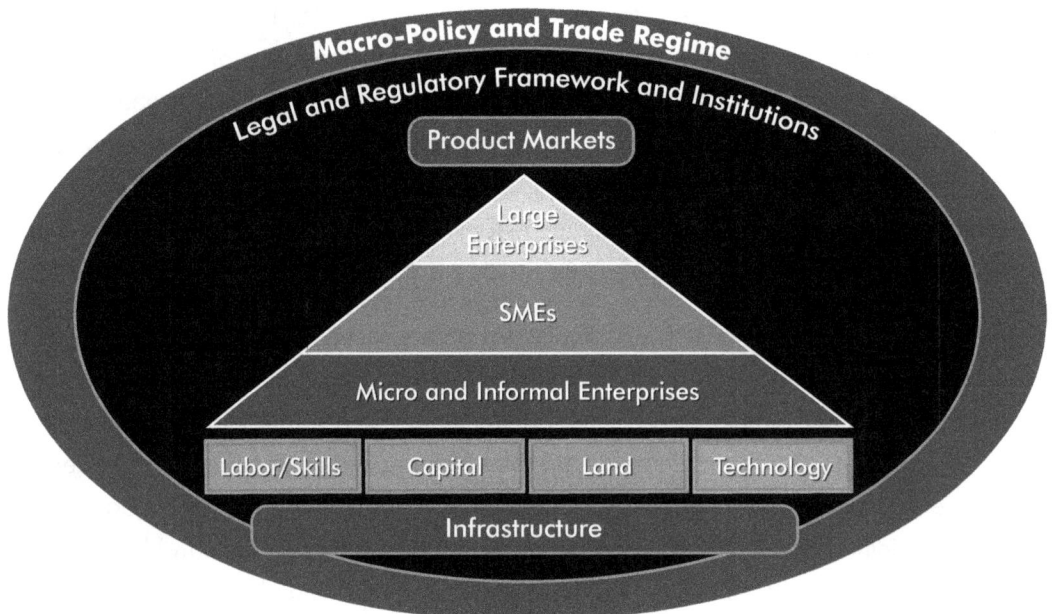

Macro-Policy and Trade Regime
Legal and Regulatory Framework and Institutions
Product Markets
Large Enterprises
SMEs
Micro and Informal Enterprises
Labor/Skills | Capital | Land | Technology
Infrastructure

SOURCE: IEG literature review.

A variety of business environment constraints—led by the burden of taxation and social security contributions, the burden of regulations, and lower quantity and quality of public goods—has been associated with a larger informal sector. Recent research suggests that a weak business environment can shift activity away from formal firms toward smaller, informal microenterprises. Impediments such as heavy business regulations, lack of access to finance, weak infrastructure, and corruption can each inhibit formal SME development (Aterido, Hallward-Driemeier, and Pages 2011). Constraints to entry are especially pertinent and limit competitive market dynamics that drive innovation and productivity growth. Excess costs and regulations are found to disproportionately discourage the survival of more productive firms while allowing less productive firms to survive (Aterido, Hallward-Dreimeier, and Pages 2011) Research also shows how financial market failures hurt small firms (Beck and Demirgüç-Kunt 2006).

A central challenge, then, is to level the economic playing field by ensuring dynamic markets; strengthening weak market-support institutions; and removing key constraints to entry, exit, and growth. Layered on top of this are targeted forms of assistance, which, as noted, are often thought to make up for deficiencies of the ecosystem (Figure 1.2). These targeted interventions may build on a foundation of more systemic reforms, may come in tandem with them, or may in fact be a means to build systemic reforms from the bottom up.

FIGURE 1.2 Targeted Support to SMEs in an Ecosystem of Policies, Institutions, and Markets

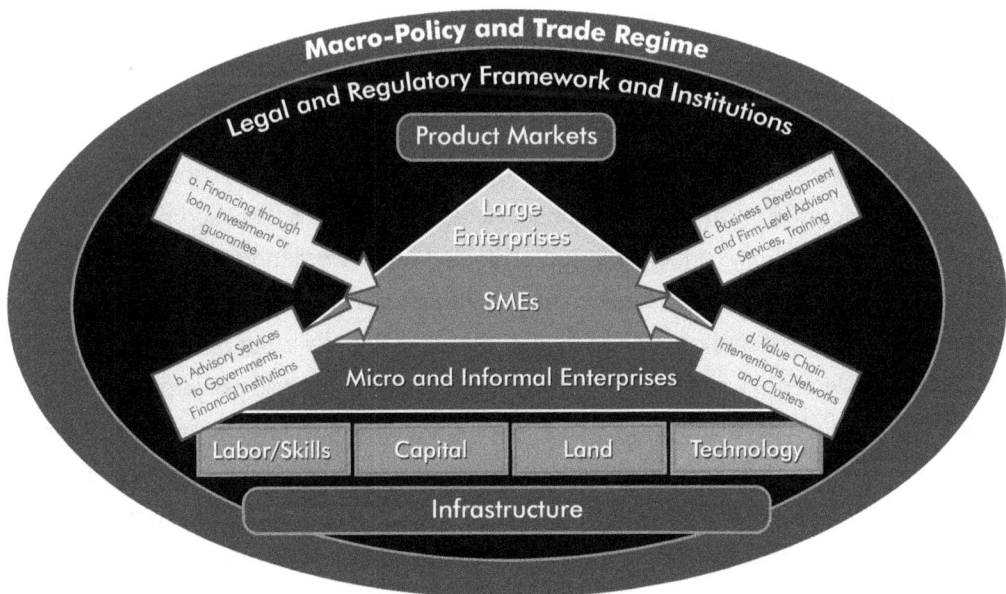

SOURCE: IEG literature review.

The IEG literature review found that financial sector development can have both a pro-growth and pro-poor impact by disproportionally alleviating SMEs' financing constraints, enabling new entry of firms and entrepreneurs and better resource allocation. In financial markets, there is both theoretical and empirical evidence that the burden of market failures falls disproportionately on smaller firms. Even in developed countries, information asymmetries—the problem of firms and banks having unequal amounts of information about the likely performance of an enterprise—tend to bias finance away from smaller firms because of credit rationing and the cost of screening.

The World Bank has found that SMEs are less likely to be able to access finance, other things being equal, where several circumstances exist: the banking sector is highly concentrated and competition limited; bank regulatory policies are inadequate; property rights protection is weak; legal systems are ineffective or rigid; or credit information is weak. On the aggregate level, there is a positive and significant relationship between financial development and job creation in developing countries. One study found that financial development helps reduce the effect of financing obstacles on firm growth, with a disproportionally beneficial effect for SMEs and for industries naturally composed of more small firms (Beck and others 2008). There is evidence that better access to finance can help firms enter the market, formalize, survive, and grow, as well as organize more efficiently. There is also an interaction of investment climate reforms with firm financing—for example, stronger property rights and better contract enforcement have been linked to easier access to credit. There is evidence that long-term institution building, including contractual and (credit) information frameworks, helps ease SMEs' financing constraints (see, for example, Beck and others 2006, 2008).

Nonetheless, access to finance is only sometimes a leading SME priority, although it is a leading microenterprise priority far more often. Access to finance is identified by about 16 percent of firms globally as their "biggest obstacle," but this ordering is not robust to examining other data collected in the surveys (see Appendix D). Globally, when comparing all the constraints on a common rating scheme, access to finance is not among the top five. Globally, enterprises with fewer than 10 employees (these are microenterprises under IFC definition) include access to finance as a leading constraint, but not firms of any larger size category (Table 1.1). In low-income countries, but not middle-income countries, SMEs identify access to finance as a leading constraint (Table 1.2). This suggests the need to adapt interventions to support SMEs to country conditions and enterprise priorities. Although finance can be a very real constraint, complementary measures may be needed to ensure that relaxing the financing constraint for SMEs does not lead firms directly into some other binding constraint to growth.

TABLE 1.1 Top Major or Severe Constraints Facing Firms, by Firm Size

	Number of Employees				
	5–9	10–19	20–99	100–299	300+
1st obstacle	Power 38.92%	Power 42.52%	Power 41.13%	Power 43.94%	Power 43.91%
2nd obstacle	Corruption 35.07%	Corruption 37.95%	Corruption 37.48%	Tax rate 35.74%	Worker skills 35.63%
3rd obstacle	Tax rate 34.87%	Tax rate 35.24%	Tax rate 35.48%	Corruption 34.87%	Corruption 33.03%
4th obstacle	Finance 33.75%	Political instability 32.80%	Political instability 32.23%	Political instability 33.32%	Transportation 32.11%
5th obstacle	Political instability 31.16%	Informal competition 32.39%	Informal competition 31.01%	Worker skills 33.28%	Tax rate 32.06%

SOURCE: Global enterprise surveys.
NOTE: 108 countries in 6 regions.

DO ALL SMES EXPERIENCE CONSTRAINTS THE SAME WAY?

In preparing this evaluation, IEG analyzed World Bank enterprise survey data[7] econometrically to determine whether there was some indication of what size definition of firms might help distinguish those that were differentially constrained by some challenges in developing economies—such as corruption or unreliable access to finance or electric power supply—and hence need targeted support. The analysis revealed that across several issues, there is a strong interaction effect between the size of firms and the income level of countries in determining how firms experience their operating environment. Accounting for this interaction improves the explanatory power of equations seeking to explain the variation in responses.

For example, the average relationship between enterprise size and its likelihood of having a loan or line of credit is that the smaller the size class of a firm, the less the likelihood is that it will get a loan (see Box 1.2). It is also true that for any size class of firm, the higher the income level of the country, the more likely the firm is to get a loan. However, if the interaction effect of country income level with firm size is controlled for, firms with 100–299 employees (those included in the IFC definition but not the World Bank definition of SME) do not significantly differ from large firms in their access.

TABLE 1.2 Top Major or Severe Constraints Facing Firms, by Country Income Group

	Country Income Group			
	Low	Lower Middle	Upper Middle	High
1st obstacle	Power 54.74%	Corruption 41.46%	Tax rate 37.38%	Tax rate 36.42%
2nd obstacle	Finance 43.44%	Political instability 36.11%	Corruption 36.47%	Skills 29.84%
3rd obstacle	Tax rate 38.21%	Power 35.49%	Skills 34.84%	Power 27.88%
4th obstacle	Corruption 36.91%	Crime, theft, disorder 32.91%	Power 33.66%	Political instability 23.44%
5th obstacle	Political instability 34.44%	Informality 31.45%	Informality 29.65%	Finance 20.67%

SOURCE: Global enterprise surveys.
NOTE: 108 countries in 6 regions.

BOX 1.2 The MSME Credit Gap: Whatever Became of Supply and Demand?

An IFC-sponsored study estimated "the total unmet need for credit" as $2.1–$2.5 trillion (Stein, Goland, and Schiff 2010). This has also been referred to as "unmet demand for credit." Although this number is eye catching, there are several methodological problems with the analysis:

"Need" is not an economic concept and in no way equates to commercially viable demand—that is, how much credit micro, small, and medium-size enterprises (MSMEs) would demand, even under ideal market conditions. Firms that say they need finance may not have viable projects to finance. The IEG literature review notes that quantifying demand would be much more difficult, as it requires detailed information on growth opportunities and productivity of enterprises that face constraints or have no access to credit.

The study uses fixed ratios to estimate unmet credit "need," based on an assumption that any firm without a loan "needing" credit needs a loan equal to 20 percent of the value of its sales, and any firm already having a loan "needing credit" needs a loan equal to 50 percent of the value of its most recent loan. A true estimate of demand would be firm specific and relate the quantity of credit demanded to the price of credit—a dynamic relationship.

Firm size distribution and the firm population itself are endogenous to financial development. Identifying a credit gap based on current firm size distribution and use of financial services is therefore necessarily a static rather than a dynamic exercise.

A "gap" implies a difference between supply and demand. To estimate the gap would require modeling the quantitative response of credit suppliers to the price of credit. Yet the article takes supply as fixed at current levels.

SOURCES: IEG literature review, interviews with IFC staff and IFC; IFC 2010; Stein, Goland, and Schiff 2010; and supporting documents on methodology provided by IFC.

However, accounting for this interaction points to a much stronger effect of size on the likelihood of getting financing for each other category of SME (Figure 1.3). It also suggests that SMEs with fewer than 100 employees are significantly and substantially worse off in low-income countries than in high-income countries, and that small firms are significantly and substantially worse off than other firms in middle-income countries. For example, a small firm with 10–19 employees in a low-income country is 56 percent less likely to get a loan or line of credit than a large firm (300 or more employees) in a low-income country (size effect) and 55 percent less likely to have a loan or line of credit than a small firm in a high-income country. However, for firms in the IFC SME category of 100–299 employees, whether in a low-, middle-, or high-income country, there is no significant difference between their odds of having a loan or line of credit and those of a large firm having one, once interaction effects (size with country and income level) have been accounted for.

In addition, as noted, some of the patterns of firms' constraints and their access to finance and services suggest that, globally, and especially in middle- and upper-income countries, the firms with 100–300 employees might better be grouped with large firms (Figure 1.4). For example, globally, firms with up to 99 employees rate informal competition as a leading constraint, whereas firms with 100 or more employees do not. Firms with 100 or more employees rate workforce skills as a top constraint, and firms with fewer than 100 employees

FIGURE 1.3 Probability of Having a Bank Loan or Line of Credit, by Firm Size (employees) and Country Income Group

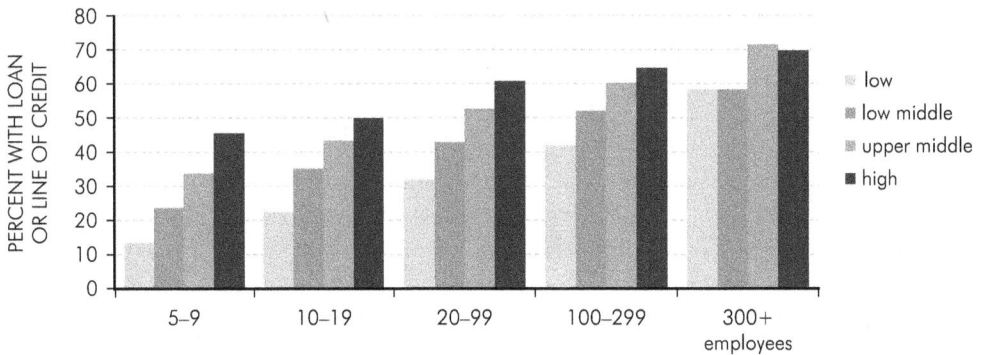

SOURCE: IEG portfolio review.

FIGURE 1.4 Tax Rates as a Constraint in Select Middle-Income Countries

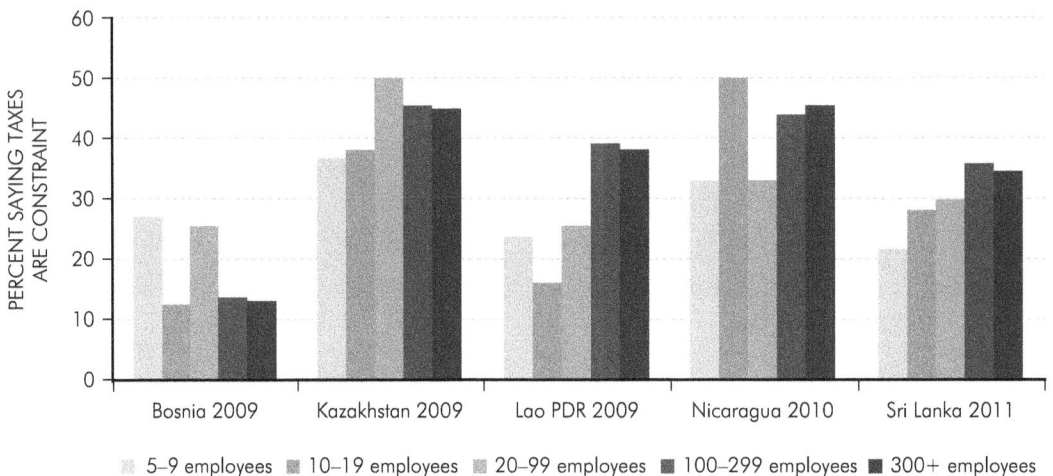

SOURCE: IEG portfolio review.

do not. For a number of constraints studied as cases for this evaluation, the responses of firms with 100–299 and more than 300 employees were highly similar across multiple constraints.

The likelihood that a firm will have a loan increases with both firm size and country income level, but when the interaction of these two factors is controlled for, the statistical difference in the rate of access for firms with 100–299 employees and firms with over 300 employees disappears.[8] This again suggests that for distinctions based on size to be meaningful, they should be grounded in relevant differences in firm attributes or experience of the local policy, institutional, and market conditions. As noted earlier, in econometric analysis, when the interaction of firm size and country income is accounted for, the statistical difference between the responses of firms with 100–299 employees and those with 300 or more employees disappears for multiple responses.

THE IMPACT AND EFFECTIVENESS OF TARGETED INTERVENTIONS

IEG's literature review searched for high-quality quantitative evaluations of the leading interventions used by the World Bank Group. The following points are among its findings:

LINES OF CREDIT: The literature review showed that this is an area that has not been properly researched. Questions regarding additionality and sustainability arise. An IEG report shed doubts on the effectiveness and quality of many of these credit lines. Beneficiary assessments showing benefits "are by their very nature partial equilibrium exercises" that do not focus on the "substantial economic cost. . . . There is a risk of pushing the system beyond the sustainable equilibrium towards fragility" (IEG 2005).

PARTIAL CREDIT GUARANTEE SCHEMES: Few rigorous impact assessments of partial credit guarantees have been done; the few that have been undertaken point to a somewhat positive effect. Yet there are questions about additionality as many firms with guarantees have obtained credit (Benavente, Galetovic, and Sanhueza 2006).

EQUITY FINANCE: The literature on the effect of private equity investment has focused mostly on developed countries. Private equity can catalyze structural changes by supporting new economic sectors and can foster industrial innovation (as measured by patenting rates). Studies have shown that venture capital can help reduce unemployment rates, mainly for skilled workers. However, other studies found no differences in employment growth between private equity-backed manufacturing companies and their control group, and no significant difference in the quantity of patents registered in the years following private equity investment. There was a higher "churn" in employment, plant growth, and investment, as well as higher productivity gains. Private equity-backed businesses have superior management practices than enterprises with family, private, and government ownership structures (Kortum and Lerner 2000; Belke, Fehn, and Foster 2003; Davis and others 2011; Bloom, Sadun, and Van Reenen 2009).

ENTREPRENEURIAL/BUSINESS TRAINING: Many of the key questions regarding justification for large-scale policy interventions in this area remain unanswered. One relevant study found some effect of training on business performance and access to finance; however, the likelihood of business survival was not affected by training. Another study found that business training combined with grant money can increase profitability for entrepreneurs in the short but not the medium term. A third study found positive effects from a business training program in three Central American countries on expansion of an existing or the start-up of a new business (Bruhn and Zia 2013; De Mel, McKenzie, and Woodruff 2008; Klinger and Schündeln 2011).

MATCHING GRANTS: "Among the problems that prevented implementation of the RCTs [randomized control trials] were project delays and political economy challenges that make it difficult to implement RCTs in a meaningful way and construct an appropriate control group" (Campos and others 2012).

In the following chapters, evaluative evidence is explored on the performance of the main types of projects in IFC, MIGA, and World Bank portfolios to shed some systematic light on the performance of these instruments in practice. However, given the limits of evaluative evidence and the general lack of counterfactual evidence and, too frequently, of baseline data, future evaluative research has great potential to contribute to the collective understanding of which instruments work best under what conditions.

WHAT IS AN APPROPRIATE DEFINITION OF SME?

How SMEs are defined establishes their relevance to Bank Group development objectives of poverty alleviation and inclusion. For SME to be a meaningful category of enterprises, it should be a group of firms that is specifically differentiated from others by the way that it experiences particular policy, institutional, or market failures or the way it benefits the economy or the poor. The literature provides little guidance on an appropriate definition, with different research using alternative definitions but little evidence of consensus.

Within the World Bank Group, IFC and MIGA have official definitions but also define SMEs in other ways. IFC and MIGA formally define SMEs as fulfilling two of three criteria:

• Having more than 10 and fewer than 300 employees

• Having between $100,000 and $15 million in sales

• Having between $100,000 and $15 million in assets.

The World Bank has many definitions—for its enterprise survey (enterprises with 5–99 employees), for its research (in some cases up to 99 employees, in others up to 250), and for individual projects (often rooted in country standards).[9]

The varying definitions of SMEs within the Bank Group create a number of challenges to evaluating its SME work:

- In many cases, it has not been consistently or appropriately defined.

- The case for SME support often depends on a mixture of definitions of SME that confuse the arguments.

- The practice of defining SME in the field bears little relation to formal definitions in Bank Group headquarters.

- For the majority of the portfolio, by design, the Bank Group cannot and does not directly monitor the benefit (or lack of benefit) for SME beneficiaries.

IFC and MIGA do not contextually adapt their definition by income level of country, size of economy, sector, or other criteria; instead, they adopt a single standard. IEG was unable to identify an empirical basis or reason for this particular definition, and the evaluation of data elicited strong counterevidence for the applicability of the current definition in many country contexts. The Bank Group's own research (http://www.ifc.org/wps/wcm/connect /9ae1dd80495860d6a482b519583b6d16/MSME-CI-AnalysisNote.pdf?MOD=AJPERES) suggests in a review of 132 country standards of what constitutes an SME that 250 employees is the most common upper bound for defining SMEs; 100 employees is the second most common upper bound and the most common in Africa (Kushnir, Mirmulstein, and Ramalho 2010).

A standard definition brings certain benefits in cross-country consistency and comparisons, but there is strong evidence that the current IFC/MIGA definition is inappropriately high for many of the countries in which it operates by two standards:

- It is inclusive of the entire, or almost the entire, formal private sector, including the largest firms in some economies (and therefore not a meaningful distinction).

- Using this as the basis for targeting misidentifies the group of firms that is differentially constrained and thus in need of special assistance.

Regarding IFC/MIGA standard, "The [United Nations Development Programme] and World Bank [IFC] definitions would include the manufacturing subsidiaries of both Nestle and Unilever in Ghana, clearly not the intended objects of development interventions. The World Bank [IFC] definition would include the majority of Ghana's top 100 manufacturers" (Gibson and van der Vaart 2008). These authors go on to point out that IFC definition would include many top 50 firms in Bolivia and Cameroon.[10] In terms of employees, the authors observe that this exceeds the limit defined by the African Development Bank by six times and the Inter-American Development Bank by three times, whereas in terms of turnover, it exceeds the latter by five times. As noted elsewhere, none of the research observing the characteristics, constraints, and contributions of SMEs actually uses the IFC/MIGA definition for SME. Thus, in any paper justifying interventions to support SMEs, the evidence does not apply to the upper end, and often the majority, of IFC definition.

The challenge is that if projects are attempting to differentiate SMEs as a group in need of special support to address special needs or disadvantages or a special contribution to the economy, it matters a great deal that they are accurately distinguished from other firms. Very few economies (in the absence of great natural resource wealth) could afford to subsidize all enterprises, and accurate targeting should improve efficiency of SME interventions. Microenterprise support is often designed quite differently from SME support, so correctly defining the lower bound of the SME definition is also important.

Another issue in much of the writing about SMEs is that the definition of SME varies within individual texts. For instance, a key IFC report for the G-20 uses definitions of SME to report on their prevalence among all enterprises, their employment share, and their share of gross domestic product (GDP) that do not conform to IFC's own definition of SMEs and, in fact, include a great many microenterprises. Another IFC work for the G-20 uses the definition of 5–250 employees—including (by IFC's definition) microenterprises and excluding many medium firms (Stein, Goland, and Schiff 2010). A recent IFC jobs study reports on SMEs' contribution to employment based on an article that defined small enterprises as those with fewer than 20 employees and medium enterprises as those with 20–99 employees (IFC 2013). The jobs study does make clear the different definitions of SMEs but shares the problem of other writing that makes reference to a literature that uses a maximum value of 99 employees to differentiate SMEs: the evidence does not pertain to the client base that IFC has defined for its SME products (and in this case includes what IFC defines as microenterprises). A number of project documents in the Bank and IFC cite literature on SMEs without noting how the parameters of the SMEs represented in the literature vary from the parameters of the designated beneficiaries of the project.

Whether the definition of SME is appropriate, few projects use the definition in practice. IEG's portfolio review found that in IFC investment project documents, 87 percent do not define SME by any criterion, and nearly two-thirds of World Bank-targeted SME investment projects do not define SME by any criterion in the concept note. Of the mainstream MIGA projects reviewed (which, according to their project descriptions, targeted SMEs), only one provided any confirmation that the beneficiaries could be classified as SMEs by MIGA standards. In the Small Investment Program (SIP), because the project enterprise is required to be an SME, almost 90 percent of project files reviewed establish the SME qualification of the enterprise into which the insured investment will go.

The literature suggests that it is difficult to arrive at any consensus definition of SME. However, the discussion here indicates that the current IFC/MIGA definition of SMEs does not consistently and effectively distinguish firms by whether they are differentially constrained by factors in the local operating environment or whether they have different levels of access to financing. The World Bank has no consistent basis for how it classifies firms. A more appropriate size distinction would, at the very least, take account of country income level and could in theory be informed by other factors (for instance, size of domestic economy, fragility, or differential costs and constraints as reflected in enterprise surveys).

Scope of This Evaluation: "Targeted" Support to SMEs

As suggested by the literature review, SMEs contend with a wide variety of institutions and factors in start-up, operation, and growth (and potentially exit). Where constraints arise from most of these, systemically improving the policy, institution, or market is generally an approach to benefiting SMEs that has benefits for other size enterprises as well.

However, systemic, universal interventions are not the focus of this evaluation. Instead, IEG focuses on the portfolio of interventions specifically aimed at delivering support to firms on the basis of their small and medium size. Clearly, by selecting activities specifically targeted to SMEs—to the exclusion of firms of other sizes—IEG excludes a large part of both the World Bank and IFC portfolios that benefit SMEs through broad systemic improvements. These range from measures to improve macroeconomic stability (where, for example, small firms are less able to hedge against inflation than large ones) to infrastructure (where there are scale economies in self-provision of power through generators) to education (where small firms may be less able to compensate for deficiencies in skills through in-house training or international recruitment) to the financial sector.

In each of these cases, systemic changes may disproportionately benefit SMEs but do not target them to the exclusion of other potential beneficiaries. Although these areas of activity are acknowledged as beneficial, they are not the focus of this evaluation. However, in the evaluation IEG considers whether such systemic interventions are important prerequisites of or complements to targeted interventions. The country case studies take into account the entirety of relevant World Bank Group interventions during the evaluation period, which should shed light on the complementarity and sequencing of nontargeted measures as they relate to targeted ones.

Targeted programs—the focus of this evaluation—are widespread in the World Bank Group as well as among other donors and many governments worldwide. Targeted programs aim to specifically benefit SMEs on the basis of their size (in terms of employees, sales or assets), the sole defining characteristic of being an SME.

As discussed below, the theory of change underlying such support is that firms benefiting from targeted support will contribute to broader development goals, especially job creation and economic growth. Empirically, any special role of SMEs in employment creation and economic growth remains an unresolved question. Therefore, IEG examines the extent to which the theory of change of the targeted interventions coheres and is followed in practice; it cannot estimate the final impact of such interventions on employment, growth, market dynamism, and inclusion.

Foremost among these targeted approaches is SME financing, which often aims either to fill the gap between SME demand for finance and the market supply or to address a market failure in SME finance, for example, by demonstrating the profitability of improved SME finance techniques to banks.

A second category of this intervention involves advice and technical assistance to government agencies, financial intermediaries, or others on how to improve services or reduce costs imposed on SMEs. Third, SME needs are also often addressed through business development services (BDS) and training designed to improve enterprise performance, either through provision of professional services (such as accounting or management consultancy) or through training of SME managers and entrepreneurs.

Finally, interventions may seek to integrate or link individual SMEs into large networks of producers. This includes vertical integration into supply chains and horizontal integration through clustering or other cooperative activity of related SMEs and supportive institutions.

With the evaluation IEG examines the extent to which the theory of change of the targeted interventions coheres and is followed in practice, but it cannot estimate the final impact of such interventions on employment, growth, market dynamism, and inclusion.

Portfolio Review: SMEs Are Big Business for the World Bank Group

SME support is big business for the World Bank Group—an important part of its portfolio. SME support overall (that is, projects coded or identified as supporting SMEs) constitutes 28 percent of IFC investment projects, 46 percent of MIGA projects, and 14 percent of the World Bank projects in the period FY06–12. This evaluation's focus on projects specifically targeting SMEs (excluding large enterprises and often microenterprises as well) still looks at 17 percent of IFC investment projects, 42 percent of MIGA projects (including the SIP), and 7 percent of World Bank projects (Figures 1.4 and 1.5).

FIGURE 1.5 SME Support in IFC Investment, MIGA Guarantee, and World Bank Investment Portfolios, FY06–12, by Number of Projects

SOURCE: IEG portfolio review.

The Bank Group's support to SMEs takes multiple forms, each aimed to support SME growth as a means to contribute to employment creation, GDP growth, market dynamism, and/or economic inclusion. The implicit (and often explicit) theory of change underlying such support is that firms benefiting from targeted support will contribute to broader development goals, especially job creation and economic growth. Sometimes, targeted support also aims to rectify market and institutional failures that negatively influence the development of SMEs, often as a complement to support for broader (and less targeted) policy, regulatory, or institutional reform efforts. The end goal is similar: to stimulate SME growth, thereby generating developmental benefits.

Collectively, the portfolio of TSME support represents a massive investment in institutional time and attention, as well as $10.5 billion in IFC investment commitments (comprising 16 percent of total portfolio value FY06–12), $2.3 billion in MIGA gross exposure (21 percent of gross exposure), and $4.9 billion in World Bank investment commitments (1.9 percent of portfolio value) over the period. On the advisory side, SME support constitutes 31 percent of IFC's advisory services projects, of which just over half are targeted. IFC advisory TSME portfolio accounted for about $170 million of cumulative expenses (Figure 1.6). In World Bank analytic and advisory activities (AAA), about 4 percent of projects are devoted to SMEs, of which only about a quarter can be classified as targeted. Similarly, only about 1 percent of the cumulative cost of its AAA work from FY06–12 can be classified as TSME work.

The World Bank Group is only one financer of SME support activities, which receive billions of dollars in developing countries from multilateral and bilateral donors, as well as from national governments. For example, a 2011 World Bank survey of development banks, which together accounted for $2 trillion in assets, found that SME support was the second leading specific mandate after agriculture and that 92 percent of the responding development banks targeted SME clients (De Luna-Martinez and Vicente 2012). The European Commission's Program for the Competitiveness of Enterprises and SMEs, which has SMEs as its main target, reported an overall budget of €3.6 billion from 2007 to 2013. The Inter-American Development Bank's Inter-American Investment Corporation approved 50 direct loans to SMEs for a total of more than $63 million between 2010 and 2012. USAID reports that its Development

FIGURE 1.6 Global Coverage of World Bank Group TSME Support by Number of Projects and Total Commitments, Expenditures, and Gross Exposure, FY06–12

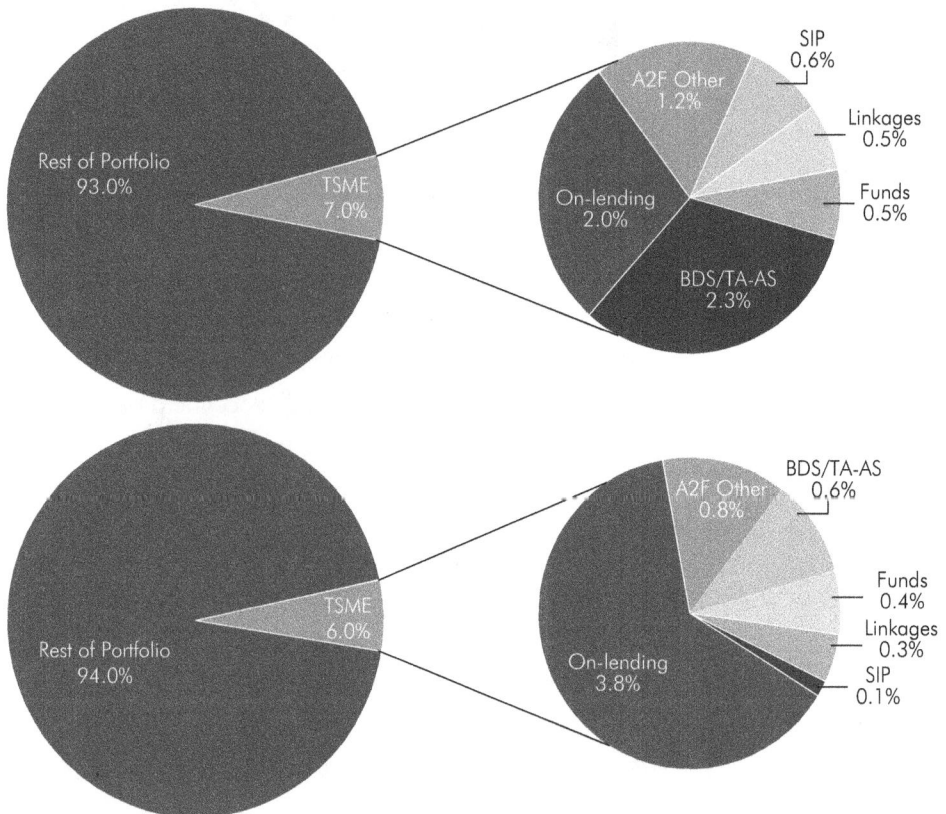

SOURCE: IEG portfolio review.
NOTE: A2F = access to finance; BDS/TA-AS = business development service/technical assistance-advisory services; SIP = Small Investment Program; TSME = targeted small and medium-size enterprise.

Credit Authority in 2012 provided guarantees that were expected to open $215 million in bank financing for small enterprises. In 2011, the African Development Bank established the Africa Guarantee Fund for Small and Medium Enterprises; this had an initial guarantee of $50 million, which was scheduled to increase to $500 million over five years.[11]

Theory of Change—Connecting Support to Outcomes

The Bank Group's support to SMEs takes multiple forms, each aimed to support SME growth as a means to contribute to employment creation, GDP growth, market dynamism, and/or economic inclusion. Each project justification (where it is offered) describes how the project will help overcome market, policy, or institutional failures in a particular country or region.[12] Some products complement others and are delivered simultaneously or sequentially. The theory of change in essence tries to capture how a particular category of intervention will change something in a developing economy and lead to desirable outcomes and impacts. In doing so, it simplifies and does not reflect all of the complementarity and sequencing issues, especially the contribution of systemic (potentially non-SME) interventions to the success of TSME intervention.

The most common form of support takes place when the Bank or IFC invests in or lends money to a financial intermediary, with the intention that the intermediary on-lend to SMEs (or in amounts only attractive to SMEs). MIGA often provides guarantees to financial intermediaries (most often banks, sometimes an equity fund) with the intention that it expands financing of SMEs; and also can directly guarantee foreign direct investment (FDI) in an SME through its SIP. In all of these cases, the intention is that the resulting finance allows the beneficiary SMEs to undertake new or expanded activities, generating employment and growth and contributing to competitive and inclusive markets.

As an example, MIGA says of its SIP program that by facilitating foreign investment into the SME sector, it will contribute to "the growth of small and medium-size enterprises" which "is critical to the creation of jobs, economic growth, and poverty reduction" (MIGA 2009). IFC explains its lines of credit to banks in Russia as follows:

> In supporting the country's market transition, IFC's financial sector strategy in Russia has been to identify reputable banks with major presence in the regions through which IFC could support the development of private SMEs. Using IFC's credit lines, these banks are able to offer longer term loans, hence supporting the growth of the SME sector, which plays an important role in employment generation, economic diversification and improved standards of living.[13]

FIGURE 1.7 Theory of Change 1a: Financing SMEs through Loans, Investments, or Guarantees

	World Bank/ IFC financing through grant, loan, investment or MIGA guarantee	The World Bank Nicaragua MSME Development project planned to disburse $5.9 million in matching grants to MSMEs.
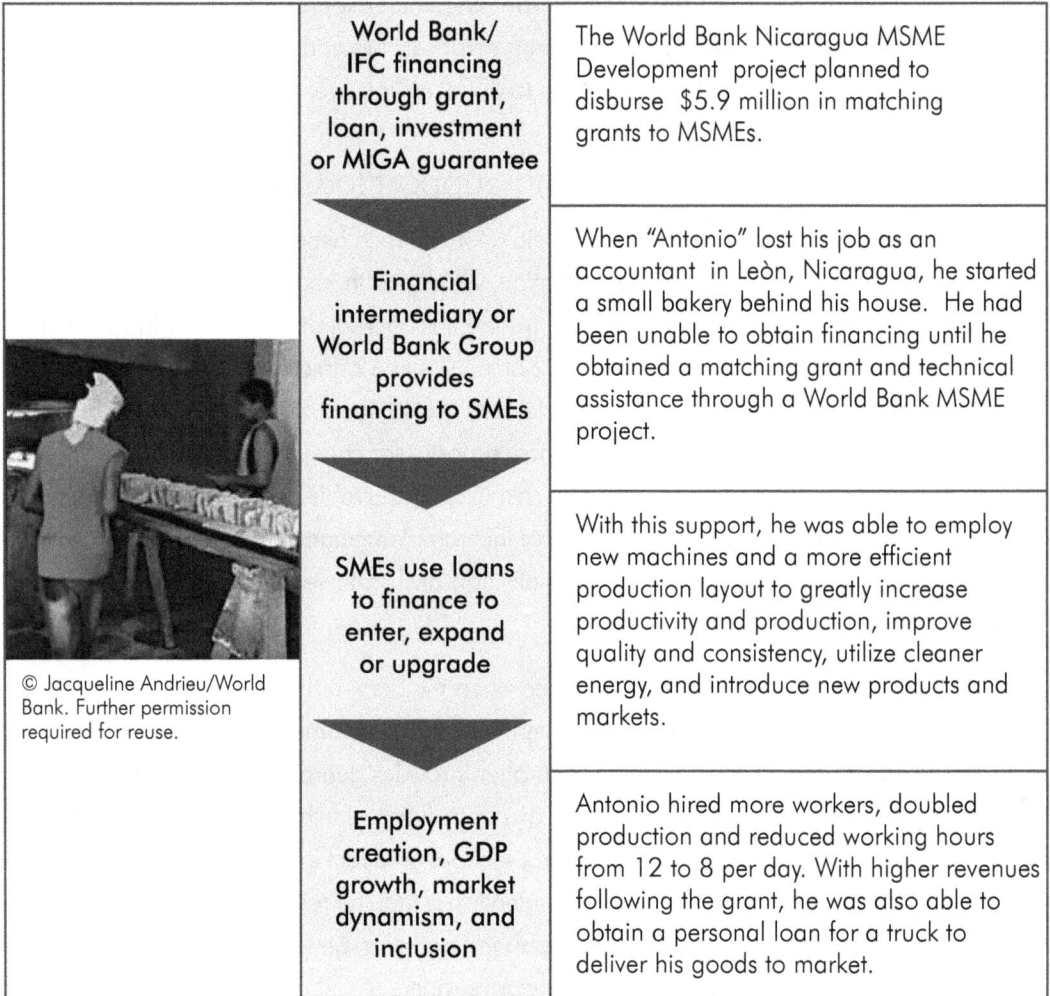 © Jacqueline Andrieu/World Bank. Further permission required for reuse.	**Financial intermediary or World Bank Group provides financing to SMEs**	When "Antonio" lost his job as an accountant in Leòn, Nicaragua, he started a small bakery behind his house. He had been unable to obtain financing until he obtained a matching grant and technical assistance through a World Bank MSME project.
	SMEs use loans to finance to enter, expand or upgrade	With this support, he was able to employ new machines and a more efficient production layout to greatly increase productivity and production, improve quality and consistency, utilize cleaner energy, and introduce new products and markets.
	Employment creation, GDP growth, market dynamism, and inclusion	Antonio hired more workers, doubled production and reduced working hours from 12 to 8 per day. With higher revenues following the grant, he was also able to obtain a personal loan for a truck to deliver his goods to market.

SOURCE: IEG portfolio review.

NOTE: GDP = gross domestic product; MSME = micro, small, and medium-size enterprise.

Figure 1.7 illustrates the logic of this theory of change, along with an example from a Nicaraguan project visited by the IEG team that was delivering nearly $6 million of financing to SMEs through matching grants.

The challenge with this model is that the project anticipated reaching only 850 Nicaraguan MSMEs, delivering an average grant of $6,000. Yet reports suggest there are 366,000 MSMEs, and the World Bank's enterprise survey indicates that nearly a quarter identify access to finance as a major or severe constraint. To deliver $6,000 to each of these firms would require more than $500 million, at least 85 times the amount actually delivered by the project.

IFC has estimated the overall "credit gap" for MSMEs in Latin America as $410 billion and the global credit gap at over $2 trillion.[14] Furthermore, there is little evidence in this case that, when the funds from this project are exhausted, a new source of matching grants will materialize. Nor did IEG see widespread evidence that the financial system was ready to finance these same firms' future needs.

Thus, except in very small economies where donors can afford to step in for a weak financial system over an extended period, a more credible theory of change for interventions that finance SMEs needs to feature the impact that interventions can have on the development of the financial sector from the bottom up. In this version of the theory of change, support delivered through financial intermediaries (often accompanied by technical assistance to the intermediaries) creates a demonstration effect or has a catalytic effect on the formation of a market for SME finance, stimulating competition, sustained institutional capacity, and the motivation for intermediaries to engage in future financing of SMEs. The intended impact is the same—SME growth with all its benefits—but the intended outcome lies more in the effect on intermediaries and financial markets than the SMEs that directly benefit from the finance.

This is exactly how IFC portrayed its strategic intervention in the Chinese banking system (Figure 1.8). Along with work on collateral and credit information systems, IFC helped a number of Chinese banks launch a sustainable SME finance practice. These banks served as role models and created both a demonstration effect and competitive pressure for other banks to supply SME finance.

A second theory of change connects the delivery of advice or technical assistance to a government body (for example, a regulator) or a financial institution with the objective of having that body act to reduce costs or improve services to SMEs (Figure 1.9). For example, IFC advisory services to banks on assessing and managing risk may complement its loan to them for SME finance.[15] The World Bank describes its MSME finance activities as "technical tools and guidance, data, lending and technical assistance" that address challenges when MSMEs—which account for a significant share of employment and GDP around the world—have limited access to finance, which restricts economic opportunity, enterprise creation, and growth while increasing vulnerability to risk.[16]

A third theory of change starts from raising the performance or bankability of enterprises through direct or intermediary-based provision of services and training (Figure 1.10). Sometimes this is linked to matching grants as a financing mechanism for the services and is often combined with other components that are regarded as complementary. For example,

FIGURE 1.8 Theory of Change 1b: Catalyzing Financial Sector Development, Deepening through IFC/World Bank Finance or Technical Assistance or MIGA Guarantees to Financial Intermediaries

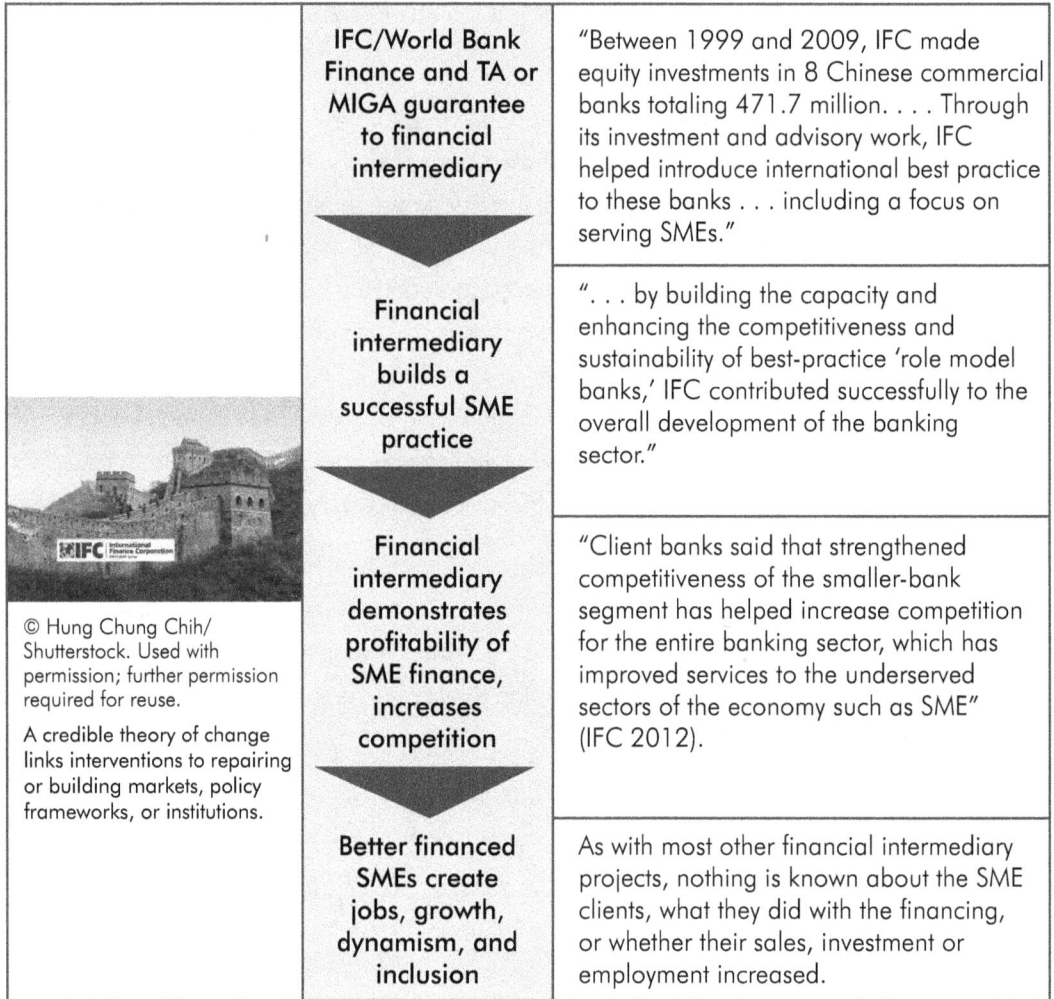

© Hung Chung Chih/ Shutterstock. Used with permission; further permission required for reuse. A credible theory of change links interventions to repairing or building markets, policy frameworks, or institutions.	**IFC/World Bank Finance and TA or MIGA guarantee to financial intermediary**	"Between 1999 and 2009, IFC made equity investments in 8 Chinese commercial banks totaling 471.7 million. . . . Through its investment and advisory work, IFC helped introduce international best practice to these banks . . . including a focus on serving SMEs."
	Financial intermediary builds a successful SME practice	". . . by building the capacity and enhancing the competitiveness and sustainability of best-practice 'role model banks,' IFC contributed successfully to the overall development of the banking sector."
	Financial intermediary demonstrates profitability of SME finance, increases competition	"Client banks said that strengthened competitiveness of the smaller-bank segment has helped increase competition for the entire banking sector, which has improved services to the underserved sectors of the economy such as SME" (IFC 2012).
	Better financed SMEs create jobs, growth, dynamism, and inclusion	As with most other financial intermediary projects, nothing is known about the SME clients, what they did with the financing, or whether their sales, investment or employment increased.

SOURCES: IEG portfolio review; IFC 2012.
NOTE: TA = technical assistance.

the multicomponent India Additional Financing for the Small and Medium Enterprise Financing and Development Project aims to achieve its objective through multiple "prongs," including policy, regulatory and institutional reform, bank finance, and risk mitigation and "strengthening business development services and market linkage programs for SMEs . . . thereby helping SMEs to improve profitability and competitiveness, and become more creditworthy" (World Bank 2004).

FIGURE 1.9 Theory of Change 2: World Bank Group Advisory Services to Governments and Financial Institutions

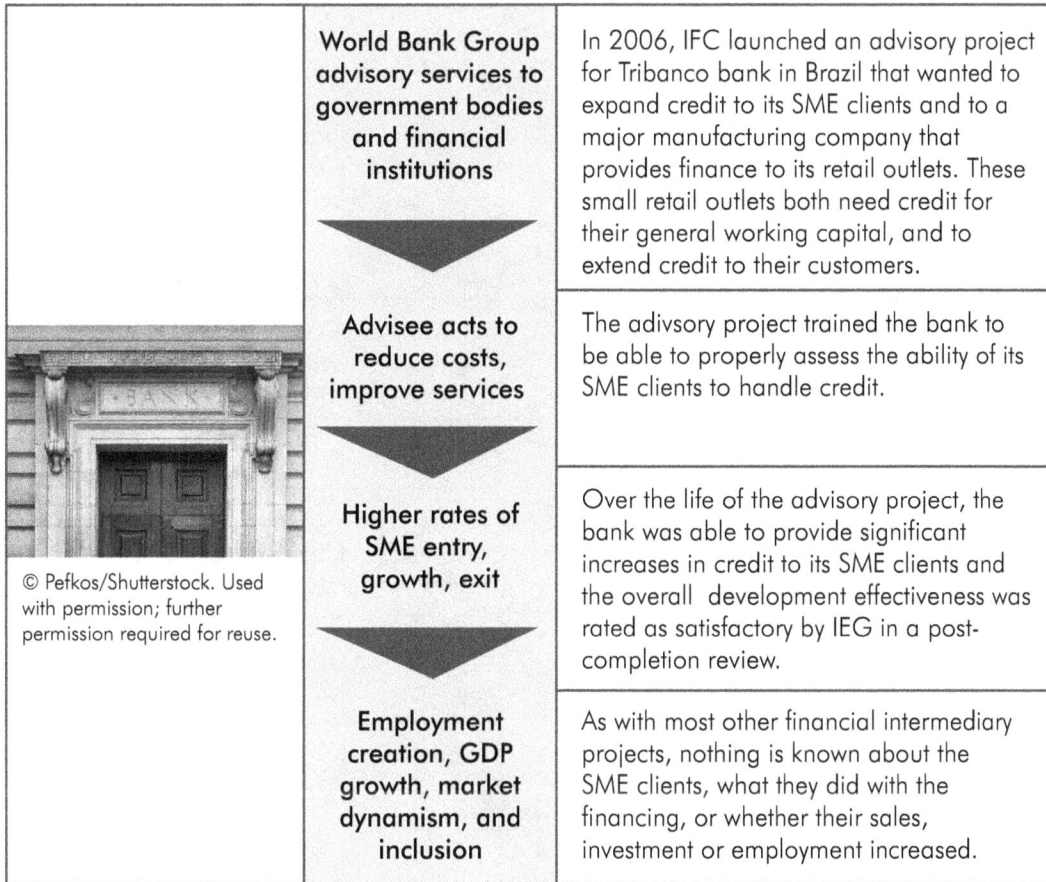 © Pefkos/Shutterstock. Used with permission; further permission required for reuse.	**World Bank Group advisory services to government bodies and financial institutions** ▼	In 2006, IFC launched an advisory project for Tribanco bank in Brazil that wanted to expand credit to its SME clients and to a major manufacturing company that provides finance to its retail outlets. These small retail outlets both need credit for their general working capital, and to extend credit to their customers.
	Advisee acts to reduce costs, improve services ▼	The adivsory project trained the bank to be able to properly assess the ability of its SME clients to handle credit.
	Higher rates of SME entry, growth, exit ▼	Over the life of the advisory project, the bank was able to provide significant increases in credit to its SME clients and the overall development effectiveness was rated as satisfactory by IEG in a post-completion review.
	Employment creation, GDP growth, market dynamism, and inclusion	As with most other financial intermediary projects, nothing is known about the SME clients, what they did with the financing, or whether their sales, investment or employment increased.

SOURCES: IEG portfolio review.
NOTE: GDP = gross domestic product.

A fourth model is intended to address the scale diseconomies, lack of connections, and lack of information of small enterprises by linking them in clusters or networks to value chains involving large firms (Figure 1.11). This is often achieved through advisory services. For example, IFC can provide training and technical support to a large enterprise to encourage use of SME suppliers. Such support is often combined with SME training and sometimes is also linked to trade credit or other financing to enable SMEs to upgrade and meet the quality standards of the larger firm. For example, IFC's West Bank and Gaza Olive Oil Supply Chain Development Project aims to enhance the performance of a group of SMEs that "lack knowledge of required skills and performance standards to operate effectively," to enhance their performance in terms of product quality and export growth to accelerate

FIGURE 1.10 Theory of Change 3: World Bank Group Finance for Business Development and Firm-Level Advisory Services and Training to SMEs

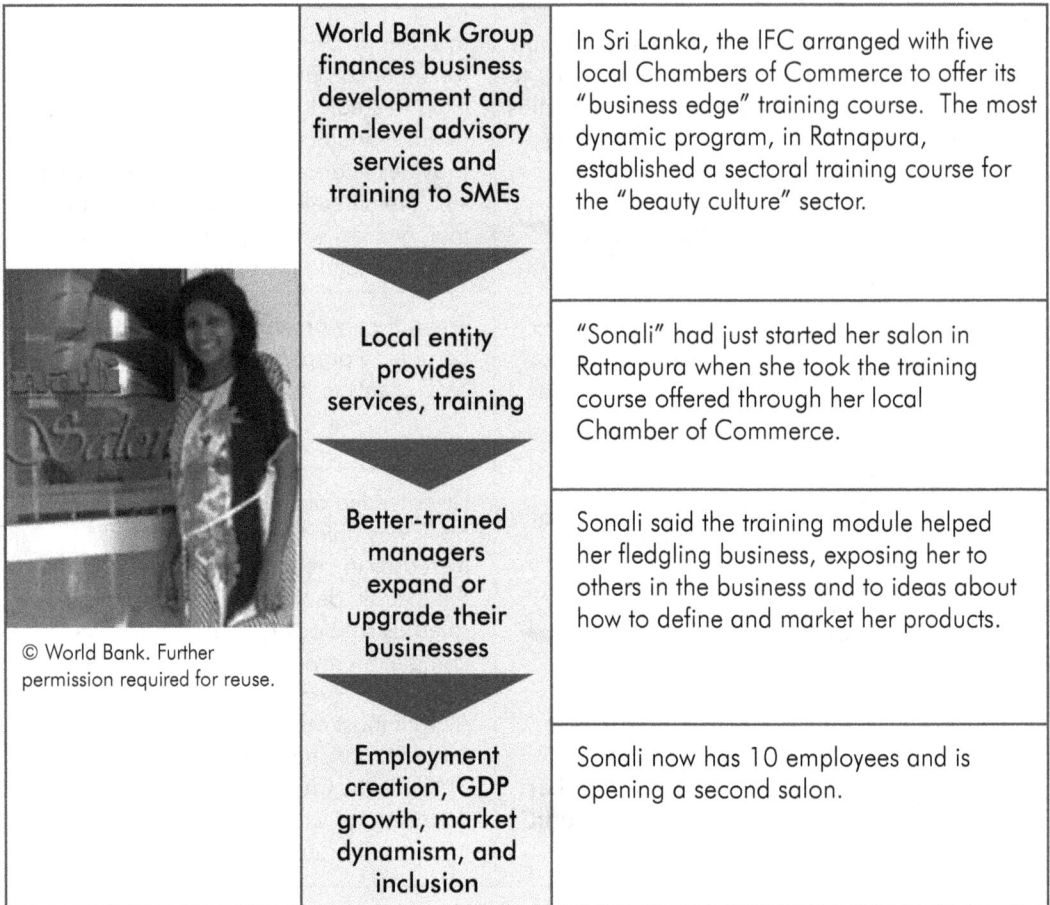© World Bank. Further permission required for reuse.	**World Bank Group finances business development and firm-level advisory services and training to SMEs**	In Sri Lanka, the IFC arranged with five local Chambers of Commerce to offer its "business edge" training course. The most dynamic program, in Ratnapura, established a sectoral training course for the "beauty culture" sector.
	Local entity provides services, training	"Sonali" had just started her salon in Ratnapura when she took the training course offered through her local Chamber of Commerce.
	Better-trained managers expand or upgrade their businesses	Sonali said the training module helped her fledgling business, exposing her to others in the business and to ideas about how to define and market her products.
	Employment creation, GDP growth, market dynamism, and inclusion	Sonali now has 10 employees and is opening a second salon.

SOURCES: IEG portfolio review.
NOTE: GDP = gross domestic product.

economic growth and support the development of a productive private sector that will attract investment, encourage economic integration, introduce new technologies, expand economic opportunities, and create new jobs.

MAPPING THE WORLD BANK GROUP PORTFOLIO TO THE THEORIES OF CHANGE

The various activities of the World Bank Group can be mapped into these theories of change. Table 1.3 provides some examples. For example, IFC, MIGA, and the World Bank each have products that fit the first theory of change, through which financing or guarantees benefit SMEs.

FIGURE 1.11 Theory of Change 4: Value Chain Interventions in Networks and Clusters

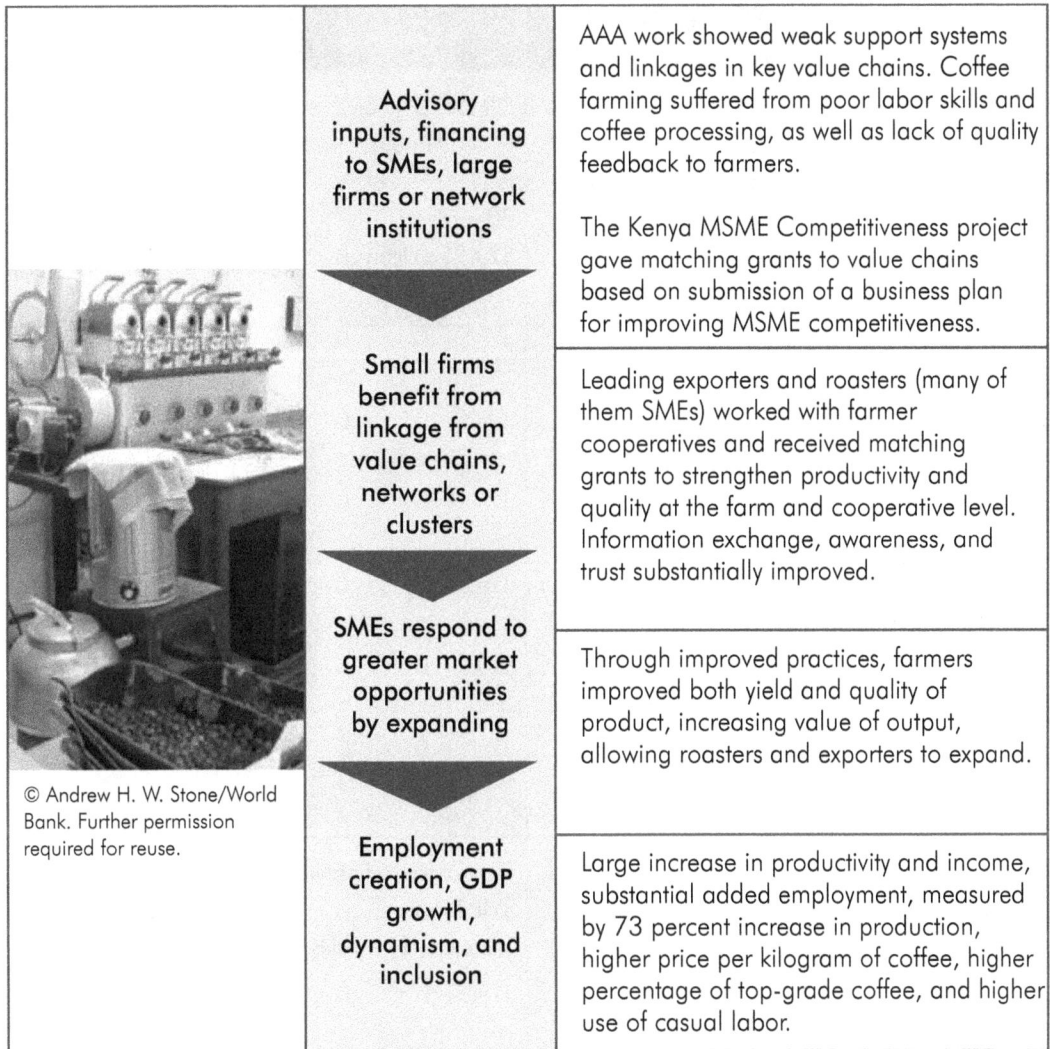 © Andrew H. W. Stone/World Bank. Further permission required for reuse.	**Advisory inputs, financing to SMEs, large firms or network institutions** ▼ **Small firms benefit from linkage from value chains, networks or clusters** ▼ **SMEs respond to greater market opportunities by expanding** ▼ **Employment creation, GDP growth, dynamism, and inclusion**	AAA work showed weak support systems and linkages in key value chains. Coffee farming suffered from poor labor skills and coffee processing, as well as lack of quality feedback to farmers. The Kenya MSME Competitiveness project gave matching grants to value chains based on submission of a business plan for improving MSME competitiveness. Leading exporters and roasters (many of them SMEs) worked with farmer cooperatives and received matching grants to strengthen productivity and quality at the farm and cooperative level. Information exchange, awareness, and trust substantially improved. Through improved practices, farmers improved both yield and quality of product, increasing value of output, allowing roasters and exporters to expand. Large increase in productivity and income, substantial added employment, measured by 73 percent increase in production, higher price per kilogram of coffee, higher percentage of top-grade coffee, and higher use of casual labor.

SOURCES: IEG portfolio review.
NOTE: AAA = analytic and advisory activity; GDP = gross domestic product; MSME = micro, small, and medium-size enterprise.

IEG examines the extent to which experience conforms with these logical sequences, although it cannot validate the final economy-wide impact. Clearly, not all projects elaborate this sequence fully, and some do not reflect much thinking about a theory of change at all. The underlying theme is that if benefits or services are to be targeted to one group of enterprises and not to others, several elements must be present:

• A good explanation of why the intervention addresses that group's needs and promotes broader development goals

TABLE 1.3 Mapping World Bank Group Portfolios and Products to Theories of Change

Product	IFC	MIGA	World Bank
Financing through loan, investment, or guarantee	On-lending, leasing, direct investment, partial risk guarantee, and more. 384 projects, $10,078 million	SIP for FDI in SME or FI, regular guarantee to FI. 88 projects, $2,495 million	FILs, partial risk guarantees, matching grants (as financing mechanism). 103 projects, $3,801 million
Advisory services to government, financial institutions	Advisory services to financial institutions, public and private bodies. 134 projects, $77 million		Technical assistance to governments, financial institutions and others. 71 projects, $380 million
Business development services/advisory services/training	Business Edge, SME Toolkit, other BDS, training and advisory. 87 projects, $53 million		BDS, training and advisory services, sometimes linked to matching grants. 25 projects, $372 million
Value chain interventions, networks, and clusters	SBA/linkages work. 51 projects, $41 million	Guarantee to firm with SME linkages. 1 project, $14 million	Value chain AAA and projects (cluster development, growth pole, and so forth). 18 projects, $383 million

SOURCE: IEG portfolio review.

NOTE: With number of projects and aggregate of commitment value, expenditure and gross exposure. AAA = analytic and advisory activity; BDS = business development service; FDI = foreign direct investment; FI = financial intermediary; FIL = financial intermediary loan; SBA = Sustainable Business Advisory; SIP = small investment program; SME = small and medium-size enterprise.

- A good identification of the targeted group

- Effective and efficient means of assuring the targeted group benefits from the intervention (delivering benefits or addressing market failures impeding that group)

- Enough information to know whether the problem the intervention sought to address has been addressed.

Evaluation Design

The remainder of the evaluation reviews IFC, MIGA, and World Bank TSME support activities since 2006, assessing their relevance, efficacy, and efficiency, as well as the work quality evidenced by each institution. The final chapter considers the World Bank Group's performance as a whole and draws lessons and recommendations to improve future development effectiveness. The chapters draw lessons from the World Bank Group's experience and make recommendations to help enhance the achievement of the Bank Group's development mission, specifically, to enhance the impact of its SME support in contributing to growth, employment, and shared prosperity.

IEG intends the report to inform the discussion of the extent and nature of the World Bank Group's future engagement in TSME support activities. It will complement other work on broader systemic reforms in support of private sector development, including IEG analyses of work on the investment climate and the financial sector.

IEG asks one overarching question in this evaluation, supported by four supporting questions, each in turn informed by a number of subordinate questions:

Has the World Bank Group effectively promoted inclusive growth through its targeted support of SMEs aimed to address constraints relating to access to finance, to services, to information and to markets?

- **Relevance:** Has there been a persuasive rationale for the World Bank Group to offer targeted support to SMEs?

- **Efficacy:** Have the World Bank Group's targeted support programs for SMEs met their objectives and reached their desired outcomes?

- **Efficiency:** Are TSME support programs efficient instruments, from both a program and institutional perspective?

- **Work Quality:** Is the World Bank Group effectively managing factors within its control?

▶ Information sources. IEG used a range of different information sources and methods of analysis in the evaluation, building on standard IEG methodology. These include internal and external literature and document reviews to identify:

- The role and significance of SMEs in development, including their contribution to employment, innovation and growth

- The theoretical underpinnings of and rationale for support for SMEs—including what specific needs, constraints, and market failures are especially important for this firm size

- The role of financial sector development in promoting SME growth, and any tradeoffs between SME-specific needs and broader growth needs

- The pertinent policy and institutional variables

- The record of success or failure of different approaches to SME support.

▶ World Bank Group portfolio review of the project databases, including all projects approved in FY06–12. To further focus on outcomes, the team also examined projects that closed during the same period, which yielded a much richer set of projects that had been subject to self- and IEG evaluation, allowing for more systematic and even econometric analysis.

▶ Enterprise survey database and other database analysis. The team undertook an extensive analysis of enterprise survey data to better understand the behavioral characteristics of SMEs, their constraints and costs, as well the relationship of size characteristics of firms to firms' access to finance and their propensity to create employment. These data were also used to understand the interactions of firm size with other firm characteristics and with country characteristics such as income level and region. IEG also used external databases (Berne Union, Bankscope).

▶ World Bank Group staff interviews. The IEG team interviewed relevant World Bank Group staff and management in headquarters and in each field visit.

▶ Beneficiary and stakeholder interviews. Opinions and insights were gathered from clients, beneficiaries, and other major stakeholders in field visit countries, including donors, business associations, government counterparts, and other interested parties. In addition, IEG conducted a broad discussion and social outreach to interested stakeholders through social media (Facebook, LinkedIn, and Twitter), including two opinion polls.

▶ Special focus and microevaluation of MIGA SIP. As part of this evaluation, IEG agreed with MIGA to conduct a programmatic evaluation of SIP. For SIP, there is little project-specific evaluatory information available, so IEG conducted a desk review of all SIP project files for the covered period, completing pending project evaluation reports and conducting additional analyses of a sample of the portfolio of mature projects in accordance with a template agreed with MIGA. Field work allows onsite information gathering for a small subsample of projects, contributing to the macroevaluation.

▶ Country case studies. Country case studies were prepared based on missions to six purposively selected countries reflecting a diversity of conditions (for example International Development Association [IDA]/non-IDA, postconflict, different regions), with a diversity of

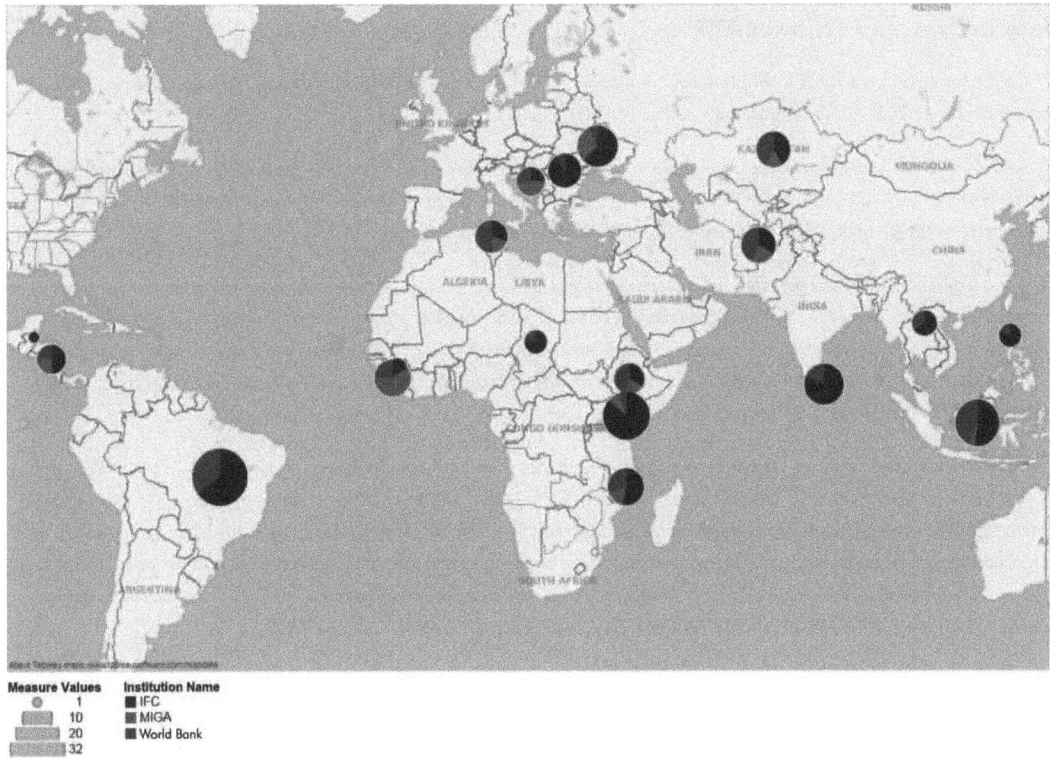

Measure Values   Institution Name
- 1 — IFC
- 10 — MIGA
- 20 — World Bank
- 32

SOURCE: IEG portfolio review.

project performance characteristics, where multiple institutions of the Bank Group had been active. In addition, a stratified, random sample of 14 additional countries was drawn for desk-based country case studies, to expand the range of country experience included in the evaluation (Figure 1.12).

Finally, IEG conducted a detailed desk review of available underwriting and monitoring documents of 41 operationally mature SIP projects and conducted site visits to 7 SIP projects. The IEG team reviewed findings and ratings from six SIP Project Evaluation Reports (PERs), cancellation data, and reports from MIGA's Legal Department on claims and pre-claims using a standard template to assess the relevance, effectiveness, and efficiency of the program in supporting SME investments. In a number of cases, interviews with MIGA staff involved in underwriting SIP projects and reviewing claims or pre-claims also helped inform IEG's evaluation of the program's relevance, effectiveness, and efficiency.

Notes

[1] "Rapid and sustained poverty reduction requires inclusive growth that allows people to contribute to and benefit from economic growth. Rapid pace of growth is unquestionably necessary for substantial poverty reduction, but for this growth to be sustainable in the long run, it should be broad-based across sectors, and inclusive of the large part of the country's labor force" (Ianchovichina and Lundstrom 2009).

[2] On the contribution of SMEs to employment creation in developing countries, see, for example, Ayyagari, Demirgüç-Kunt, and Maksimovic 2011, 2013; World Bank 2011a, 2011b; IFC 2013.

[3] Definitions of SME vary widely (see Box 1.1). In this evaluation IEG uses IFC's definition—having 10–300 employees and assets between $100,000 and $15 million or sales in the same dollar range. However, the research cited here used the criterion of firms with up to 250 employees (Beck and Demirgüç-Kunt 2006).

[4] In the World Bank, this was reflected in Klein and Hadjmichael (2003): "Establishing an equal playing field for all types of enterprises is often one of the most politically difficult parts of reform. Neither large nor small or medium-size firms should be favored. What should be favored are competition and the rule of law." In IFC it was reflected in a study by Hallberg (2000): "[T]he justification for SME interventions lies in market and institutional failures that bias the size distribution of firms, rather than any inherent economic benefits provided by small firms."

[5] These justifications appear in a great deal of literature but also in many Bank Group project documents. For example, the Executive Vice President and CEO of IFC stated in 2011, "[SMEs] are . . . engines of job creation and growth in emerging markets that are central to the larger equation of development. The dynamic, fast-moving firms make a special contribution to local economies. It can be measured in many ways—levels of new business formation; job creation and retention; increased productivity, innovation, and value added; or links with global value chains, to name a few" (IFC 2011). http://www.ifc.org/wps/wcm/connect/409734804c561178926edaf12db12449/TOS_SME.pdf?MOD=AJPERES.

[6] In a comparison of the 15 constraints rated on a scale of 0–4 on the World Bank's enterprise surveys, power supply, corruption, tax rates, political instability, and informal competition generally figure among the top constraints of SMEs across regions and income levels of countries. Using IFC's definition of SMEs, medium-size enterprises also report needing more skilled and educated workers. Access to finance is often identified as the "biggest obstacle" when firms are allowed to identify only one.

[7] Enterprise surveys provide firm-level data from over 135,000 establishments in more than 135 countries. Data are used to create over 100 indicators that benchmark the quality of the business environment across the globe. Firm-level data are available to registered users on the enterprise surveys site: http://www.enterprisesurveys.org/.

[8] In a logistic regression, the dependent variable—having a bank loan or line of credit—was regressed on firm size categories (5–9 employees, 10–19 employees, 20–99 employees, 100–299 employees, and 300+ employees), on country income level (low, middle, and high), on interaction terms for each size category with country income level, and on control variables for sales, firm age, and firm sector. Without interaction terms, each size category below 300 and each country income level below high had a significant negative coefficient. Once interactions were accounted for, the coefficients for firms with 100–299 employees and the interaction terms for these firms with country income level became insignificant. The coefficient for middle-income countries also became insignificant. One interpretation is that targeted interventions should focus on all SMEs in low-income countries and only on firms with fewer than 100 employees in middle-income countries.

[9] For example, the World Bank's Global Financial Development Report uses the less than 100 employee threshold, whereas some of the leading Financial and Private Sector Development/Development Economics Vice Presidency research uses a 5–250 employee bracket to define SMEs (see Ayyagari, Demirgüç-Kunt, and Maksimovic 2011).

[10] In Nicaragua, IEG was informed that only about a dozen private firms nationwide would exceed IFC's SME threshold.

[11] For details on these donor programs aimed at SME support, see http://ec.europa.eu/cip/index_en.htm. http://www.iic.org /en/media/news/iic-announces-us80-million-initiative-sme-development-latin-america-and-caribbean. http://www.usaid.gov /news-information/press-releases/usaid-mobilizes-record-amount-private-capital-support-small and http://www.afdb.org/en /topics-and-sectors/initiatives-partnerships/african-guarantee-fund-for-small-and-medium-sized-enterprises/.

[12] For example, in the first theory of change, IFC or the Bank would identify a financing gap (potentially indicated by a low credit-to-GDP ratio, a low "financial penetration ratio," or evidence of substantial unmet SME demand for credit) driven by a market or institutional failure it knows how to address. This market failure may have to do with ignorance on the part of the banking community of the potential profitability of SME lending (an information failure) or of appropriate screening and risk management techniques or it may be rooted in systemic problems in the financial sector.

[13] Based on the Expanded Project Supervision Report for line of credit.

[14] [T]he total unmet need for credit by all formal and informal MSMEs in emerging markets today is in the range of $2.1 trillion to $2.5 trillion (Stein, Goland, and Schiff 2010).

[15] IFC explains its SME banking program by stating that "access to financial services for SMEs remains severely constrained" and that SMEs "play a major role in creating jobs and generating income for low income people; they foster economic growth, social stability, and contribute to the development of a dynamic private sector." It goes on to state that "IFC uses both investments and technical assistance to support financial intermediaries outreach to the SME sector more effectively and efficiently." http://www.ifc.org/wps/wcm/connect/Industry_EXT_Content/IFC_External_Corporate_Site/Industries /Financial+Markets/MSME+Finance/SME+Banking/

[16] http://fpdweb.worldbank.org/units/fpdvp/ffidr/Documents/FI%20One%20Pager%20Nov%202012.pdf.

References

Aterido, Reyes, Mary Hallward-Driemeier, and Carmen Pages. 2011. "Big Constraints to Small Firms' Growth: Business Environment and Employment Growth Across Firms." *Economic Development and Cultural Change* 59(3):609–47.

Ayyagari, Mehghana, Asli Demirgüç-Kunt, and Vojislav Maksimovic. 2013. "Size and Age of Establishments: Evidence from Developing Countries." World Bank Policy Research Working Paper 6718, Washington, DC.

———. 2011. "Small vs. Young Firms across the World: Contribution to Employment, Job Creation, and Growth." World Bank Policy Research Working Paper 5631, Washington, DC.

Batra, Geeta, and Syed Mahmood. 2003. "Direct Support to Private Firms: Evidence on Effectiveness." World Bank Policy Research Working Paper 3170, Washington, DC.

Beck, Thorsten, and Asli Demirgüç-Kunt. 2006. "Small and Medium-Size Enterprises: Access to Finance as a Growth Constraint." *Journal of Banking and Finance* 30 (11): 2931–43.

Beck, Thorsten, Asli Demirgüç-Kunt, Luc Laeven, and Ross Levine. 2008. "Finance, Firm Size, and Growth." *Journal of Money, Credit and Banking,* 40(7): 1379–1405.

Beck, Thorsten, Asli Demirgüç-Kunt, Luc Laeven, and Vojislav Maksimovic. 2006. "The Determinants of Financing Obstacles." *Journal of International Money and Finance,* 25(6): 932–52.

Beck, Thorsten, Asli Demirgüç-Kunt, and Ross Levine. 2005. "SMEs, Growth, and Poverty: Cross-Country Evidence." *Journal of Economic Growth* 10(3) 199–229.

Belke, A., R. Fehn, and N. Foster. 2003. "Does Venture Capital Investment Spur Employment Growth?" Working Paper 197, Center for European Policy Studies, Brussels.

Benavente, Jose Miguel, Alexander Galetovic, and Ricardo Sanhueza. 2006. "Fogape: An Economic Analysis." Mimeo.

Biggs, T., and M. Shah. 1998. "The Determinants of Enterprise Growth in Sub-Saharan Africa: Evidence from the Regional Program on Enterprise Development." RPED Discussion Paper 103, World Bank, Washington, DC.

Bloom, Nicholas, Raffaella Sadun, and John Van Reenen. 2009. "Do Private Equity-Owned Firms Have Better Management Practices?" CEPOP24. Centre for Economic Performance, London School of Economics and Political Science, London.

Bruhn, Miriam, and Bilal Zia. 2013. "Stimulating Managerial Capital in Emerging Markets: The Impact of Business Training for Young Entrepreneurs." *Journal of Development Effectiveness* 5(2): 232–66.

Campos, Francisco, Aidan Coville, Ana Maria Fernandes, Markus Goldstein, and David McKenzie. 2012. "Learning from the Experiments That Never Happened: Lessons from Trying to Conduct Randomized Evaluations of Matching Grant Programs in Africa." World Bank Policy Research Working Paper 6296, Washington, DC.

Dalberg. 2011. *Report on Support to SMEs in Developing Countries through Financial Intermediaries.* Luxembourg: European Investment Bank.

Davis, Steven J., John Haltiwanger, Ron Jarmin, Josh Lerner, and Javier Miranda. 2011. "Private Equity, Jobs and Productivity." Harvard Business School Working Paper 12-033, Cambridge, MA.

De Luna-Martínez, José, and Carlos Leonardo Vicente. 2012. *Global Survey of Development Banks.* World Bank Policy Research Working Paper 5969, Washington, DC.

De Mel, Suresh, David McKenzie, and Chris Woodruff. 2008. "Returns to Capital in Microenterprises: Evidence from a Field Experiment." *Quarterly Journal of Economics* 123: 1329–72.

Gibson, T., and H. J. van der Vaart. 2008. *Defining SMEs: A Less Imperfect Way of Defining Small and Medium Enterprises in Developing Countries.* Washington, DC: Brookings Institution.

Hallberg, Kristin. 2000. *A Market-Oriented Strategy for Small and Medium-Scale Enterprises.* Washington, DC: World Bank.

Haltiwanger, John C., Ron S. Jarmin, and Javier Miranda. 2010. "Who Creates Jobs? Small vs. Large, Large vs. Young." NBER Working Paper No. 16300, Cambridge, MA. http://www.nber.org/papers/w16300.

Hsieh, Chang-Tai, and Peter J. Klenow. 2012. "The Lifecycle of Plants in India and Mexico." NBER Working Paper No. 18133, Cambridge, MA.

Ianchovichina, Elena, and Susanna Lundstrom. 2009. *What Is Inclusive Growth?* Washington, DC: World Bank.

IEG (Independent Evaluation Group). 2005. "Review of Bank Lines of Credit." Report No. 31131, World Bank, Washington, DC.

IFC (International Finance Corporation). 2013. *Jobs Study: Assessing Private Sector Contributions to Job Creation and Poverty Reduction.* Washington, DC: World Bank.

———. 2012. *Road Map FY13–15: Creating Innovative Solutions in Challenging Times.* Washington, DC: World Bank.

———. 2011. "SME Banking." http://www. ifc.org/wps/wcm/connect/Industry_EXT_Content/IFC_External_Corporate_Site /Industries/Financial+Markets/MSME+Finance/SME+Banking/

———. 2010. "Scaling-Up SME Access to Financial Services in the Developing World." Financial Inclusion Experts Group, SME Finance Sub-Group, G20 Seoul Summit.

Klapper, Leora, and Christine Richmond. 2011. "Patterns of Business Creation, Survival and Growth: Evidence from Africa." World Bank Policy Research Working Paper 5828, Washington, DC.

Klein, Michael. 2010. *Promoting Small and Medium Enterprises: Their Importance and the Role of Development Finance Institutions in Supporting Them.* DEG, KfW Bankengruppe: The Atrium Dialogues.

Klein, Michael U., and Bita Hadjmichael. 2003. *The Private Sector in Development.* Washington, DC: World Bank.

Klinger, Bailey, and Matthias Schündeln. 2011. *Can Entrepreneurial Activity Be Taught? Quasi-experimental Evidence from Central America, World Development, 1592–1610.* Klinger and Schündeln.

Kortum, S., and J. Lerner. 2000. "Assessing the Contribution of Venture Capital to Innovation." *RAND Journal of Economics* 31: 674–92.

Kushnir, K., M. Mirmulstein, and R. Ramalho. 2010. *Micro, Small and Medium Enterprises around the World: How Many Are There, and What Affects the Count?* Washington, DC: World Bank.

Levine, Ross. 2005. *Does Firm Size Matter for Growth and Poverty Alleviation?* Washington, DC: Brookings Institution.

Lundström, Anders, and Lois Stevenson. 2005. *Entrepreneurship Policy: Theory and Practice.* New York: Kleuwer Academic Publishers.

McMillan, J., and C. Woodruff. 2002. "The Central Role of Entrepreneurs in Transition Economies." *Journal of Economic Perspectives* 16 (3):153–70.

MIGA (Multilateral Investment Guarantee Agency). 2009. "Small Projects, Big Impact." Press Release, April 22.

OECD (Organisation for Economic Co-operation and Development). 2004. *The Istanbul Ministerial Declaration on Fostering the Growth of Innovative and Internationally Competitive SMEs.* Paris: OECD.

——. 2000. *The Bologna Charter on SME Policies.* Paris: OECD.

Page, John, and Måns Söderbom. 2012. "Is Small Beautiful? Small Enterprise, Aid and Employment in Africa." Working Paper 094, UNU-WIDER.

Reinecke, Gerhard, and Simon White. 2004. *Policies for Small Enterprises: Creating the Right Environment for Good Jobs.* Geneva: International Labor Organization.

Stein, Peer, Tony Goland, and Robert Schiff. 2010. *Two Trillion and Counting: Assessing the Credit Gap for Micro, Small and Medium Enterprises in the Developing World.* Washington, DC: World Bank.

Storey, D. J. 2008. *Entrepreneurship and SME Policy.* World Entrepreneurship Forum.

——. 2003. "Entrepreneurship, Small and Medium Sized Enterprises and Public Policies." In *Handbook of Entrepreneurship Research,* ed. Z. J. Acs and D. B. Audretsch. London: Kluwer Academic Publishers.

World Bank. 2011a. "JERP: Financing Reporting by Small and Medium Enterprises in Kazakhstan: Current Status and Policy Options." World Bank, Washington, DC.

——. 2011b. "Turkey Improving Conditions for SME Growth Finance and Innovation." Washington, DC. World Bank Report No. 54961-TR https://openknowledge.worldbank.org/handle/10986/12211.

——. 2004. "India—Additional Financing for the Small and Medium-Size Enterprise Financing and Development Project." Project Appraisal Document, World Bank, Washington, DC.

2 IFC Support for SMEs

CHAPTER HIGHLIGHTS

- IFC identifies SME support is a strategic objective based on job creation potential.

- IFC's TSME portfolio is significant, constituting 17 percent total projects and 16 percent of commitments.

- Most IFC investment projects do not define SMEs or root SME support in a clear theory of change that would connect the intervention to correcting a market failure.

- The most credible theory of change underpinning much of IFC's TSME support lies in its contribution to developing sustainable private markets for SME finance, rather than the direct benefits it delivers to firms. IFC is most effective when it works strategically through its targeted investments, often in conjunction with more systemic approaches, to expand the supply of SME oriented financial (or other) services, increase competition, and improve market functioning.

- IFC's relevance is greater when it operates at or near the frontier.

- Many clients value IFC's support, professionalism, and standards, especially when it is able to tailor its products to their needs

- TSME projects were generally less successful than the overall portfolio and the rest of the financial markets portfolio. However, these projects improved their performance over time.

- In general, IFC lacks sufficient monitoring and evaluation information about its TSME projects to truly understand their development impact, both in terms of beneficiary impact and impact on market development.

- IFCs TSME advisory services overall have performed better than the rest of the advisory portfolio, except in low-income countries.

Rationale

IFC has had a long-standing commitment to the support of SMEs, starting with the establishment of its first project development facility more than 30 years ago, and most recently manifested in its Roadmap for FY14–16. Over the course of three decades, it has shifted its focus from direct assistance to SMEs to indirect assistance to financing SMEs through commercial banks and financial institutions.

IFC began providing direct technical assistance to SMEs in the 1980s through its donor-funded project development facilities, and then started financing them directly in several parts of the world. The technical assistance was tailored to help SMEs access finance by helping companies develop sound investment projects and find financing from banks for these projects. In parallel with the project development facilities, IFC set up small pools of funds (about $100 million in total) to support direct SME investments mainly in Africa and the South Pacific.[1]

IFC learned several lessons from its experience in providing direct assistance and financing for SMEs. From a financial standpoint, IFC's experience was disappointing. Although the amounts involved were relatively small, their gross non-accrual rates were much higher than IFC's portfolio as a whole. Also, the success rate of advisory services offered through the project development facilities and cost recovery were limited (Cohn 2004). Generally, only a small proportion of clients provided contributions, which were often very small compared to the overall costs of the programs. Even though the services were essentially free, IFC's SME clients were dissatisfied with the lack of local knowledge of many IFC technical consultants, and donors funding these programs were uncomfortable about use of their funds to assist what IFC defined as SMEs but what they saw as large companies in many developing countries and the high overhead costs of IFC's advisory operations.

With regard to facilitating SME finance through financial institutions, IFC first started investing in banks in FY94, mainly in the Latin America and the Caribbean Region. IFC's Global Financial Markets Department used the SME focus to justify its assistance to commercial banks in middle-income countries, especially in their frontier markets, and in IDA countries. IFC made the case that frontier markets existed even in large middle-income countries, given regional disparities, and that investing in financial institutions that targeted SMEs in specific areas had an important development impact. Working with financial intermediaries allowed

IFC to support far more MSMEs than it would be able to support on its own, and it enabled IFC to meet its targets on reach indicators such as the number and volume of loans to SMEs. In addition, portfolio performance improved.

To further address these concerns, IFC introduced the Private Enterprise Partnership (PEP) model in the former Soviet Union countries in 2000 and then expanded it to other regions. PEP consolidated IFC's existing large Advisory Services program in the Commonwealth of Independent States to install a more specialized management structure and to address donor requests for a long-term IFC commitment to the region. PEP management was organized by core product areas; their objective was to deliver Advisory Services in financial markets, corporate governance, business enabling environment, linkages with large firms, and SME development. PEP became a model for a number of multidonor, regionally focused project development facilities. In recent years, IFC has done much to mainstream facility staff and standardize core products in its advisory services.

STRATEGIC UNDERPINNINGS

IFC's FY14–16 Roadmap states as one of its five objectives developing local financial markets through institution building, the use of innovative financial products, and mobilization, focusing on MSME. It emphasizes the job creation potential of SMEs, which "may account for up to four-fifths of job creation and two-thirds of employment in developing countries." This has become an often repeated phrase used to justify SME interventions by IFC, yet its own jobs study arrives at a much more nuanced conclusion, characterized in the Roadmap as follows:

> In general, while MSMEs tend to have higher rates of job growth in developing countries, larger companies provide more sustainable jobs, are typically more productive, offer higher wages and more training, and support a big multiple of the direct jobs they provide through their supply chains and distribution networks (which in particular provide opportunities for the poor) (IFC 2013).

Read through the lens of longitudinal research on job creation, this means that although MSMEs create more jobs, net job creation is not necessarily higher because more firms exit the market. The jobs study provides no grounds on which to differentiate firms by size beyond addressing systemic constraints that may disproportionately handicap a particular class of firms' ability to generate employment.

In this regard, access to finance, power supply, and informal competition are especially highlighted as constraining SMEs, based on enterprise surveys. In particular, the Roadmap states that SME finance can result in significant job growth. It calls for a customized strategy: "Using a job lens in country, regional, or sectoral strategies can help identify key constraints to job creation in specific contexts, since jobs challenges differ." Only some of the key constraints to SMEs will be connected to the TSME portfolio, whereas others, such as support for broader financial sector reforms, electric power investments, and regulatory reform, may not. Many of these constraints, though, are addressed through other IFC or Bank Group instruments.

Looking forward, from the point of view of jobs creation, this suggests the need for country-specific diagnostics to identify leading constraints to job creation in firms of all sizes, in multiple sectors, and in both leading and lagging regions. It also highlights the importance of amending existing metrics such as enterprise surveys and subnational Doing Business reports to provide sufficient information to shape strategy and project interventions.

IFC Investments for Targeted Support to SMEs

INVESTMENTS PORTFOLIO OVERVIEW

The portfolio review, which covers projects approved FY06–12 (see Figure 2.1), finds that 17 percent of IFC's overall portfolio in terms of number of investment projects and 16 percent in terms of value can be classified as targeted SME. IFC investments that supported SMEs during this period were primarily indirect—by financing institutions (banks, funds, risk guarantee facilities, and so forth) that support SMEs, IFC has increased access to finance for

FIGURE 2.1 Distribution of IFC TSME Portfolio, by Number of Projects

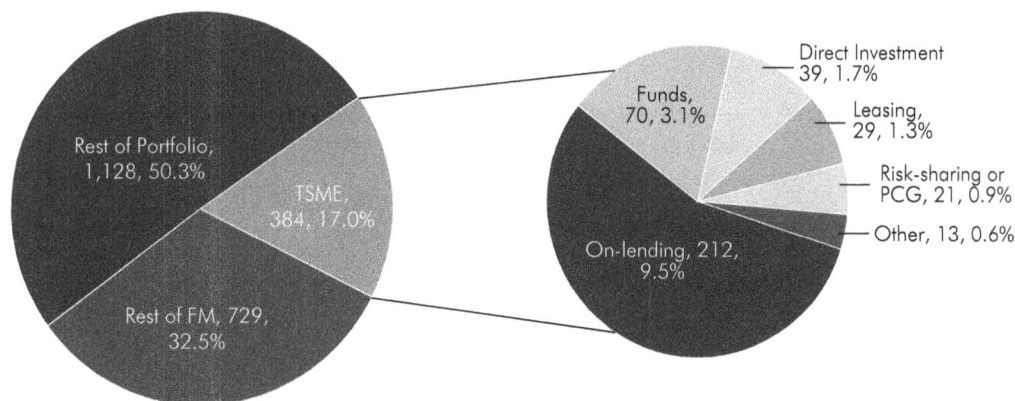

SOURCE: IEG portfolio review.
NOTE: FM = financial markets; PCG = partial credit guarantee; TSME = targeted small and medium-size enterprise.

SMEs, enhanced the financial system's capacity, and built or strengthened financial markets in SME financing. This product line, which facilitates SME finance through financial institutions, constituted 55 percent of projects and 74 percent of net commitments for targeted SME support in dollar terms.

Within this product line, loans to banks accounted for 73 percent of projects (representing 65 percent of commitments), equity investments in banks accounted for 15 percent of projects (representing 18 percent of commitments), and the remaining 12 percent of projects (representing 18 percent of commitments) were combined loan and equity investment projects. Other significant product lines include equity and venture capital funds aimed at financing SMEs (representing 18 percent of targeted SME projects and 14 percent of TSME net commitments), partial credit guarantees (representing 6 percent of TSME projects and 4 percent commitments), and leasing (representing 8 percent of TSME projects, and 5 percent of TSME net commitments). Direct investments in SMEs, largely rejected in the early 2000s as a strategy for targeting SME support, has dwindled to less than 1 percent of TSME net commitment value, although numerically it still accounts for 10 percent of projects.

In terms of industry composition, TSME investments were overwhelmingly focused in the financial markets industry group, which accounted for 97 percent of the total value of commitments to TSMEs. By number, 10 percent of projects were in manufacturing, agriculture, and services (MAS), but these accounted for only 2 percent of commitment value (see Figure 2.2).

FIGURE 2.2 Distribution of IFC TSME Portfolio, by Commitment Value ($ millions)

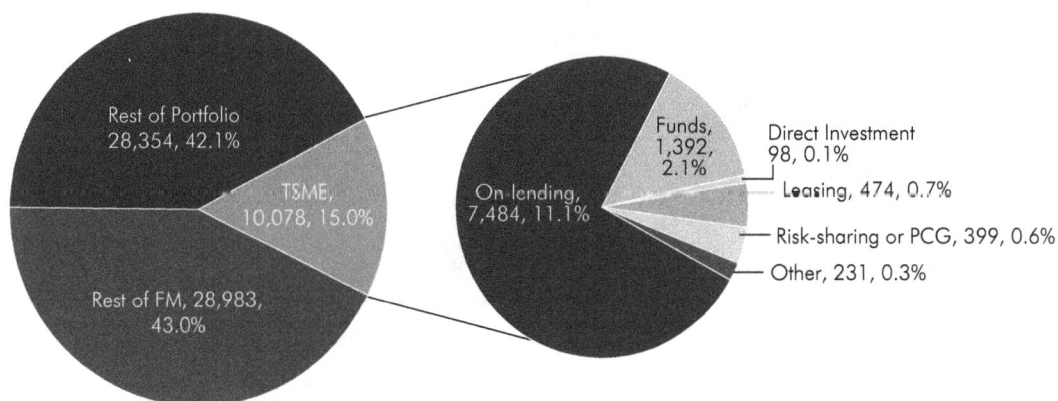

SOURCE: IEG portfolio review.
NOTE: FM = financial markets; PCG = partial credit guarantee; TSME = targeted small and medium-size enterprise.

FIGURE 2.3 Distribution of IFC TSME Investment Portfolio by Industry Group, Region, and Income Level, by Commitment Value ($ millions)

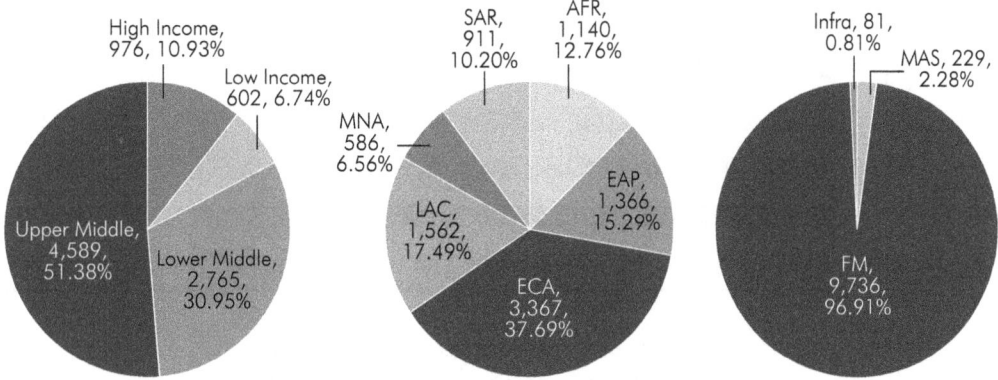

High Income, 976, 10.93%
Low Income, 602, 6.74%
Upper Middle, 4,589, 51.38%
Lower Middle, 2,765, 30.95%

SAR, 911, 10.20%
AFR, 1,140, 12.76%
MNA, 586, 6.56%
LAC, 1,562, 17.49%
EAP, 1,366, 15.29%
ECA, 3,367, 37.69%

Infra, 81, 0.81%
MAS, 229, 2.28%
FM, 9,736, 96.91%

SOURCE: IEG portfolio review.
NOTE: For Figures 2.3 and 2.4, country income status is determined as of 2013. The "high income" countries category includes mostly countries that "graduated" to high income status from upper-middle-income status after project initiation, including Chile (2012 graduation), Lithuania (2012), Oman (2007), Russia (2012), and Uruguay (2012). Saudi Arabia graduated in 2004.

Income level and regional figures exclude "regional" projects ($1,116 million) and industry figure excludes GDP ($1 million). FM = financial markets; Infra = infrastructure; MAS = Manufacturing, Agriculture, and Services. **Regions:** AFR = Africa; EAP = East Asia and Pacific; ECA = Europe and Central Asia; LAC = Latin America and the Caribbean; MNA = Middle East and North Africa; SAR = South Asia.

The product mix is somewhat different in different countries. Most IFC TSME commitments were in upper-middle-income countries and heavily focused in the Europe and Central Asia Region (Figure 2.3). Low-income countries benefited from less than seven percent of TSME investments committed in the 2006–12 period, whereas lower-middle-income countries received 31 percent of commitment value. Overwhelmingly, the TSME investment portfolio is focused on financial markets.

The story by number of projects is somewhat different: Europe and Central Asia remains the region with the most projects (32 percent); Africa is the second leading region with 21 percent of projects. Over two-thirds of projects are in middle income countries, roughly evenly divided between upper- and lower-middle-income. Seventeen percent were in low-income countries and 11 percent in high-income countries. Eighty-six percent of projects were in financial markets.

Organized by income level and as measured by either number of projects or commitment value, leasing, financing of banks to on-lend to SMEs, and risk sharing facilities levels are the highest in upper-middle-income countries. By contrast, the prominence of projects utilizing equity or venture capital funds is highest in lower-middle-income countries (Figure 2.4). This may indicate that the legal and financial regulatory systems in higher-income countries are

FIGURE 2.4 Portfolio Distribution by Country Income Level (commitment value, $ millions, FY06–12)

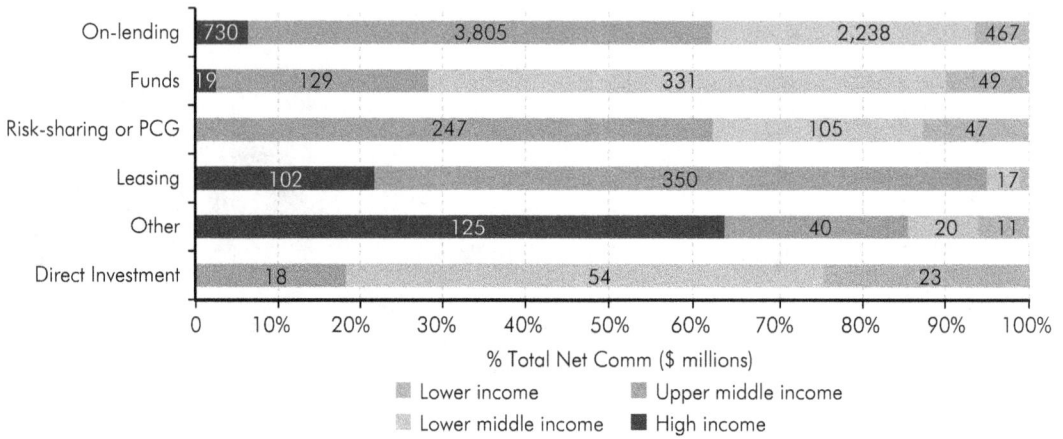

SOURCE: IEG portfolio review.
NOTE: See note for Figure 2.3. PCG = partial credit guarantee.

more amendable to risk-sharing facilities and lease finance. However, the heavy emphasis on on-lending in high- and upper-middle-income countries seems to be in direct contravention to the logic of using resources to redress poorly developed capital markets.

Although even wealthy countries may have lagging regions, banking is generally far more developed in upper-middle- and high-income countries. Survey data indicate that SMEs in these countries are much more likely to already have access to bank finance. The likelihood of crowding out private sources of capital is also greater in these better-developed capital markets. Furthermore, it is not clear how providing longer-term foreign exchange financing to banks—often on terms better than those prevailing in local markets—helps in the development of the financial markets or increases the availability of local currency funding for SMEs.

RELEVANCE OF INVESTMENT PORTFOLIO

WHO IS TARGETED? For the TSME investment portfolio to be relevant, projects should be relevant to the defined beneficiaries and connected to some defined challenge they are seeking to resolve. IFC has clearly defined its standards for what constitutes an SME, although that standard has questionable relevance in some country contexts. However, whether or not the standard is ideal, IEG's review finds that it is generally not applied (see Table 2.1). An IEG review of 250 Board documents of TSME investment projects found that 82 percent contained no definition of SME.[2] A further 7 percent had a definition higher than the standard IFC criteria, and 4 percent contained a definition with thresholds lower than IFC official criteria. For example, for an on-lending project for a Brazilian bank, IFC's loan agreement defined eligible subborrowers as companies with sales of no more than 300 million Brazilian reals

TABLE 2.1 Definition of SME in IFC TSME Board Documents

SME Definition in Board Report	Number of Projects	% of Projects
Not defined	204	82
Greater than IFC criteria	18	7
IFC criteria	14	6
Less than IFC criteria	9	4
Average loan or loan proxy (<$2 million)	5	2
Total	250	100

SOURCE: IEG portfolio review.
NOTE: Percentages are rounded.

(about $140 million at current rates). Thus, only 6 percent of IFC's portfolio (14 projects) defines SMEs in accordance with IFC's established criteria.

A review of 166 legal agreements for IFC TSME investment projects in the Financial Markets line shows that only 38 percent contain a definition of SME in their legal agreement (Figure 2.5). Furthermore, 60 percent of projects that say they are targeting SMEs have no provisions mentioning SMEs as beneficiaries. Overall, only 20 percent of the targeted SME Financial Markets portfolio both define SMEs and have provisions mentioning them. Comparing 2006–09 with 2010–12, the percent of projects without definitions or provisions

FIGURE 2.5 Presence of SME Definition and Provision in Loan Agreement for IFC Financial Markets Investments, by Time Period

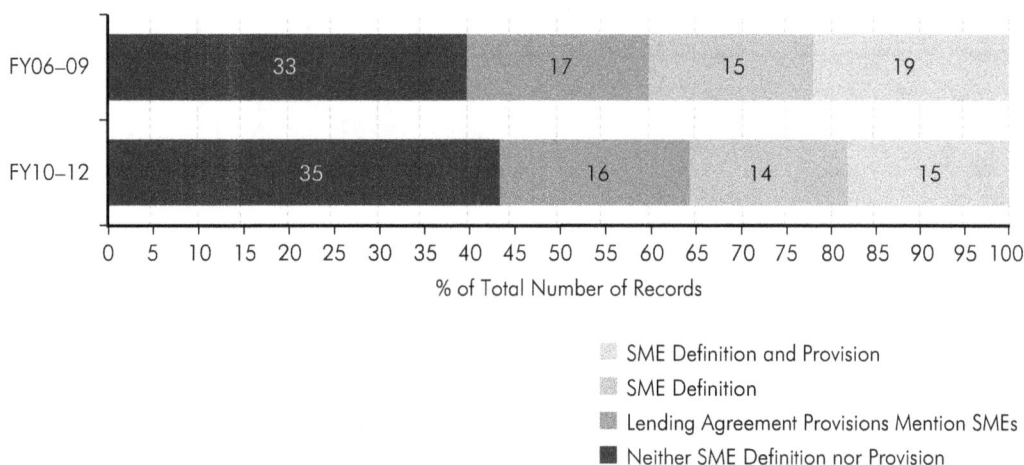

SME Definition and Provision
SME Definition
Lending Agreement Provisions Mention SMEs
Neither SME Definition nor Provision

SOURCE: IEG portfolio review.

actually increased, driven by a sharp decrease in 2010. Failing to define SMEs or add specific provisions can increase the risk that clients do not adhere to the intention of projects (Box 2.1), whereas specificity can strengthen the focus of lending on SMEs (Box 2.2).

By contrast, the use of SME monitoring indicators has grown dramatically. IEG's review of IFC investments suggests that 80 percent committed since 2006 had TSME monitoring indicators. These indicators became far more prevalent after 2005, rising from 7 percent of projects committed before 2006 to the current 80 percent level. IEG believes this reflects the widespread use of reach and Development Outcome Tracking System (DOTS) indicators, which made such monitoring mandatory in certain types of projects. For financial institutions, these indicators generally track loans of less than $1 million, although for over 20 countries, they track loans of less than $2 million.[3] However, it is not at all clear that these monitoring data are being used as a management, learning, or accountability tool.[4]

Although standardization has certain corporate benefits in reducing discretion and comparisons across projects, the risks associated with using IFC's current universal SME definition were witnessed multiple times in IEG's country case studies. In Belize, IFC engaged with a bank through a trade finance line and a targeted advisory services project that aimed to define and segment the bank's SME portfolio, revise its SME lending procedures, and design new SME products and services. The Advisory Services project conducted a thorough market analysis of the SME sector and bank's portfolio. The analysis included the SME definition of the Belize Trade and Investment Service and the Belize Chamber of Commerce: having no more than 15 employees; annual turnover up to $250,000; and having assets up to $150,000 (or investments in machinery not exceeding the same amount). In addition, the project's statement of market failure concludes that the bank's portfolio "shows a high concentration (62 percent) in the corporate loan segment (loans of greater than $500,000)." SME loans are thus defined as those of less than $500,000.

Nonetheless, according to project files, IFC recommended that the bank define its SME portfolio as loans under $1 million[5] with no other portfolio segmentation. So after conducting analytic work that defines SMEs by one standard and calling for portfolio deconcentration based on a second standard, the project then calls for segmentation by IFC standards, which it has shown to have no relevance for Belize.

ARE SME PROJECTS CREATING JOBS? In recent years, IFC has increasingly linked its TSME activities to job creation, yet the evidence for this link is not robustly established. First, although SMEs employ a large number of people, it is hard to isolate any special importance based on net job creation that would justify supporting them while excluding microenterprises and large firms. Second, no systematic evidence is being collected, much less analyzed, to indicate whether on-lending to banks is creating employment.

In the case of the leading product—on-lending to banks—the degree to which IFC financing of intermediaries results in employment creation, poverty alleviation, or even SME investment goes unrecorded. Throughout the evaluation period, IFC typically neither demanded nor received any information from financial intermediaries about their clients' level of employment and investment or other enterprise-level information. Before and during IEG field visits, IFC staff cited bank privacy concerns as the main reason they did not ask banks for information on their clients. IEG efforts to survey client bank sub-borrowers ran into the same barrier of privacy.

A second concern was adding to the considerable burden of dealing with IFC, which already required a host of covenants and practices regarding corporate governance and environmental and social (E&S) safeguards, many of which are not required by alternative financiers (see Box 2.3). Still, it is difficult to justify an intervention where an investment is warranted by its benefits to SMEs but there is no evidence of additionality at the enterprise level. IFC needs to know much more about what is done with such funds.

IS IFC WORKING AT THE FRONTIER? There is substantial historical and anecdotal evidence that, in some countries, IFC has been tremendously effective at ramping up the SME practices of banks that became major players in domestic financial markets. There was also substantial indication from client interviews that IFC is favored as a long-term business partner, and that many partner banks welcome its high environment and corporate governance standards, although the associated paperwork is regarded by some clients as imposing a high compliance cost.

However, the case studies suggest that IFC's relevance has been greater when it operates near the frontier—that is, in countries (especially low-income and fragile and conflict-affected states) where the financial sector had not yet developed to serve SMEs; with intermediaries that had not yet firmly established an SME practice and or could not raise capital privately to do so; and for regions or markets within countries where SMEs are not served.

Indonesia provides a good example. IFC's interventions in Indonesia were highly relevant in the post-1998 financial crisis period, and a number of the banks became IFC's long-term partners, benefiting from multiple injections of capital and credit lines, often for TSME projects. However, during the evaluation period, there were a number of banks that had both access to international capital and expertise in serving SME clients. In recent years, the Indonesian banking community was actively competing for SME clients, knew how to assess risk and manage portfolios, and had access to private capital. However, IFC continued to finance these banks on favorable terms, even though several of them had grown and are now among the country's leading banks. A more relevant strategy might have been to move to second- or third-tier banks; focus on underserved regions, locations, and clients; and/or shift capital to countries with less mature capital markets. Indeed, a discussion with a country manager in Indonesia indicated that IFC did intend to move its portfolio farther toward the "frontier"—second-tier banks, remote regions, and environmental and gender-oriented lending—but had done relatively little to date.

Similarly, in Kenya, IFC continued to partner with a bank it had financed for more than 20 years and provided with its full range of SME technical advisory services. An informed expert suggested that the bank's SME portfolio was mature and unlikely to expand. Remembering that the objective of SME finance is to build institutions, markets, and capacity, rather than simply to find conduits for IFC finance to small firms, a more relevant strategy would have been to operate closer to the frontier. Part of this frontier may lie in second-tier banks, in outlying regions, or in lending to neglected population groups, including women (Box 2.4).

BOX 2.4 Gender and IFC Projects

A 2012 IFC Women and Business Issue Brief notes that small and medium enterprises (SMEs) with female ownership represent 30–37 percent (8 million–10 million) of all SMEs in emerging markets. Despite the segment's significant size, relatively little assistance has focused on them. Historically, targeted assistance has focused primarily on women-owned micro and informal enterprises, rather than SMEs.

IEG's portfolio review identified 14 Investment and 20 Advisory Services TSME projects that aim to address these challenges faced by women-owned SMEs. Nine of the 14 investment projects provided on-lending targeted to SMEs or MSMEs without accompanying technical assistance; the client bank's existing support to women-owned SMEs ranged from 15 to 50 percent. The remaining five projects included finance for on-lending combined with technical assistance to help banks set up or expand lending programs from women-owned enterprises.

In Nigeria, IFC provided a bank with a $15 million investment to on-lend to 300 women entrepreneurs, supported by technical assistance and BDS to equip women entrepreneurs with financial and business skills. Both investment and the advisory services were evaluated as successful. The bank loaned a total of $35.5 million to 476 women entrepreneurs and grew its SME loan portfolio for women from 3 percent of SME loans in 2006 to 15.8 percent in 2009, with very few nonperforming loans. The bank loaned an additional $20.5 million to women from its own resources. Several of the beneficiaries reported significant benefits including higher sales and employment.

For Advisory Services, of 20 projects, 14 were combined with investments, with mixed results. In addition to the Nigeria project described above, there were similar projects implemented in Cameroon, Tanzania, and Uganda. In Tanzania, traditional BDS and technical assistance support was complemented by a $5 million line of credit as well as some innovative services. The project exceeded output and outcome targets, expanding the portfolio from 24 to 178 loans.

In Uganda, although results achieved were satisfactory, the project experienced delays from high staff turnover and then a restructuring of the bank, requiring a project extension. The remaining projects were not combined with investments. IFC Advisory Services knowledge products have helped to inform other projects supporting the growth of women's businesses by analyzing regional trends and best practices while other projects combined technical assistance and BDS to banks but were not linked to investment. For example, in the Democratic Republic of Congo, 40 staff of a client bank were trained on customer service to women entrepreneurs and 562 women were trained in business skills using IFC's Business Edge.

SOURCES: IEG portfolio review; IFC 2012c.

TABLE 2.2 IFC Investment Portfolio Evaluated (FY06–12) by Category—Percent with Satisfactory Development Outcome

TSME Classification	Number with Rating	% Successful (DO)
Targeted SME	92	59
Rest of FM	122	69
Rest of portfolio	263	73
Total	477	69

SOURCE: IEG portfolio review.
NOTE: Successful denotes a "moderately satisfactory" or a "satisfactory" or a "highly satisfactory" rating. DO = development outcome; FM = financial markets.

INVESTMENT PORTFOLIO EFFICACY

To gauge the efficacy of the TSME portfolio, the evaluation team reviewed all IEG-evaluated projects that were evaluated between 2006 and 2012. TSME projects generally had a lower rating than the overall portfolio and a lower rating than the rest of the financial markets portfolio (Table 2.2). However, when broken down by time period, targeted SME projects approved since 2006 performed better than those approved earlier. Sixty-seven percent of financial market projects evaluated 2010 to 2012 were rated successful, a significant increase from the 50 percent that were rated successful between 2006 and 2009.

Not surprisingly, development effectiveness varied substantially depending on product line, industry group and country type (Figure 2.6). Based on IEG ratings, the most successful category of project in the targeted SME portfolio was on-lending to commercial banks, with a 71 percent success rate, followed by leasing (50 percent) and funds (47 percent). Direct investments in SMEs had the lowest success rate—25 percent—in part because they were more concentrated in low income countries. By industry group within the targeted SME investment portfolio, financial markets were by far more successful (62 percent) than MAS (38 percent). However, in a regression controlling for such characteristics as income level and fragile and conflict-affected status, some of these categorical differences in development outcomes lost their statistical significance.

Within the TSME portfolio of projects committed 2006–12, 262 projects are entirely targeted (68 percent) and 122 have a substantial component that is targeted. About 13 percent of TSME investment projects specifically include microenterprises as intended beneficiaries—the rest do not.[6] For projects with a TSME component it is possible for the component and the

FIGURE 2.6 IFC Investment Portfolio by Product Line—Percent with Satisfactory Development Outcome (evaluation FY06–12)

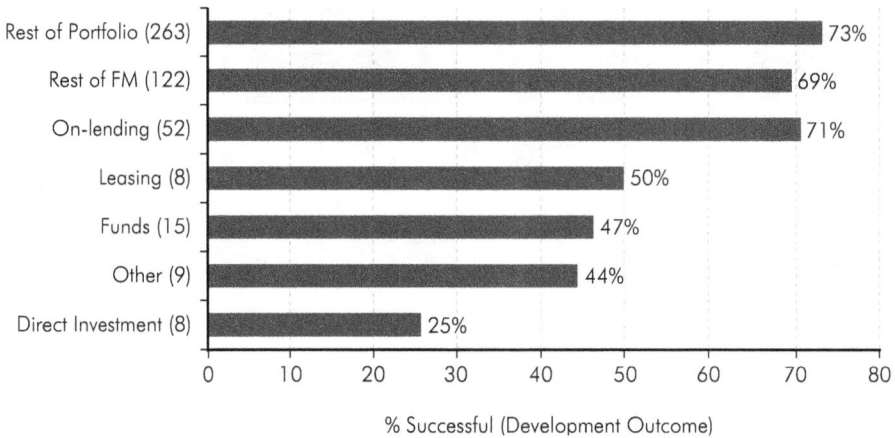

SOURCE: IEG portfolio review.
NOTE: Successful denotes a "moderately satisfactory" or a "satisfactory" or a "highly satisfactory" rating.
FM = financial markets.

project to perform differently. For example, within the body of IEG-evaluated TSME projects, of 52 that "reached SMEs," 37 (71 percent) had successful development outcome ratings and 15 (29 percent) had negative IEG development outcome ratings. Of these 15, one-third were direct investments in SMEs. By contrast, of nine projects with unsuccessful development outcomes, four succeeded in reaching SMEs.

One example of how components can perform differently from overall projects can be seen in an IFC project with a Russian bank project. Although the project received a positive development outcome rating, the share of SMEs in the Bank's portfolio plummeted over the life of the loan. IEG's evaluation found that the goal to expand the SME client base was not achieved. By contrast, a project in Vietnam rated as mostly unsuccessful was acknowledged by IEG as succeeding in reaching SMEs, allowing more individuals and enterprises to reach financial services and resources necessary for business development.

ON-LENDING On-lending to SMEs through financial intermediaries constitutes the lion's share of value of IFC's TSME investments. According to its SME Banking website:

> IFC works to increase access of SMEs to financial services in developing countries by providing funding for equity, loans, and mezzanine finance to financial intermediaries focusing on SME financing, and by building capacity of financial intermediaries and raising awareness on best SME Banking practices. IFC uses both investments and technical assistance to support financial intermediaries outreach to the SME sector more effectively and efficiently.

For SME loans, IFC collected two indicators from banks it financed: nonperforming loans, which it collects for all bank finance, and SME loans, generally defined as loans of less than $1 million. The latter indicator is used both as a "Reach" indicator to monitor how many SMEs its investments in financial intermediaries are reaching and as a development effectiveness indicator in the DOTS. These reach data provide a potentially useful measure of the extent to which IFC clients are reaching SMEs and the extent to which, through them, IFC is also reaching SMEs. IEG notes that it would be even more useful to know (i) the exact characteristics such as sales, assets and employment of the borrowing firms and changes in those characteristics before and after receiving a loan; and (ii) some counterfactual information by which the impact of IFC's SME financing could be judged, including the trend in financed bank portfolios prior to SME financing, the performance of comparable banks that did not receive IFC financing, the trend in SME loan beneficiary performance prior to receiving IFC-supported financing, and the performance of comparable SMEs that did not receive IFC-supported financing.

IEG analyzed these reach data for recent years with the intention of learning the extent to which the data provide insight into the outcome of targeted SME interventions as observed in client loan portfolios. A first look at the data summarized all clients for which there are data for the years 2010 and 2012. Although the reach data are available for several years, the number of clients reporting has increased in recent years, and this, combined with a decision to avoid the worst years of the financial crisis, led to a decision to examine changes in client portfolio composition over the period 2010–12. This produced a sample of 111 clients, divided between those with targeted projects (76 clients) and those without targeted projects (35 clients).

During this period, clients with targeted projects were somewhat less likely to produce nominal increases in the size of their SME portfolio than clients with non-targeted projects, although both groups saw increases for a majority of clients: 66 and 71 percent, respectively. Note, however, that 34 percent of targeted clients experienced a nominal decline in their SME portfolios over this period. The average growth rate for the nontargeted banks' SME portfolios was 24 percent, nearly double the value of 13 percent growth for the targeted banks' SME portfolios, although the two values are not statistically different.

Targeted clients were also less likely to produce growth in their SME portfolio in excess of the growth in their non-SME portfolio—that is, an increase in the share of their portfolio that is SME. The relative share of SMEs in the portfolio declined for 63 percent of targeted clients, compared to 51 percent of nontargeted clients. Moreover, targeted clients were slightly more likely to experience a nominal decline in their SME portfolio even when there was nominal growth in the overall portfolio.

These results hold generally for the period 2009–11 as well. IEG also reviewed summary statistics for the size of the SME portfolio relative to the total loan portfolio for projects committed in 2010. That review showed that in the two years following commitment, the nominal size of the SME portfolio remained nearly constant for the 22 targeted clients that had targeted projects committed in FY10, but the SME portfolio declined relative to the total portfolio (from 22 to 19 percent). Only 4 of the 22 clients experienced a relative increase in their SME portfolio over the period. In conclusion, the Reach Data examined during the period 2010–12 do not provide support for the idea that SME-targeted projects produce an increase in the recipient's SME portfolio that is distinguishable from the impact of non-targeted projects on non-targeted clients. The one exception is among a small group (7) of microfinance institutions, where support to help them "scale up" to SMEs is more clearly associated with absolute and relative increases in their SME portfolios.

Although this evidence is not positive, it is possible that IFC is focusing its lending on banks that would otherwise do little for SMEs and improving on a poor base. The most important conclusion is that when there are monitoring data like this, it should be used to signal problems and adjust the program to improve its efficacy.

As one example, IFC began its relationship with a mid-size Brazilian bank in 2006 to help the bank expand its SME lending business. Although the number of bank borrowers surpassed established targets, and despite IFC's significant engagement with the bank through a combination of equity investments, loans, and trade finance guarantees, DOTS indicators show the number of SME borrowers declining every year since 2008 at an average rate of 33 percent. And as noted, IFC's experience with the Russian bank provides a second example of a shrinking SME loan portfolio.

For this evaluation, IEG reviewed 82 IFC investment projects that sought to support SME through financial intermediaries (banks, funds, and financial service companies). Of these, around 40 percent (33 projects) did not meet their SME financing targets. Projects fell short of expectations when the SME portfolio decreased in size; the SME portfolio increased in size but had fewer clients (which means larger clients); or the increase in SME financing fell short of targeted portfolio increases. The two primary reasons identified in the closing evaluations for projects falling short of expectations were the macroeconomic environment and the financial intermediary changing its strategy. Banks were especially prone to strategic changes. Funds, by contrast, often did not meet expectations because they could not meet their fundraising targets.

Equally problematic in gauging efficacy is the secrecy surrounding the clients of banks supported by IFC. It is, therefore, unclear what impact these investments are having at the firm level and, in spite of its importance as a share of the total portfolio, there has been no attempt to assess impact through a systematic study. IFC officers with whom IEG spoke in headquarters and the field visits said that demanding any more information through banks would be too imposing and deter the banks from doing business with IFC. However, studies conducted by IFC and lending programs at other institutions suggest that it is possible to gather such information. For example, in IFC's gender baseline study (Khodakivsk 2013), IFC was able to obtain specific information, including employment data, from 3,100 firms that received SME loans from 34 banks in 25 countries. Additionally, the European Investment Bank requires its clients to grant it access to data on subborrowers, including employment and sales, and access to the subborrowers directly for monitoring and evaluation (M&E) purposes.

FUNDS Between FY06 and FY12, IFC invested $1.4 billion in 70 TSME funds. According to IFC's 2012 funds strategy, investments in small businesses foster the creation of new industries and promote job growth in frontier regions. In addition, the strategy states that growth equity funds that invest in SMEs as part of a diversified portfolio have better returns and development impact than funds exclusively focused on SMEs. South Asia and Sub-Saharan Africa host the most projects overall, with India alone hosting 15 IFC-financed funds. In addition, about 43 percent of the regionally focused funds (which spread risk across a group of countries) can be found in Sub-Saharan Africa. IFC often participates in the funds' advisory or investment committees and provides advice to the funds' managers.

Fifteen TSME fund projects were evaluated between FY06 and FY12. These invested more than $1 billion in 196 companies, with investments ranging from $100,000 to $2.2 million. Of these projects, seven were successful. The most commonly identified factors of success include the fund's focus on its SME strategy (six projects); the successful transfer of knowledge and development of management and corporate governance to investee companies (five projects); and project impact on private sector development (four projects). Overall, however, TSME fund projects were less successful than non-TSME funds and performed worse over time.[7]

LEASING IFC has identified leasing as a "powerful product to provide SMEs with much needed term-financing to invest in productive and logistic equipment" (http://www.ifc .org/wps/wcm/connect/Industry_EXT_Content/ IFC_External_Corporate_Site/Industries /Financial+Markets/MSME+Finance/Leasing/). Leasing obviates the need for collateral, which is a common constraint to SME finance, as the leased asset itself acts as collateral. Leasing comprises 8 percent of the number of TSME investment projects and 5 percent of commitment value.

As noted, of eight leasing projects evaluated by IFC between 2006 and 2012, half succeeded in achieving their development objectives. IEG found an example of a leasing project in the Nicaragua case study, where IFC had successfully financed the start-up of a leasing company. IEG rated the investment as moderately satisfactory. Unfortunately, an earlier IFC project to establish a legal framework for leasing had not resulted in new legislation or regulations (and IEG rated its development outcome as unsuccessful). After the IFC projects concluded, and in the absence of a supportive legal framework, the company found difficulties enforcing leasing agreements. By the time of IEG's country visit in early 2013, it was winding up its leasing operations. This points to a broader challenge of appropriate sequencing of advisory work and investment.

INVESTMENTS EFFICIENCY

The main efficiency concern for IFC's TSME investments is whether its strategy of working with individual banks is the most efficient method of addressing systemic problems in countries' financial sectors, given that the magnitude of IFC financing is nothing close to the estimated gap in SME financing. Therefore, efficient use of IFC's limited resources would focus on building sustainable and competitive commercial financial markets that serve SMEs, focusing on markets that are underdeveloped and poorly served.

Another challenge is the potentially distortionary effect on markets that IFC may have if it is "crowding out" private actors in reasonably functioning financial markets. It is not always clear whether IFC's financing is priced at or near the market, as it often offers credit on a longer-term basis. If it is priced below competing sources of finance, it has the potential to distort markets and subsidize favored partners or clients, giving them a competitive advantage.

For example, an officer of a major donor in Kenya charged with financial sector work stated that his agency does not engage in SME finance, because IFC and several other donors were supplying the market with financing below the market rate. In Indonesia and Kenya, IEG met with management at banks who said they could have financed their SME portfolio from alternative sources, but preferred the terms of IFC financing (as well as, in some cases, the reputational benefits offered by working with IFC).

Additionally, with regard to product standardization, IFC designed and implemented successful standard business models, which contributed to operational economies of scale in delivery. In some cases, however, products may not have been sufficiently tailored to country conditions and client needs. For instance, instruments used for first-tier banks in well-developed financial markets are unlikely to be successfully replicated for noninvestment grade banks in poorly developed financial markets (or vice versa).

BOX 2.5 DOTS Challenges for Tracking SMEs

DOTS plays a potentially vital role in monitoring and evaluating the reach of IFC investment activities. It provides a unique source of timely and consistent monitoring data. It does this by reporting on an annual basis selected indicators of reach at the project and client level, without assessing the extent to which changes in those indicators over time were a direct result of IFC investment activities. In the case of targeted SME investments in the financial sector, their "reach" is monitored by annual reports of the amount of the client's loan portfolio consisting of individual loans of less than $1 million. (In a few countries, the threshold used is $2 million.)

To assess the extent to which TSME projects succeed on the basis of DOTS indicators, IEG examined a sample of all bank clients in three countries: Brazil, Egypt and Kenya. The analysis included a review of the data provided in DOTS, how actual results compared with baselines and targets, how those data compared with DOTS ratings, and how the DOTS data compared with reach data reported elsewhere. The analysis revealed the following:

There is no consistent correspondence between the DOTS SME loan data and IFC reach data, although they have the same title and appear to come from the same sources. In some cases the two databases simply disagreed; in others there were data in one source but not the other.

Although a number of projects were "Not Rated" in DOTS (in some cases because it was too soon to tell), the DOTS ratings that exist do not appear to be consistent with the reported data and the reported target. For example, a Brazilian client was rated as having achieved its SME target when the DOTS data report an actual decline in the level of SME lending by the client.

Also, SME lending ratings in DOTS are not always important components of the overall project ratings reported in Expanded Project Supervision Reports. The broader portfolio review noted two projects, one in Croatia and one in Russia, for which the client actually reduced its SME lending, but where the overall project assessment in the reports was mostly satisfactory. For a TSME project, it is difficult to understand how these projects can be regarded as successful when their objective has been defined as expanding lending to SMEs.

The recent IEG Biennial Report on Operations Evaluation (IEG 2013a) pointed to systemic challenges for the DOTS in tracking on-lending. First, short-term finance projects are not covered at all in the DOTS results framework. Second, IFC generally lacks information on final beneficiaries, and substitutes with "proxy" measures—specifically, loans of under $1 million in value. This report observes that

continued on page 60

INVESTMENT PORTFOLIO WORK QUALITY

In general, IEG found that clients, especially bank clients, were happy with the professional quality and high standards of IFC. In some cases, the dedication of individual staff or teams in adapting products to specific project needs was seen as critical to a successful outcome. In client interviews, IEG heard specific compliments about investment officers who had put in extra effort and long hours to meet the needs of the client. Nevertheless, there are multiple dimensions of work quality that could be strengthened:

• Weakness in the project preparation, especially the failure to use evidence to show a need for IFC's interventions, in defining SMEs, and in presenting a credible model of how the project addresses needs and represents a sustainable solution to the identified market failure.

• Weaknesses in tailoring global products to local needs.

• In spite of the increasingly well-developed DOTS, a systematic weakness in collecting indicators to gauge whether projects are achieving their stated development objectives (see Boxes 2.5 and 2.6).

• Failure to use information collected to "correct course"—as exemplified by the data suggesting that, in many cases, SME on-lending is not increasing SME access to loans, and evidence that the Global Trade Finance Program (GTFP) (Box 2.7) is serving SMEs to a far smaller extent than has been indicated.

To better understand the ways that work quality may influence development outcomes in IFC's TSME investment portfolio, IEG conducted a regression analysis of projects evaluated between 2006 and 2012 to identify factors associated with better outcomes. The analysis revealed that, controlling for a variety of factors, development outcome is significantly related

Excepted from *Results and Performance of the World Bank Group 2012:*

[T]he wholesaling approach poses several challenges. First, measuring the development results of financial sector projects, in particular those involving wholesaling of IFC funding via a financial intermediary, is inherently difficult. This is because IFC and MIGA have no relationship with, access to, or often even knowledge of the companies or microenterprises that are borrowing or leasing from the financial intermediary. . . . Moreover, the level of funding provided by IFC (or insured by MIGA) relative to total assets of the intermediary, and the fungibility of funds, means that the intermediary's sub-portfolio can, at best, be only notionally attributed to IFC or MIGA intervention.

Second, IFC and MIGA need to rely on financial intermediaries to adopt and implement policy mandates that are aligned with those of the Bank Group in their choice of sub-borrower and to apply rigorous safeguards. However, there is inevitably less control afforded to IFC, and therefore little assurance that an intermediary is addressing the real development needs of the country. . . . MIGA financial sector projects rarely carry any requirement for reporting on how the MIGA-insured shareholder loan was deployed and who the end beneficiaries are. . . .

Above all, it is essential that both IFC and MIGA seek a deeper understanding of the development impact of financial sector projects and use such knowledge to calibrate their intervention strategies. This, in turn, will call for indicators that can measure effects beyond the financial intermediary itself and gauge development progress among its clientele.

SOURCE: IEG 2013b.

to longer length of project in years (which ranges from three to seven years from commitment to evaluation), often a feature of project design. Additionally, IEG found that projects in upper-middle-income countries received better ratings for project supervision, adequacy of technical design, and adequacy of risk assessment.[8] This suggests that development outcomes for TSME projects can potentially be improved by strengthening the technical design of projects, more active engagement in project supervision, and better risk assessment.

IFC Advisory Services for Targeted Support to SMEs

IFC's Advisory Services have been transformed in the last decade from a weakly standardized set of products to a narrower and far more standardized business line. The business practice continues to undergo dramatic changes as part of the change process in the World Bank Group. During the portfolio review period, IFC launched 272 TSME advisory projects

BOX 2.7 Is the GTFP an SME Program?

IFC's Global Trade Finance Program (GTFP) offers confirming banks partial or full guarantees to cover payment risk on banks in emerging markets for trade-related transactions. It intends to expand trade finance by providing risk mitigation in new or challenging markets where trade lines may be constrained.

Although this financing is open to firms of all sizes and therefore does not constitute targeted SME support, IFC has often portrayed this program as primarily aimed at SMEs. In its 2012 annual report, IFC states that 80 percent of trade finance guarantees benefit SMEs, based on the percentage of transactions it guarantees that are worth less than $1 million.

For several reasons, IEG finds that it is incorrect to portray GTFP as an SME finance program. First, as noted in a recent evaluation (IEG 2012), these 80 percent of transactions comprise only 23 percent of the volume of guarantees. Second, the proxy of $1 million has never been tested for trade finance or for any type of working capital finance, so there is no evidence of any correlation of this proxy to SME status. Third, there is a great deal of counter-evidence to the current way of counting SMEs. In case study countries examined in the GTFP evaluation, it was relatively easy to find large firms associated with GTFP financing of less than $1 million. Further, because IFC tallies an SME loan for each transaction under $1 million and some firms finance multiple transactions through GTFP, there are numerous instances of firms whose total volume of GTFP financing would exceed the proxy. In one case, a single large firm had financed nine transactions under GTFP, seven of which were counted as SME by IFC.

This raises an additional concern about the counting system—that there were firms counted by IFC as both SMEs and non-SMEs. In Brazil, 46 percent of "SME" transactions were undertaken by firms that also engaged in non-SME transactions, and 37 percent of alleged "SME" clients turned out to be simultaneously classified as non-SME clients by virtue of larger transactions. Looking at several of the case study countries it is clear that the $1 million proxy is particularly subject to error in middle-income countries.

A more accurate approach would be to develop and test proxies for working capital adapted to country characteristics, to better differentiate the size of firms, as well as to count the total value of transactions by a given firm. However, this is also potentially problematic, as there is substantial evidence that large firms are interested in financing small trade transactions, and client banks maintain an interest in financing large firms. Thus, considerably less than 23 percent of the volume of guarantees goes to SMEs.

Country	% of SME Transactions Where Client Is Both SME & Non-SME	% of SME Clients Reported as Both SME & Non-SME
Afghanistan	0	0
Brazil	46	37
Kazakhstan	17	16
Kenya	10	8
Mozambique	0	0
Nicaragua	11	8
Romania	29	17
Sierra Leone	2	6
Sri Lanka	2	3
Ukraine	35	31

SOURCES: IEG portfolio review and GTFP records.

(Figure 2.7), representing expenditures of around $170 million (Figure 2.8). Nearly half of those projects took the form of technical assistance to financial institutions and governments. Of these, 74 percent (99 projects) provided advice to financial institutions, 18 percent provided advice to governments, 4 percent to both, and 4 percent provided advice to other relevant institutions. About a quarter of the projects related to business development services (BDSs); nearly another quarter was for linkage products, often focused on upgrading production of suppliers to large firms.

Advisory dollars were focused largely on poorer countries (IDA and IDA blend), and 40 percent of expenditures took place in Africa. Fifty-one percent of expenditures focused on small business advisory activities, 36 percent on access to finance, and 12 percent on investment climate reforms targeted at SMEs.

Advisory Services projects often offer a mix of several related product lines. The most prevalent in the FY06–12 TSME portfolio are within the Access to Finance and Sustainable

FIGURE 2.7 IFC Advisory Services, by Expenditure Value ($ millions)

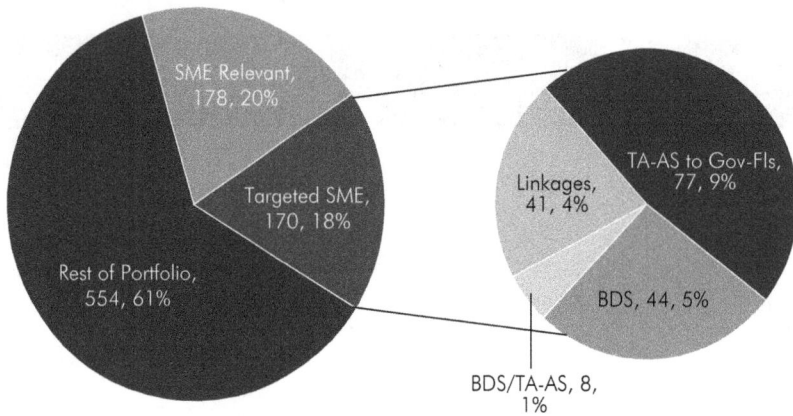

SOURCE: IEG portfolio review.
NOTE: BDS = business development service; FI = financial institution; TA-AS = technical assistance – advisory service.

FIGURE 2.8 IFC Advisory Services, by Number of Projects

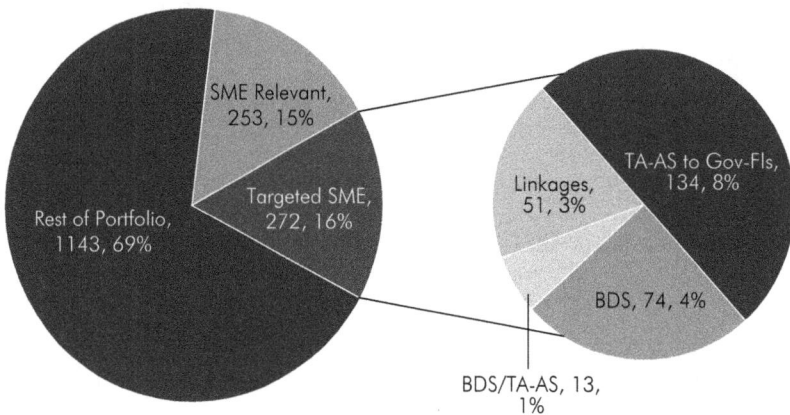

SOURCE: IEG portfolio review.
NOTE: BDS = business development service; FI = financial institution; TA-AS = technical assistance–advisory service.

Business Advisory business lines, more specifically the "SME Banking" and "Farmer and SME Training" product lines (Figure 2.9). These two product lines are present in 30 percent of the 272 TSME projects; the rest are each present in less than 10 percent of projects.

In many cases, Advisory Services projects focus on interventions that aim to benefit firms of all sizes, though they may disproportionally benefit SMEs. In some cases, however, otherwise size-blind activities are designed to specifically benefit SMEs. For example, 43 projects contain access to finance product line "credit bureaus," of which 4 are specifically targeted to SMEs. Of these four, one project focused entirely on supporting a credit bureau, and the other

FIGURE 2.9 TSME Advisory Portfolio, by Product Line

By Main TSME Product Lines (top 9)

By Business Line

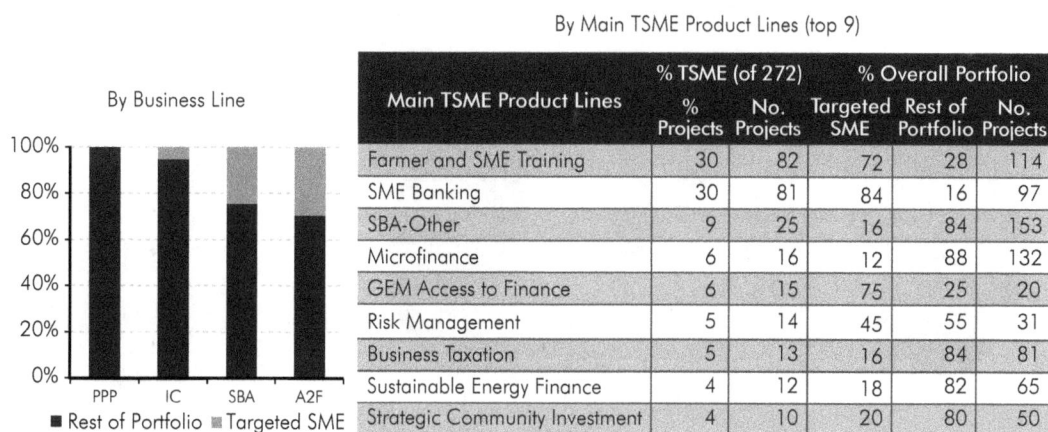

Main TSME Product Lines	% TSME (of 272)		% Overall Portfolio		
	% Projects	No. Projects	Targeted SME	Rest of Portfolio	No. Projects
Farmer and SME Training	30	82	72	28	114
SME Banking	30	81	84	16	97
SBA-Other	9	25	16	84	153
Microfinance	6	16	12	88	132
GEM Access to Finance	6	15	75	25	20
Risk Management	5	14	45	55	31
Business Taxation	5	13	16	84	81
Sustainable Energy Finance	4	12	18	82	65
Strategic Community Investment	4	10	20	80	50

■ Rest of Portfolio ■ Targeted SME

SOURCE: IEG portfolio review.
NOTE: A2F = Access to Finance; GEM = Global Economic Monitor; IC = Investment Climate; PPP = public-private partnership; SBA = Sustainable Business Advisory; TSME = targeted small and medium-size enterprise.

three combined work on a credit bureau with other SME banking activities. For example, in South Africa, an SME banking project aimed to support and accelerate SME lending by working with financial institutions, credit reporting companies and bureaus, and existing BDS providers. Similarly, a total of 81 projects contain the investment climate product line "Business Taxation," of which 13 (16 percent) are TSME. All 13 of these projects combine business taxation activity with other activities such as business regulation (7 projects) and trade logistics (3 projects). For example, in Uzbekistan's SME Policy Development Project IV, business regulation reform accounted for 75 percent of project activities; Business Taxation accounted for the remaining 25 percent.

ADVISORY SERVICES RELEVANCE

Many IFC Advisory Services projects are highly relevant to the countries and conditions where they are delivered, and some of them are also linked in complementary ways to investment projects. In fact, TSME Advisory Services projects achieved slightly higher relevance ratings than the rest of that portfolio (76 percent and 72 percent, respectively). IEG found other projects to be too standardized and neglected to establish their relevance in addressing specific market failures in the country where they were delivered. Although the standard template that IFC staff complete asks them to identify a market failure (before 2011, it asked the "intended development result of the project to address client need/market failure") the advisory work will address, more than half fail to do so (Table 2.3). Of those that do, 78 percent refer to some type of information failure or asymmetry, one project (4 percent)

FIGURE 2.10 TSME Portfolio by Business Line, Region, and IDA Classification, by Cumulative Expense ($ millions)

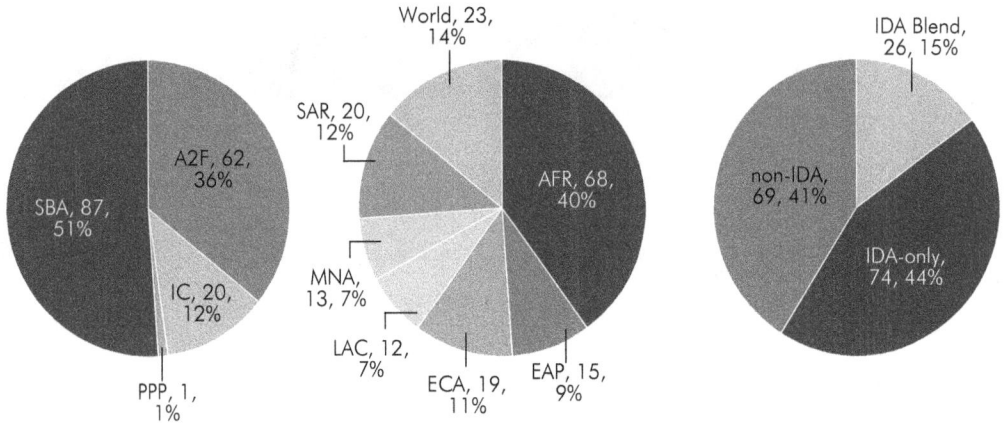

World, 23, 14%
SAR, 20, 12%
A2F, 62, 36%
SBA, 87, 51%
AFR, 68, 40%
IDA Blend, 26, 15%
non-IDA, 69, 41%
IDA-only, 74, 44%
IC, 20, 12%
MNA, 13, 7%
LAC, 12, 7%
ECA, 19, 11%
EAP, 15, 9%
PPP, 1, 1%

SOURCE: IEG portfolio review.
NOTE: IDA = International Development Association. **Business Lines:** A2F = access to finance; IC = investment climate; SBA = Sustainable Business Advisory; **Regions:** AFR = Africa; EAP = East Asia and Pacific; ECA = Europe and Central Asia; LAC = Latin America and the Caribbean; MNA = Middle East and North Africa; SAR = South Asia.

TABLE 2.3 Market Failure Claims in Evaluated Projects Based on Documents of IFC TSME Advisory Projects Closed, FY06–12

Market Failure Claim?	Number of Projects	% Projects
Yes	27	45
No	33	55
Total	60	100
Type of Market Failure		
Information asymmetry	21	78
Noncompetitive markets	1	4
Just claim (no details)	5	19
Total	27	100

SOURCE: IEG portfolio review.

points to noncompetitive markets, and 19 percent claim market failure but do not specify the type. Projects evaluated in 2010 and beyond maintained this trend.

Additionally, country visits suggested that simply identifying the right *type* of advisory service may be insufficient. Some clients complained that certain products were too standardized for their needs. For example, a bank in Kenya said that IFC at first had offered expertise based on Eastern European experience, when the bank sought experts with knowledge of East Africa. Once IFC tailored the advisory program to its needs, however, the client was highly satisfied. Other clients complained that the use of Business Edge[9] was not tailored to their needs or to the sector or context in which it was offered.

Conversely, some of the work with the greatest traction was tailored. The team observed an interesting IFC project in Kenya helping local authorities use small private sector operators to provide clean water. The engagement was designed taking the local factors into account, including the work done by the World Bank. One fascinating product was a highly readable customized training manual for potential private water suppliers, with detailed information on business planning, market research, suppliers, appropriate technologies, and Kenyan regulatory and tax requirements and authorities. It is too early to assess the development outcome of this project, but it was interesting to observe the care and expertise with which the task team configured the project to local conditions.

In addition to projects that were successfully tailored or contextualized, many advisory projects were linked with complementary investment projects (Table 2.4). According to IEG's portfolio analysis, roughly 20 percent of TSME investment projects have accompanying advisory services. Nearly a quarter of on-lending projects had parallel advisory services projects, which often provided advice on aspects of SME lending such as risk and portfolio management. Within the portfolio of on-lending, IEG was able to match 46 advisory service projects to 39 TSME investment clients. The most common form of complementary advisory services was intended to improve or extend a client's MSME operations or strategy (56 percent); fewer projects (22 percent) aimed to assist clients in a new MSME operation or strategy. Interestingly, stand-alone TSME advisory services actually perform somewhat better on average than those linked to investments.[10]

According to IEG's portfolio analysis, advisory services may help establish conditions for project success. TSME investment projects[11] with associated advisory services for the same clients during or after the investment commitment achieved successful development outcomes 76 percent of the time, compared with a 55 percent success rate for projects not accompanied by such services. For on-lending specifically, 79 percent of projects

TABLE 2.4 Parallel Advisory Services Projects

Product Line Summary	Number of Projects	% with Advisory Services
Rest of portfolio	1,128	10
Rest of FM	729	25
On-lending	212	28
Funds	70	0
Direct investment	39	15
Leasing	29	28
Risk sharing or PCG	21	10
Other	13	23
Total	2,241	17

SOURCE: IEG portfolio review.
NOTE: FM = financial markets; PCG = partial credit guarantee.

accompanied by advisory services achieved success, but only 68 percent of on-lending projects not accompanied by advisory services achieved success.[12]

Although this complementarity is looked on as best practice within IFC, it is not always clear whether clients agree to the advisory services project as valuable in themselves or as a means of securing attractive IFC financing. In some cases, IEG found clear indications that IFC's advisory work was an important component of the realignment of the client's strategy toward SME financing. However, IEG also met client bank officials (in Indonesia, Kenya, and Sri Lanka; see Box 2.8) who were primarily interested in IFC's financing and did not give much credence to IFC's advisory work, as they had been in the field of SME financing for several years. In contrast, some IFC staff justified lines of credit as an incentive for banks to follow their advice on portfolio and risk management, E&S standards, or gender or "green" lending. There the question was, if it is only a behavioral incentive, could it not be attached to a smaller amount of financing, for example, would $10 million be sufficient instead of $50 million?

IFC helped a bank in Sri Lanka learn to analyze business profiles of potential SME clients from the details of transactions in their savings and checking accounts. Using the SME Toolkit, IFC trained entrepreneurs and built up the bank's capacity in scenario analysis and in developing a risk management system to help the bank in its thrust to reach out to SME customers. IFC's advisory work helped close gaps in the bank's organization to deal with SMEs, the development of a risk rating system, guidance on pricing and linking the bank's capital requirements to its changing risk profile, and operational details on key performance indicators.

SOURCE: IEG case study.

TARGETED SME ADVISORY SERVICES EFFICACY

Overall, the TSME advisory portfolio has been more successful than the rest of the advisory portfolio (Figure 2.11). When advisory work is well timed and targeted, it can be catalytic in building markets, as it was in Ghana (Box 2.9). However, in low-income countries, targeted SME advisory work is not only dramatically less successful than targeted SME in middle-income countries, but is also less successful than the rest of the advisory portfolio in low-income countries.

In particular, projects in the Sustainable Business Advisory product line (as well as the Investment Climate product line) have proved more successful for TSMEs than for the rest of

FIGURE 2.11 Success Rate of IFC's Advisory Services, TSME versus Rest of Portfolio

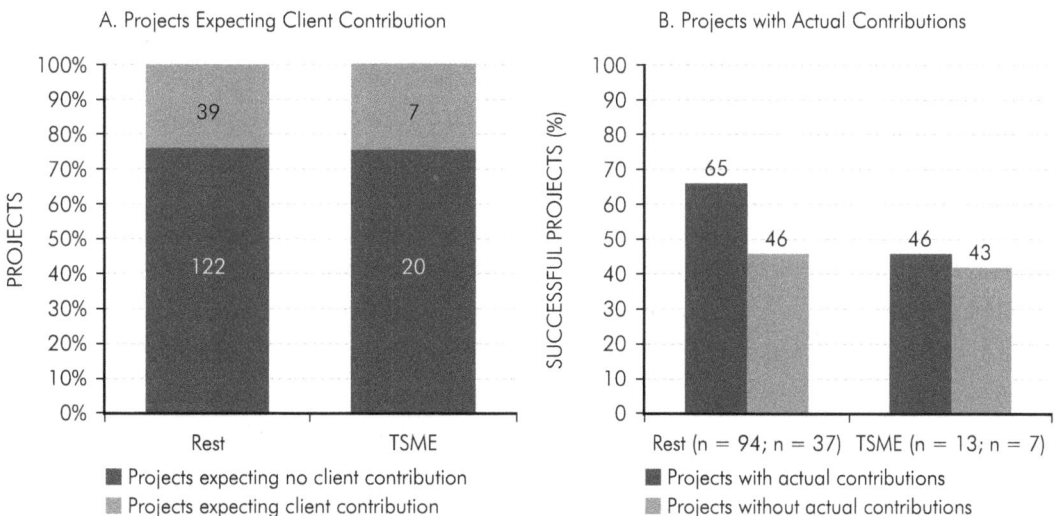

A. Projects Expecting Client Contribution

B. Projects with Actual Contributions

■ Projects expecting no client contribution
■ Projects expecting client contribution

■ Projects with actual contributions
■ Projects without actual contributions

SOURCE: IEG portfolio review.

IFC's technical assistance to Ghana, launched in 2004, was found by IEG to be excellent both in its strategic relevance and IFC's role and contribution. According to the IEG Evaluation Note, IFC was the only player in the leasing space and IFC's role and contribution was essential to the development of leasing that took place. Although some of the targeted legal and regulatory changes did not materialize by the time of closure, there was a dramatic increase in leasing transactions and contracts, and the legislative framework supported by the project could be credited with the creation of 12 new leasing institutions in Ghana and increased investment (including foreign investment) in the leasing business. IFC brought in the United States Trade and Development Agency to support leasing association sustainability.

SOURCE: IEG 2010b.

the portfolio.[13] However, within the Access to Finance line, the opposite pattern is seen, with 61 percent of TSME projects receiving successful development outcomes compared with 70 percent of projects in the rest of the portfolio. By primary product line, TSME projects in Farmer and SME Training, Resource Efficiency, and Gender Entrepreneurship Markets were top performers.

In general, it is very difficult to attribute impact to advisory services, and few are able to demonstrate direct impact. In fact, in IEG evaluations, 93 percent of TSME Advisory Services (and 97 percent of the general Advisory Services portfolio) either had no measurement of impact or no counterfactual or lacked the quasi-experimental or experimental basis to evaluate impact. It is possible that some projects that were too early to judge may later have been subject to some kind of robust measurement. For example, in the Mozambique SME supply chain linkage project, IEG found poor quality data from the client that failed to provide evidence of impact.

TARGETED SME ADVISORY SERVICES EFFICIENCY

Standardization of products brings certain efficiencies from economies of scale and the ability to control quality in a uniform way. In addition, use of highly skilled and well-trained local staff in country offices appears to be a highly efficient way to adapt to local conditions while maintaining quality. At the same time, as already mentioned, if projects are not tailored to local demands and needs, resources may be wasted. Furthermore, as IFC seeks to make its Advisory Services more self-sustaining, it is finding it difficult to make reasonable returns on certain products. In East Africa, for example, IEG was told that the licensing fees being collected for Business Edge were insufficient to cover the cost of the project managers who marketed, distributed, and oversaw quality. In Kenya, an unsuccessful business model for an SME incubator scheme was allowed to continue at a significant loss and without many successful business launches. Meanwhile, in Afghanistan, high marginal costs made the program uneconomic in its early years (see Box 2.10).

As IFC moves to increase cost recovery and assure client commitment to services provided, information on pricing and cost recovery becomes highly relevant. Based on IEG's database of evaluated advisory work, the proportion of TSME Advisory Services projects expecting a client contribution was nearly the same as that for the general Advisory Services portfolio (Figure 2.11a). However, unlike the rest of the portfolio, TSME projects expecting contributions were not substantially more successful than those not doing so (Figure 2.11b). TSME projects were more likely to expect (56 percent) and collect (41 percent) cash fees to be used for the

---

BOX 2.10 Afghanistan Business Edge—Effective, How Efficient?

Relevance: The Business Edge project in Afghanistan aimed to enhance the business performance and competitiveness of Afghan enterprises, especially SMEs. It did so by building the capacity of local training providers to meet the increasing demand for management skills training.

Effectiveness: An impact assessment of Business Edge training found that most participants (91 percent) expressed positive impacts on their company performance; 51 percent were able to increase their revenues, and 25 percent hired additional workers (between 1 and 5).

Efficiency: Although Business Edge was able to establish itself as a good-quality, value-adding training platform for SMEs in Afghanistan, the cost per training seat has been quite high relative to other countries (for example, only $50 per seat in the Republic of Yemen). However, the cost has decreased substantially over the years, from $2,766 during the second year to $149 during the fifth year. The relatively high cost in the beginning of the project is attributable to several factors, including the investment made in the translation of training materials, higher operational costs because of the country's security situation, and the need to identify and build the capacity of trainers in the early stages of the project.

Work Quality: Approximately 32 percent of trainees responding to a quality evaluation identified the need for "better" trainers and improvements in training delivery. It appears that the training providers need more customized training to enable them to better serve MSMEs.

SOURCES: IEG portfolio review, project completion report and IFC commissioned impact assessment.

project than was the rest of the Advisory Services portfolio (35 percent expect, 34 percent collect), but the ratio of actual to expected contributions was lower for TSME Advisory Services.

Country case studies revealed other sources of inefficiencies, such as from insufficient coordination, including with the World Bank. In Kenya, the IEG evaluation team noted that a project with a late entrant to coffee exporting largely repeated work that the World Bank had just completed with the entire coffee value chain (see Chapter 4). Finally, as mentioned previously, without better M&E to provide meaningful indicators of development impact, it is not possible to fully know the efficiency of development projects.

ADVISORY SERVICES WORK QUALITY

IFC has refined its major products to reflect lessons from experience and has strengthened staff training as well. Although work quality has shown signs of improvement—due to more training of staff in the major product lines, improvements in the tailoring of standard products, and greater strategic focus of products—more still needs to be done with regard to providing more tailored advisory services as well as improving M&E.

IEG used a database of evaluated Advisory Services projects to examine the characteristics of successful TSME advisory activities. Overall, TSME Advisory Services were rated lower (51 percent successful) on their design characteristics than the rest of the portfolio (62 percent successful) was. Of TSME Advisory Services projects that were successful, 65 percent clearly stated their objectives with realistic project outcomes and impacts; 52 percent had an appropriate mix of components or activities to achieve their objectives; and 48 percent identified appropriate and committed counterpart or partner. The biggest difference between TSME Advisory Services and the rest of that portfolio (where TSME was better) was in having SMART indicators with indicators with baseline data collected and an appropriate mix of components/activities to achieve components and activities to achieve intended objectives.

Identifying committed counterparts and flexible implementation can help sustain a project through difficult times. One example reflecting this lies in a TSME Advisory Services project in Guinea, which was focused on developing SME linkages in the mining sector by helping build the capacity of local SMEs suppliers (using Business Edge training) and improving mining companies' ability to increase their consumption from such SMEs. Over the course of the project, conflict forced the project team to evacuate three times. Despite this, the project maintained quality services through flexible and creative implementation methods. A key aspect was maintaining effective communications with business service providers, key local partners who took ownership of their consulting relationship with SMEs and continued to carry out their activities in spite of flare-ups.

Similarly, though less pronounced, TSME Advisory Services received slightly lower ratings (67 percent successful) on their implementation than the rest of that portfolio did (72 percent successful). Of TSME Advisory Services projects that IEG rated as successful in their implementation, 43 percent had proactive client engagement and follow-up, 35 percent had good consultant work, and 33 percent encouraged project ownership by keeping local stakeholders engaged. The main differences between TSME Advisory Services and the rest of the portfolio were in the categories: "right mix of local/ international expertise," where TSME was higher, and "results-based project management," where TSME was lower.

In field visits to countries with more developed financial sectors or visits to more sophisticated banks, IEG was often informed that the bank had access to alternative, more tailored advisory services, and there were several instances where IFC's offered assistance had been rejected. Where local staff or their capable local partners had adapted products to local needs, the results were generally superior. Where staff simply pursued volume or replication through standard approaches, results sometimes suffered. Positive examples include:

- In Sri Lanka, Business Edge was used by a local Chamber of Commerce to inform businesses about the best practices from Colombo. Participants welcomed the opportunity to benchmark themselves against other businesses and appreciated the hands-on business training.

- In Kenya, IFC helped a bank develop a strategy for providing longer-term lending to its existing SME clients, primarily for supporting investments. Although a nationwide credit scoring system is not in place, IFC advisory team helped design a system to integrate the bank's credit scoring models into such a system when it is ready. IFC's advisory work also helped the bank design its due diligence process tailored for SMEs.

- In Sri Lanka, a telecommunications company with national coverage saw the SME Toolkit (an IFC online resource to help SME owners and managers start and grow their business) as a way to transform single prepaid phone card retailers into social entrepreneurs and change agents. The company adopted IFC's program and particularly appreciated the rigor IFC brought to establish baselines and define treatments and its use of control groups.

- In Afghanistan, farmers and SMEs in the green raisin and pomegranate food value chains lacked basic knowledge on best practice and therefore were generating very low incomes. IFC conducted a successful 10-month pilot project on production designed to enhance the performance of a group of SMEs in terms of product quality, productivity, sales, and export growth. The aim was to create a sustainable, long-term comparative advantage in these two key exportable goods. Given initial success, a second project was designed and implemented. This project also met or exceeded its planned objectives. Specifically, it identified two markets for fresh and processed products, improved the operations of three SMEs, helped farmers build new drying houses, trained more than 1,475 (goal was 1,200) farmers, and established the planned extension worker association.

However, when staff design projects that do not have sufficient adaptation or that use less capable local partners, results can fall short of expectations. Examples include a case where IFC staff had to thoroughly rethink their approach to a Kenyan bank on advisory services (noted above), quality problems of delivering Business Edge in Afghanistan (see Box 2.10), and a case encountered in Irian Jaya, where a partner company reported to IEG that it threw out large parts of the standard SME Toolkit/Business Edge-based curriculum and worked with IFC to develop more relevant material to the local SMEs it was training.

In other cases, it appears the advisory services needed to engage local stakeholders better to have more impact. An advisory project to support the introduction of a warehouse receipts project in Indonesia that IFC took over from a major donor was undertaken based on IFC experience with the product in Eastern Europe. Unfortunately, the Indonesian banks pulled out of commodity financing because of ambiguities in the local laws. In spite of a fresh framework law and regulations, major commodity players and banks remained skeptical about the product and it did not take off. Thus the technical advisory work had no impact. In Nicaragua, IFC's advisory work on a leasing law failed to win over the banking community, so a law drafted under the activity in accordance with global best practice was never approved.

Throughout, there were difficulties in monitoring and evaluating impact and performance, even with DOTS. Often, the only impact documented from advisory services was a client satisfaction survey, which did not provide any evidence of developmental impact. Meanwhile, in some cases, the outcomes and impacts of some of IFC's advisory projects were undervalued, as only those benefits that occurred before project closing were captured. In Indonesia, for example, IEG follow-up on two advisory projects suggested that their benefits became apparent after their closure, as the processes they set in motion came to fruition in subsequent years. This suggests a need both for more substantive indicators and approaches to evaluation and a need for a more longitudinal approach to evaluation that establishes the baseline conditions and pattern at the outset, and can monitor outcomes over the expected life of benefits of the activity undertaken. This may not be possible or affordable in all cases, but where IFC maintains a long-term presence, relevant information may be obtainable. The experience with a series of Global Environment Facility (GEF)-financed projects supporting small-scale renewable energy enterprises projects (Box 2.12) suggests that product design can be adapted to incorporate the lessons of evaluation.

BOX 2.11 Ukraine TSME Food Value Chain Advisory Project

In Ukraine, to promote the food processing industry, which had the potential to offset imports of processed food and add value to agricultural exports, IFC undertook an advisory project that worked in conjunction with local retailers and provided food safety training to interested processing companies, many of which are SMEs. The concept originated in 2008, with most training taking place over 2010–12. In the initial phase of the project IFC arranged for training to raise participants to international standards for food safety. Of 17 participants in the initial phase, IEG arranged to interview 6, of which 4 met IFC SME definitions.

Participants were willing to incur what most of them characterized as significant costs, mostly for the training itself, but in some cases for the physical investment needed to comply with international standards. Participants rated the training as either good or excellent. All reported better hygiene and/or food safety following the program.

Five reported that the training provided special benefits, including improved product quality. Four companies thought that sales would have been lower without the program; two thought that employment would have been lower; and one thought that investment would have been lower without the program. Three companies reported increased employment as a result of the project. Three also reported improved productivity and reduced waste. Two reported the introduction of new products as an outcome. Only one company reported a new client as a result of the program, although two reported that the program allowed them to retain old clients. None reported any improvement in access to finance as a result of the project. All of the respondents foresaw further improvements over time arising from the training.

SOURCE: IEG field survey of food value chain advisory beneficiaries in Ukraine.

During the period under review, the World Bank Group provided support for 47 TSME projects that intended to benefit the global environment through the conservation of biodiversity and natural resources and reductions in greenhouse gas emissions (see figure). These projects cover a wide array of topics, including fisheries, tourism, water resources, recycling, agriculture, forestry, renewable energy, and energy efficiency.

Many projects are based on the understanding that SMEs require access to finance and capacity development to confront environmental challenges. They do this by investing in technologies to comply with environmental regulations, increase their use of renewable energy, and enhance their energy efficiency. In communities that exploit natural resources, SME development is sometimes used to generate alternative livelihoods that help preserve ecosystems. In Argentina, World Bank matching grants to SMEs for investments in cleaner production processes and pollution abatement projects help reduce industrial pollution in the Matanza-Riachuelo River Basin. In Ethiopia, IFC is helping coffee famer cooperatives acquire wet mills to reduce water consumption and effluents by 90 percent.

With regard to access to finance, the World Bank Group is most active in financing for energy efficiency and renewable energy, including two GEF projects supported by the World Bank in India and the Pacific Islands; three World Bank projects in Ethiopia, Jamaica, and Tunisia; and 29 IFC projects, of which 13 included technical assistance to help financial institutions develop energy efficiency/renewable energy products. For example, in South Africa, IFC has extended a loan of $7.7 million to support a bank in financing eligible SME energy efficiency subprojects.

In India, a GEF project is providing grants for 500 SME energy efficiency projects. Progress to date has been marginal, with slow implementation for the first three years.

A recent IEG evaluation on climate change (IEG 2010) found that a series of GEF-financed projects supporting small-scale renewable energy enterprises was mostly unsuccessful. These projects suffer from key design flaws, supporting companies with inexperienced management, technology that is not locally known, and products that are inappropriate for the market. However, newer approaches had begun to take these challenges into account.

The review also finds that IFC needs to focus more on projects with the highest potential for energy efficiency savings. IFC's focus on small loans with low CO_2 savings potential. SME finance may not be the most efficient channel for achieving energy efficiency.

CONTINUED **BOX 2.12** SME Projects with Environmental Objectives Supported
by the World Bank Group

The World Bank Group has also provided BDS to support environmental companies. In the TSME portfolio, the Bank Group supported two BDS projects, as well as seven others that combined BDS with access to finance. In Rwanda, the World Bank supported a GEF project with a subcomponent focused on increasing SMEs' participation in the renewable energy sector through an incubation program. As of May 2013, 60 people had been trained. In Sri Lanka, the World Bank was using matching grants and BDS in the tourism sector to support SMEs such as hotels to implement energy savings to achieve a green certification.

Finally, in some countries, the Bank Group supports SMEs to provide alternative income generation opportunities for the poor to protect overexploited natural resources. In West Africa, where fish resources are overexploited, GEF is supporting youth in fishing communities to start up SMEs outside the fisheries sector.

Success Rate of IFC's Advisory Services, TSME versus Rest of Portfolio

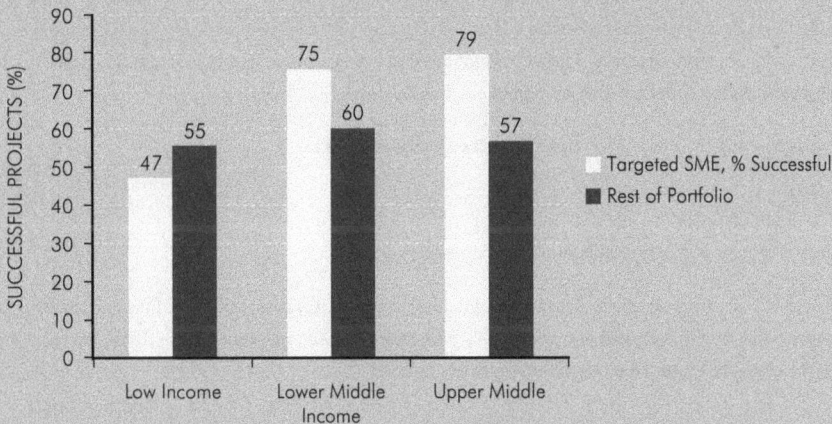

SOURCES: IEG portfolio review.

Notes

[1] The Africa Enterprise Fund, the Small Enterprise Fund, and the Pacific Islands Investment Facility.

[2] Although it is possible that investment officers assume IFC's standard definition of SME will be inferred, IEG did not encounter evidence of any mechanism other than clear definitions and provisions that would hold a client accountable to an unspecified definition. In cases where SME is defined, the variation is so substantial that no standardization can be assumed. Even monitoring uses a proxy rather than any actual measure of beneficiary characteristics, and these monitoring data are apparently not used for project ratings, which limits their value for accountability and learning.

[3] IFC's *Revised Operational Manual for Reach Data Analysis FY13* (IFC 2012b) identifies more than 20 "advanced" developing countries, including nearly half of the world's population, where a $2 million proxy for loan value will be used in place of a $1 million value.

[4] An additional problem is that these data track the client's entire portfolio, whereas IFC financing may be a small part of its capital. It is difficult to deduce the counterfactual—what would have happened without IFC financing—without additional information.

[5] Though the $1 million proxy is used only once, a $500 proxy is used in several other instances.

[6] Based on IEG evaluated projects, there is no significant difference in development outcomes between TSME and targeted MSME projects.

[7] IFC's Chief Investment Officer for Private Equity and Investment Funds Department observes, "Larger companies create significantly more jobs per company at a lower fund investment per job in IDA blend and non-IDA countries. In IDA countries, SMEs and larger companies create a similar number of jobs per company" (Wilton 2012).

[8] Looking only at significant variables [ranges in brackets]: Development Outcome [1–6] = 0.020 +0.408 * length of project in years (3–7) + 0.584 * upper-middle-income country + 0.497 * Supervision [1–4 rating] −0.670 * Inadequate Technical Design [0–1 dummy] − 1.005 * Inadequate Risk Assessment [0–1 dummy]. The R-squared of 0.468 indicates that this model accounts for almost half of all variation in development outcomes.

[9] Business Edge, a branded IFC product, is a classroom-based training program for SME and microenterprise owners and entrepreneurs that uses local trainers to deliver an interactive management curriculum covering multiple subjects, including finance and accounting, human resources, market, operations and management, and personal productivity. It is modular, and different training sessions may offer different combinations of modules.

[10] IEGPE Micro Team Master Advisory Services Evaluative Database 2013.

[11] Evaluated FY06–12.

[12] This difference is greater in TSME projects than for the rest of the portfolio.

[13] This success did not carry over to all regions. In the Africa Region, only 36 percent of TSME Sustainable Business Advisory projects were successful, and in East Asia and Pacific only 33 percent succeeded. Nonetheless, TSME Sustainable Business Advisory in Africa still outperformed the rest of that portfolio in Africa.

References

Cohn, Walter. 2004. "A Synthesis Evaluation of Four IFC-Supported Small and Medium Enterprise Facilities." http://www .ifc.org/wps/wcm/connect/8cd9c4804a9904b6bce6fe9e0dc67fc6/SME_Report-1-27-05%2Bredacted_w_annex .pdf?MOD.

IEG (Independent Evaluation Group). 2013a. *Assessing the Monitoring and Evaluation Systems of IFC and MIGA: 2013 Biennial Report on Operations Evaluation.* Washington, DC: World Bank.

——. 2013b. *Results and Performance of the World Bank Group 2012.* Washington, DC: World Bank.

——. 2012. *Evaluation of the International Finance Corporation's Global Trade Finance Program, 2006–2011.* Washington, DC: World Bank.

——. 2010. *Climate Change Phase II: The Challenge of Low-Carbon Emissions.* Washington, DC: World Bank.

IFC (International Finance Corporation). 2013. *Jobs Study: Assessing Private Sector Contributions to Job Creation and Poverty Reduction.* Washington, DC: World Bank.

——. 2012a. "Interpretation Note on Financial Intermediaries." http://firstforsustainability.org/.

——. 2012b. "Review of IFC's Role in China's Financial Sector Transformation." Summary Note, Washington, DC.

——. 2012c. "Women in Business." Issue Brief. http://www.ifc.org/wps/wcm/connect/bb0b20004d0481febbebfff81ee631cc /IFC-issue-Brief_AM12_Women-and-Business.pdf?MOD=AJPERES

Khodakivska, Alla. 2013. "Establishing a Baseline for Lending to Women-Owned SMEs among IFC-Financed Financial Institutions." IFC Factsheet, Washington, DC. http://www.ifc.org/wps/wcm/connect/d94af5004efbe3b18f07cf3eac88a2f8 /IIIFC_Factsheet_Gender_Baseline_Brief.pdf?MOD=AJPERES.

Wilton, David. 2012. "Guest Commentary: Implications for Job Creation and Achieving Good Financial Returns in Emerging Markets: An Analysis of Private Equity Funds Backed by IFC." http://www.ifc.org/wps/wcm/connect/45ff7f004f1b67e5a8a0eb 3eac88a2f8/IFC+Job+Creation+4Q12+David+and+Wilmot.pdf?MOD=AJPERES.

3 MIGA's Targeted Support to SMEs

CHAPTER HIGHLIGHTS

- MIGA is one of only three political risk insurers offering a special facility and underwriting procedures that support SME investments in developing countries. However, the extent of unmet demand for PRI from SME investors remains unclear.

- MIGA's support to SMEs takes two approaches: direct aid to foreign investors making small investments in SMEs (SIP and regular guarantees); or indirect support through foreign financial intermediaries for their investments in subsidiaries to on-lend to SMEs (wholesale).

- MIGA's support for SME has been substantial during FY06–12 and comprised 45 percent of projects and 21 percent of MIGA's gross exposure.

- SIP projects are each highly relevant to three of MIGA's operational priorities of supporting investments in IDA countries, in conflict-afflicted or fragile environments, and South-South investments.

- The viability of SIP projects is more challenging because of the location of most SIP projects in high risk countries and the inherently riskier nature of smaller firms.

- Despite efforts by MIGA to follow up on SIP projects' E&S requirements, in some cases it did not succeed in bringing projects into compliance with its requirements.

- SIP's streamlined processing of guarantees has not produced efficiency gains in terms of reduced processing time. Feedback from MIGA staff also indicates little savings in underwriting resources compared to regular guarantees.

- MIGA's regular guarantees also offer a means to channel large amounts of political risk coverage to benefit SMEs. However, as applied currently, there is no mechanism to ensure the funds will be used for the purpose stated in the Board document.

- Wholesale guarantees that target SME finance are highly concentrated on a few clients driven by regulatory provisions in their home countries. Wholesale guarantees that target SMEs underperformed relative to a comparable group financial sector projects in terms of business performance, economic sustainability, and contribution to private sector development. In addition, there is no evidence that the long-term tenor was passed on to end-borrowers.

- Overall, the lack of systematic tracking of project performance makes it difficult to determine project results or whether the expected project objectives were achieved.

Rationale

Support to SMEs has its roots in MIGA's mandate to promote foreign direct investment in developing countries. MIGA was established to facilitate the flow of foreign investment to developing countries, and complement (public and private) providers of political risk insurance (PRI) especially in serving clients and markets not served by other providers. Promoting FDI in the SME sector in developing countries was expected to bring important economic (for example, job creation, technology transfer) and social (building local markets and community development) benefits (MIGA 2000). PRI from MIGA was expected to meet the demand for political risk coverage in small projects unavailable from commercial insurers because of smaller premium income, higher insurance and reputational risks, and the larger underwriting resources required for smaller projects (MIGA 2000). These considerations underpinned the inclusion of SME support as one of four MIGA priority areas in the strategy document.[1]

Support to SMEs has not been an explicitly stated priority in MIGA's recent strategies[2] but MIGA has continued engagement with SMEs. MIGA's Strategic Directions for FY05–08 subsumed support to SME investments as an integral part of MIGA's frontier market strategy. Recent strategies do not mention support to SMEs as an operational priority or focus area.[3] However, MIGA has continued to support investments in SMEs through the SIP and its regular (that is, non-SIP) guarantees.

MIGA is one of three[4] political risk insurers[5] with a special facility and underwriting procedures for supporting SME investments in developing countries. There are few options available in the PRI market for foreign investors seeking insurance against noncommercial risks for investments in SMEs. Thirty Berne Union members—the international association of credit and investment insurers—reported the absence of a targeted facility for SMEs, and two members noted their organizations have not covered and have no future plans to underwrite SME investments (Figure 3.1). Among the reasons for the reluctance to support SME investments were: SMEs' limited financial and human resource capabilities to deal with long-term problems associated with overseas investments; the complex structuring of investment insurance products may be less useful to SMEs; and transaction sizes are often too small to generate sufficient premium revenues, especially for private sector insurers.

FIGURE 3.1 Berne Union Investment Committee Members' Underwriting of SME Investments

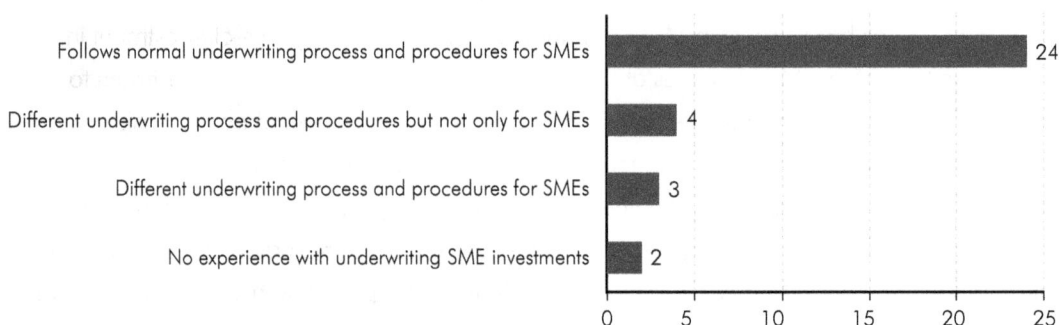

Follows normal underwriting process and procedures for SMEs	24
Different underwriting process and procedures but not only for SMEs	4
Different underwriting process and procedures for SMEs	3
No experience with underwriting SME investments	2

Horizontal axis: 0, 5, 10, 15, 20, 25

SOURCE: Berne Union website, see Berne Union Investment Insurance Committee Spring Meeting. April 23, 2012. "SMEs: Special Opportunities."

Most PRI providers underwrite investments in SMEs according to normal underwriting procedures, though several (four) Berne Union members have a simplified underwriting process that does not limit the streamlined process to SMEs. For the majority of members, SMEs and large projects face the same noncommercial risks and the scale of the investment matters more than the size of the enterprise. Still, the extent of unmet demand for PRI from SME investors remains unclear. It is also difficult to assess whether foreign investors into SMEs in developing countries use other risk mitigation tools such as self-insurance or engaging an experienced local partner or do not insure at all due to cost, lack of information, or lack of interest.

MIGA Guarantee Portfolio Overview for Targeted Support to SMEs

MIGA supports foreign investments into SMEs in developing countries through its regular guarantees and the SIP. MIGA has been supporting SME investments directly through its regular underwriting process since 1991, a year after it issued its first guarantee. The SIP was established in 2004 to support direct foreign investments in SMEs. Project underwriting under the SIP started in 2006. SIP provides a fixed menu of PRI to eligible cross-border direct investments in SMEs using an expedited process while granting a premium subsidy to the investor.

At the same time, MIGA support to SMEs through its regular guarantee program takes two approaches: retail (direct) and wholesale (indirect). MIGA's retail approach consists of providing PRI coverage directly to foreign investors making small investments in SMEs in developing countries that do not qualify for SIP. Through the wholesale approach, it mainly provides guarantees to foreign financial intermediaries for their investments in subsidiaries in developing countries for on-lending to SMEs or for other financial services to SMEs. In another but rarely used model, the guarantee is provided for an investment in a large company with upstream linkages to SMEs.

Approved by MIGA's Board of Directors in March 2004, SIP was established to encourage cross-border investments into SMEs by facilitating access to MIGA guarantees in MIGA member countries in a cost-effective way. The program was initially designed for small and medium investors (SMIs) making investments into SMEs in developing countries but was later expanded to support large investors into SMEs. The project was intended to apply only to relatively simple projects that did not raise environmental or social concerns.

In an effort to reduce transaction costs and streamline procedures, MIGA designed a standardized contract of guarantee that combined coverage against currency transfer restriction and inconvertibility, war and civil disturbance and expropriation and streamlined the underwriting and approval procedures. MIGA Board approval was waived and project approval delegated to the MIGA Director of Operations.[6] MIGA adopted what it describes as standardized, marginal cost basis premium pricing for SIP projects (excluding fixed administrative costs reflected in the pricing for all other guarantees), effectively lowering premium rates compared to MIGA regular guarantee projects. MIGA also waived the guarantee application fee for SIP SMI investors.

SIP was intended for small, "plain vanilla" but highly developmental projects. Guarantees of up to $5 million linked to cross-border investments into SMEs were eligible under the 2004 SIP policy. Although SIP would especially focus on SMEs in the MAS sectors, in practice, the program was open to investors of all sizes and to all sectors. Projects classified as Category A under MIGA's environmental and social policies and investments requiring coverage for breach of contract risk were ineligible under the SIP.

MIGA has adopted IFC's definition of SMEs. The SIP guidelines state that MIGA needs to ensure that investments supported by the SIP meet the SME definition. For investments through financial intermediaries, 50 percent or higher of the borrowers must meet the SME definition under direct investments.

MIGA expanded the program scope but no annual volume targets were set. At the end of the SIP's pilot phase in 2007, MIGA increased the threshold of guarantee amount eligible under SIP from $5 million to $10 million and restricted eligible projects to those within the financial and agribusiness, manufacturing, and service (AMS) sectors only (MIGA 2007). In all other respects, the eligibility criteria remained unchanged, including the definition of SMEs. No restrictions were imposed on the size of the investors or on the overall project amount.

MIGA's SME Portfolio: FY06–12

MIGA's support to cross-border investments into SMEs has been substantial. SME-related projects during FY06–12 comprised 45 percent of the number of projects issued, representing 21 percent of MIGA's gross exposure (Figure 3.2). Projects that directly identified support of SMEs as an objective in the underwriting document accounted for 45 percent of projects. These include projects insured under the SIP and regular guarantee projects that intended to stimulate upstream linkages with SMEs (Figures 3.2 and 3.3). IEG identified targeted projects as those with language in their project briefs that stated that "the project enterprise would contribute to SME development" and/or "the expansion of the SME sector" but excluded those with reference to supporting large firms. In some cases, projects contained targeted components as well as untargeted components. Fifty-seven percent of the TSME projects were underwritten under the SIP, but these account for less than 8 percent of MIGA's gross exposure amount in support of SMEs.

SIP projects account for a substantial share of the number of projects supported, but only a small fraction of MIGA's guarantee volume. Although guarantee coverage to SIP projects is small (2 percent of gross exposure), these projects account for a large number of projects (26 percent of projects) that MIGA underwrote FY06–12. The number of SIP projects supported annually varied (Figure 3.3) over the seven-year period. However, the share of SIP projects has increased over the last three years: 17 percent in FY10, 24 percent in FY11, and 26 percent in FY12.

FIGURE 3.2 MIGA Portfolio, by Number of Projects and Gross Exposure Value ($ millions), FY06–12

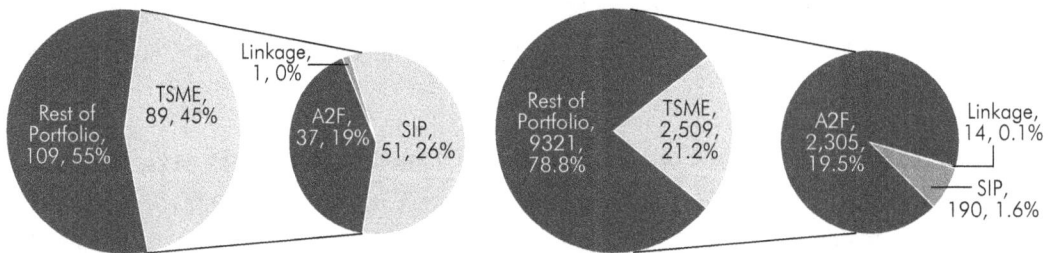

SOURCE: IEG portfolio review.
NOTE: A2F = access to finance; SIP = Small Investment Program.

FIGURE 3.3 MIGA Portfolio Trend, by Number of Projects Approved

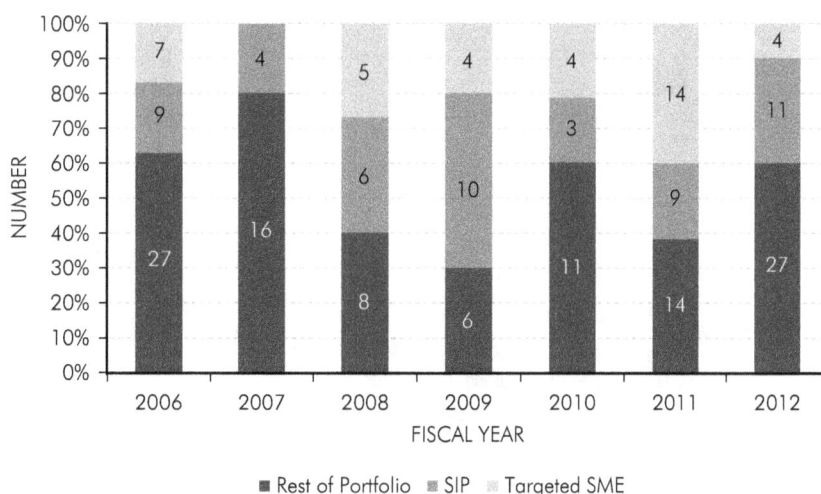

SOURCE: IEG portfolio review.
NOTE: SIP = Small Investment Program.

SIP Portfolio

The SIP portfolio is diversified within its target sectors by number of projects or by gross exposure (Figure 3.4). The portfolio included investments in development banks, micro-lending institutions, leasing companies, an insurance company and electronic payments companies. Small manufacturing enterprises accounted for 24 percent of the portfolio and included the manufacture of metal parts, tin cans, PVC pipe, polypropylene containers, polyethylene terephthalate bottles, vegetable oil, and wood chips. Seventeen percent of the SIP projects were in agribusinesses, including wineries, cotton production, cocoa production, fruit juice, and a fisheries project. The SIP portfolio also included 5 hotel projects (12 percent), and the remainder consisted of investments in various service providers (20 percent), including Internet services, data center hosting, cargo screening, automobile inspection, transport services, and truck maintenance (Figure 3.5).

In practice, not all SIP projects have had simple, "plain-vanilla" structures. Twenty-two percent of operationally mature projects reviewed involved privatizations. These included the full or partial privatization of government holdings in hotels, financial institutions, cargo screening and agribusiness. In each case, the investee company qualified as an SME according to IFC/MIGA criteria or involved a financial services company that serves a customer base that is at least 50 percent MSME firms.

FIGURE 3.4 MIGA Portfolio Trend, by Gross Exposure

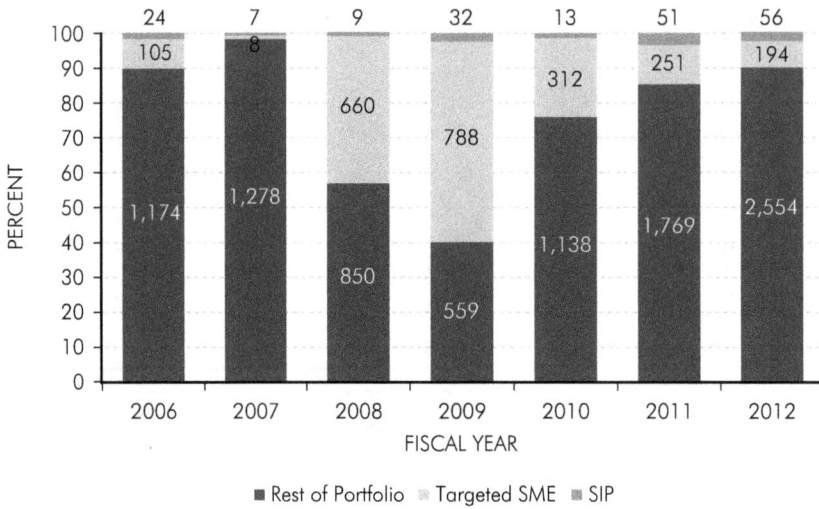

SOURCE: IEG portfolio review.
NOTE: SIP = Small Investment Program.

FIGURE 3.5 Number of SIP Projects, by Sector

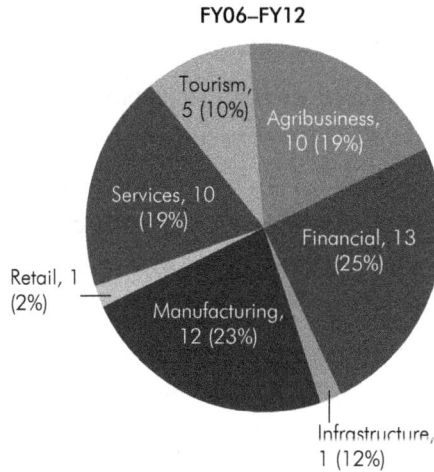

FY06–FY12

SOURCE: MIGA, IEG portfolio review.
NOTE: SIP = Small Investment Program.

RELEVANCE OF SIP PORTFOLIO

SIP interventions are consistent with three of MIGA's operational priorities: investments in IDA countries, investment in conflict-afflicted or fragile environments, and South-South investments. During the FY06–12 period, MIGA insured 52 investment projects under the SIP, of which 63 percent are located in IDA countries, 59 percent in Africa, and 33 percent in fragile and conflict-affected states (see Figure 3.6). Thirty-four percent involved South-South investments. Of the 41 SIP projects supported during the FY06–11 period and reviewed in-depth for this evaluation, 56 percent were relevant to two of three MIGA operational priorities, 22 percent were consistent with at least one of three MIGA operational priorities and 7 percent of the projects supported all three MIGA operational priorities.

Most SIP projects are located in high risk countries that have not attracted substantial FDI or where PRI providers have little presence. SIP has allowed MIGA to support investments in member countries that typically do not attract large amounts of FDI, hence where it was not previously involved. Public and commercial investment insurers have little to no exposure in these high risk countries, which tend to be off-cover for political risk insurers. Examples include Afghanistan, Burkina Faso, Sierra Leone, and Madagascar, among others.

SIP has allowed MIGA to support cross-border ventures by small and medium-size foreign investors. Cross-border investors insured by MIGA through the SIP fall into four types: (i) SMIs investing in SMEs;[7] (ii) private equity funds;[8] (iii) financial institutions investing in bank subsidiaries and financial services companies;[9] and (iv) Large companies or subsidiaries of large multinationals.[10] Sixteen of 41 SIP projects reviewed (39 percent) were investments by SMIs. An additional three initially identified as SMIs turned out to be wholly owned by either large multinational corporations or national development agencies. In eleven projects, the guarantee holders are either wholly-owned by large corporations or government entities that MIGA supported with subsidized premium rates. In another 11 projects, MIGA insured the investments of global private equity funds investing in SME projects.

FIGURE 3.6 Number of SIP Projects, by IDA Status, Region, and FCS Status, FY06–12

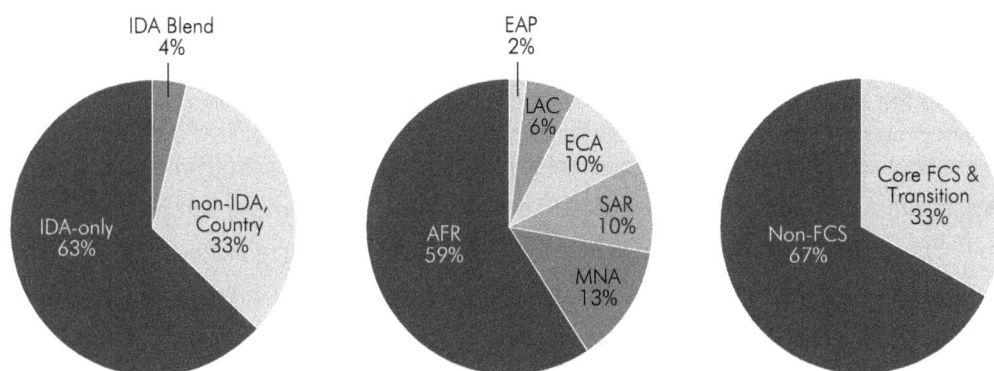

SOURCES: MIGA, IEG portfolio review.
NOTE: FCS = fragile and conflict-affected situation; IDA = International Development Association; SIP = Small Investment Program. **Regions:** AFR = Africa; EAP = East Asia and Pacific; ECA = Europe and Central Asia; LAC = Latin America and the Caribbean; MNA = Middle East and North Africa; SAR = South Asia.

The SIP has been relevant to smaller size projects in AMS sectors typical for fragile and conflict affected states. In some fragile and conflict-affected situations, MIGA's early engagement and focus on projects in these sectors have been relevant to developing small and medium enterprises and consistent with supporting employment and economic growth objectives.

MIGA's contribution to SIP projects is mainly through the provision of PRI and assisting SIP investors in dealing with governments on potential disputes. In at least seven SIP projects, SIP investors requested MIGA assistance in resolving potential disputes between the investors and the host country government. MIGA's affiliation with the World Bank is considered to be one of the agency's comparative advantages for small investors because of their lack of experience and resources in dealing with host governments. In at least four projects, the project sponsors insisted on a MIGA guarantee before they would disburse the funds. In addition, eight SIP projects involve investments by private equity funds that required PRI for their entire portfolio of investments and entered into a master contract with MIGA. These funds cite MIGA PRI coverage as a key part of their cross-border risk mitigation strategies and important to raising and deploying funds in their target markets.

The SIP has only marginally increased MIGA's deal flow to SMEs compared to similar projects underwritten as regular guarantees prior to the introduction of SIP. There is a marginal difference between the number of projects and MIGA's exposure to projects with less than $10 million coverage in the manufacturing, agribusiness, services, tourism and finance sectors under its regular non-subsidized guarantee program before the SIP and those projects issued under the SIP. Forty-seven "small projects" were underwritten under MIGA's regular guarantee program during the period FY99–05, or seven years before the SIP became operational. MIGA provided coverage to 52 projects under the program since the first SIP guarantee was issued in FY06 until FY12 (Figures 3.7 and 3.8). However, the amount of MIGA's exposure to small projects during the seven year period before the SIP's implementation was similar ($193 million) to the exposure to SIP projects over the last seven years ($189 million).

The regional composition of MIGA guarantees to small projects before SIP implementation was somewhat more diversified: Africa—30 percent; Asia—11 percent; Europe and Central Asia—35 percent; and Latin America and the Caribbean—24 percent. Since the SIP's activation in FY06, MIGA has focused more on higher risk countries in Africa and to some extent the Middle East and North Africa, whereas its exposure to Asia, Europe and Central Asia, and Latin America and the Caribbean have declined. In Africa, prior to SIP, MIGA had provided coverage to investments in small projects through regular guarantees in Angola, Guinea, Kenya, Mozambique, Nigeria, Senegal, Tanzania, Togo, Uganda, and Zambia.

FIGURE 3.7 Comparing MIGA Support to SMEs, Before and With the SIP—by Number of Projects

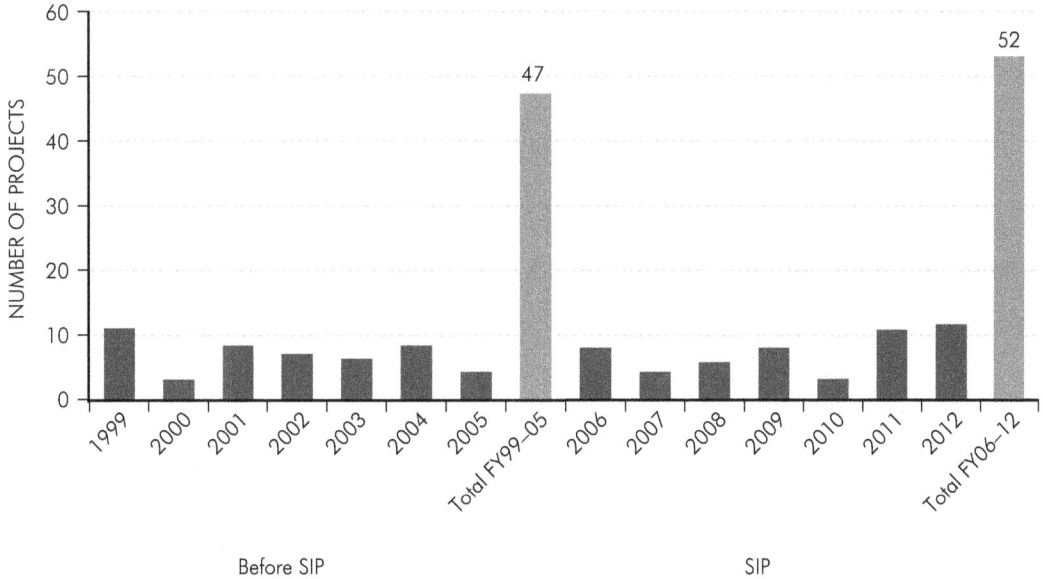

SOURCE: MIGA and IEG portfolio analyses.
NOTE: SIP = Small Investment Program.

FIGURE 3.8 Comparing MIGA Support to SMEs, Before and With the SIP—by Gross Exposure Amount

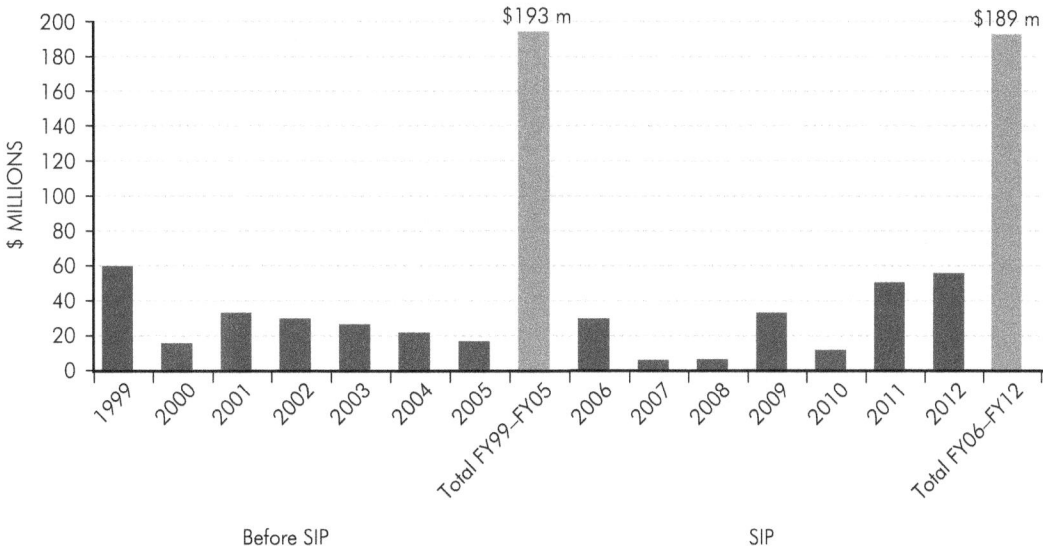

SOURCE: MIGA and IEG portfolio analyses.
NOTE: Includes projects targeting SMEs in the finance, manufacturing, agriculture, services, and tourism sectors with gross exposure of ≤ $10 million. SIP = Small Investment Program.

Employment creation was the primary stated project development objective in nearly three-quarters (73 percent) of the SIP projects reviewed. Estimated employment numbers tend to be under 50 persons, although 12 of the 41 projects expected to hire 50–500 new and temporary employees. For agribusiness projects, potential employment that would be created included a large number of farmers who would benefit from SIP agribusiness projects. In addition, SIP projects were expected to provide new, improved, or expanded services; local training and skills development; government and export revenues; procurement of significant amounts of local goods and services; and, in the case of financial intermediary projects, loans for on-lending or other financial services to MSMEs.

SIP projects have a high potential contribution to local private sector development because they are mostly located in IDA and fragile countries. Although the amount of SIP coverage is typically in the $1 million to $10 million range, the potential upstream and downstream effects as well as demonstration effects are higher. Ex ante, according to IEG's programmatic review, 16 of the 52 SIP projects supported by MIGA had a high potential for contribution to private sector development given host country conditions. Among the 41 SIP projects subjected to in-depth reviews, 12 projects may have wider private sector development effects, either positive or negative, beyond the small investment amounts covered by MIGA. For example, an investment in a privatization of an agribusiness company was insured for $1.5 million, yet the project covered nearly the entire country; an ice-making factory was insured for $1.2 million but the company provides small fishermen in several fishing villages with ice to keep their catch fresh. A mobile payment system, insured by MIGA for $1 million, pioneered the mobile payment system in a country with an underdeveloped banking system. The sponsor of privatized hotel guaranteed by MIGA invested capital and know-how to staff resulting in financial profits, increased hotel occupancy and set high standards of hotel service in the country. MIGA's coverage of the sponsor's equity and debt under the SIP totaled $1.8 million.

Achievement of project development objectives in a majority of SIP projects could not be determined because of the lack of data on project performance. However, two projects had high development outcome (DO) ratings and met their objectives. Only 15 of the 41 operationally mature projects reviewed for this evaluation in depth had information about their development results and performance.[11] The lack of systematic tracking of project performance makes it difficult to determine project results or whether the expected project objectives were achieved. Two SIP projects achieved a successful outcome rating notwithstanding their location in conflict-affected areas (see Box 3.1). These projects had robust business models, sponsors with relevant experience, and considerable upstream

BOX 3.1 Privatizing a State-Owned Hotel in Burkina Faso: A SIP Success Story

In 2007, MIGA provided €2.2 million PRI coverage to the equity investment and corporate guarantees of a Malian hotel developer for the 15-year lease, management, renovation and expansion of Hotel Independence in Burkina Faso. In addition to the sponsor funds, IFC, Banque Ouest Africaine de Développement and Bank of Africa provided loan financing.

Background

The privatization of Hotel Independence was part of the government's efforts to attract foreign private investment to rehabilitate and operate inefficient state-owned assets. Before the group's takeover, the hotel was poorly managed, with occupancy rates as low as 20 percent, and no significant investments or renovations since its construction in 1960. The importance of proper hotel accommodations for doing business in the country's capital Ouagadougou prompted the government to lease to an experienced operator. After refurbishment, the hotel was expected to have 168 upgraded rooms, new restaurants, shops, and a conference center. This was the first hotel to be privatized in the country.

Project Outcomes

Significant progress was made in reversing the long-term decline of Hotel Independence. Renovation was fully completed in February 2009 with 178 rooms, along with conference facilities. The updated rooms and improved general infrastructure and services combined with its prime location in the city center have contributed to the hotel's performance. Operating revenues, margins and gross profits have improved significantly due to increased occupancy rates from 42 percent before the renovation to 78 percent in 2012. Average daily room rates have increased from €56 to €83. Employee productivity also improved because of the positive effect of the performance evaluation system the company introduced. Relationships established with a trade union, a comparable wage structure, and training programs focused on instilling a service and client-oriented environment contributed to improved performance. Customer satisfaction surveys were introduced. Local suppliers benefitted from the revitalization of the hotel, though less than expected.

The sponsor's extensive knowledge gained as an experienced hotel operator in West Africa contributed significantly to performance improvements. Issues of management and staff turnover detract from the project achievements, as does the project's non-compliance with IFC/MIGA's reporting requirements, particularly an overdue life and fire safety audit.

SOURCES: MIGA and IEG.

and downstream benefits for the local economy and invested in improving staff skills and technical knowledge. One project achieved efficiency gains and gained market share over its competitors. The magnitude of employment effects was minimal, but staff earned higher wages and better benefits than local peers and received training on a regular basis to upgrade skills.

Financial and operational difficulties and management weaknesses have hampered the achievement of the SIP projects' development potential. Unsuccessful SIP projects are characterized by financial losses or have not been implemented and therefore did not realize their development potential.

Although SIP projects were mostly located in fragile, conflict-affected countries, these projects also share inherent weaknesses such as lack of financing, management problems, and unrealistic business plans relative to country and market contexts. Twelve SIP projects that had poor results have one or two of the following factors in common. Two of these twelve projects were not implemented, and the others had been experiencing losses since starting commercial operations. One project company folded because of a dispute with the government.[12] Another project also shut down after a year because it had a flawed business model;[13] two other projects received inferior equipment. Two projects faced financial difficulties although their potential to contribute to improved living standards remained high. Two bank projects also experienced financial losses, negative margins, and high incidence of nonperforming loans; and one was in breach of the bank regulator's minimum capital requirement.

The viability of SIP projects is challenging because of the location of most SIP projects in high-risk countries. SIP projects operate under difficult business environments with underdeveloped physical and social infrastructure, governance issues, weak judicial systems, large poor population, low skill levels, and uncertain regulatory regimes—in addition to the high risks small investments face regardless of their location. One-third of SIP projects were in countries that emerged from conflict. Ensuring viability and business success under these circumstances can be challenging. An agribusiness project in a fragile or conflict-affected country could not enforce production and sales contracts signed with local farmers who received free inputs and know-how from the project. Local farmers opted to sell their output to a competitor instead.

But MIGA is required to ensure that the SIP projects it supports would meet its viability benchmark. The SIP Checklist requires that the real sector project must have at least a 10 percent financial rate of return,[14] the threshold for financial viability. At underwriting, MIGA must attest that the project meets this benchmark in the SIP Checklist. IEG's in-depth review of 41 SIP projects showed most project underwriters had ticked the box largely based on sponsor's representation, without indicating the projected financial rate of return or any accompanying explanation of the assumptions.

The weaknesses in the compliance with this requirement suggest both a work quality problem in terms of the underwriting and an efficacy problem of projects from the start. For nine real sector SIP projects the box was ticked to indicate that the projects have at least a 10 percent fiscal rate of return, without having an indication of the estimated rate of return or an explanation of the assumptions. Calculations of the fiscal rate of return also varied, particularly in the projects where MIGA relied on the investor's calculations. The average ex ante estimated rate of return for the remainder of the projects was 30 percent, but this may be an unreliable indicator for the reasons already stated.

The nine real sector SIP projects that have some information on their ex post financial performance also underperformed relative to the expected internal rate of returns. Most of these projects are located in fragile states with weak economies and had steep learning curves. Poor sponsor quality, flawed business models, and management problems also caused financial difficulties. A telecom project in a post-conflict country relied solely on high tariffs extracted from the diplomatic corps and international nongovernmental organizations, but service quality was poor and equipment often broke down because of inferior quality, according to regulators. It continues to hold on to its telecom license even though its clientele abandoned the company in favor of new Internet providers that entered the market. Only one project among this cohort has financial information, indicating that it is viable and generating returns for the investor.

So far, support to private equity funds' (PEF) investments in SMEs under SIP has had mixed results. MIGA supported two private equity funds' planned investments into SMEs under the SIP that made use of a master contract of guarantee to provide coverage to the funds' investee companies.[15] Providing guarantees to equity funds, whose priorities are aligned with MIGA, has the potential of reaching more SMEs efficiently.[16] And with PEFs as partners, MIGA is able to share its portfolio risk.

However, in spite of the fund manager's oversight, partnering with PEFs does not ensure that investee companies will be profitable and sustainable. In the case of a PEF focused on investing in financial services companies in Sub-Saharan Africa, only one among the fund's four investee companies was expanding, and the others faced problems ranging from the withdrawal of the proposed equity investment, cost cutting, to problems with the partial privatization agreement with the government. Another PEF supported by MIGA also had four investee companies, of which only one has the potential to become viable but will take longer than expected. All are struggling financially, and two of the PEF projects have ceased operations. The difficulties of this PEF stemmed mainly from the inexperience of its fund managers in operating a business and the fund's flawed business model.

SIP projects can have big E&S footprint. Four projects may have substantial environmental and social effects although they are SIP projects. These projects also have a high potential for adverse reputational risk to MIGA and the World Bank Group more broadly. Despite MIGA's efforts to thoroughly monitor and follow up with a company on their environmental and social requirements, one SIP project has been the subject of intense national and international scrutiny because of the local investor's adverse conduct and the foreign investor's inability to improve performance of the company.

EFFICIENCY

Minimal efficiency gains came from the SIP streamlined process. The streamlined process was intended to make the SIP cost-effective, enabling MIGA to offer lower premiums. In interviews, MIGA management and staff estimated a 20 percent potential cost savings in underwriting SIP projects because a Board paper and approval are not required.

IEG could not validate the efficiency gains from the SIP projects because MIGA has not provided data on the actual cost of underwriting and managing the program. Thus, the actual cost of underwriting a SIP project or even at the program level could not be determined. Also, interviews with MIGA staff indicated little difference in time and due diligence effort involved in processing SIP projects compared to regular guarantees, despite the streamlined underwriting process. SIP projects need to meet all of MIGA's policies and guidelines including environmental, social, and integrity; investors are often less experienced and information and data are less readily available, resulting in more, not less, intensive underwriting processes. IEG's review of the SIP in 2007 noted that there had been no significant time savings in conducting E&S due diligence, with many smaller investors needing time-consuming support. Even where MIGA attempted to attain efficiencies using master contracts, it is unclear whether savings were realized (Box 3.2). On the revenue side, the average MIGA exposure for a project was $3.24 million, with an average premium rate of 0.9 percent per annum. The average first-year premium for these projects was about $19,000.

SIP projects have a substantial cancellation rate. Of the 41 SIP projects reviewed, 59 percent were cancelled by the investor prior to the full term of the insurance coverage. Of these 59 percent, 45 percent were cancelled by the end of the third year of coverage and 28 percent were cancelled by the end of one year of coverage. Reasons for early cancellation of the SIP guarantees included cost-cutting measures; early repayment of a loan; the sale

MIGA has insured investments into SMEs both directly and through intermediaries through the SIP using two types of investment structures: (i) supporting investments in banking and financial services institutions, which themselves provide financing to SMEs or microenterprises, and (ii) offering a master contract guarantee structure to a private equity fund which then proposes subinvestments for approval by MIGA.

In 2009, MIGA developed the master contract structure to support a private equity fund, to raise risk capital for future investments in East Africa in the banking and information technology sectors. Under the structure, MIGA reviews the Fund's structure and social and environmental processes and provides guidance on MIGA's underwriting requirements. MIGA then reserves political risk insurance coverage capacity, for a fee, and reviews prospective investments proposed by the Fund. Investments must meet MIGA's requirement to be covered under the master contract. This structure has provided greater certainty of MIGA support of the Fund's goals as it raises and deploys capital. This approach has been used under SIP in two instances, totaling eight individual investments.

MIGA's Master Contract for an African Private Equity Firm

A specialty private equity firm in Africa focused on investing in companies within the financial sector with potential for turnaround or growth in certain Sub-Saharan African countries. It sought MIGA's support to raise funds for several planned investments. This modality allows MIGA to partner with an investment company whose priorities are aligned with MIGA's, in this case to promote developmental long-term investment in promising sectors in Sub-Saharan Africa. The master contract originally anticipated MIGA political risk coverage for up to 20 of the firm's planned investments—up to a total of $150 million, but this was reduced significantly later because of lack of investment opportunities.

MIGA insured four of the firm's investments through the SIP underwriting procedure, with a total investment amount of about $11 million. These projects are all related to financial services and electronic payments technology and included investments in a local bank and payment system company in Rwanda, one in an electronic payments card company in South Africa, and an insurance processing company in Kenya. Guarantees to two of the projects were cancelled early by the investor. In the first instance, the proposed equity investment did not proceed because the bank was being privatized. The MIGA coverage financial services project in South Africa was terminated to reduce costs, although the enterprise continues to operate.

continued on page 98

MIGA's Master Contract with an Investment Fund in Africa

In 2009, MIGA entered into master contracts of guarantee with an investment fund to provide coverage of up to $16.2 million to be invested in Sierra Leone. Investment will be made in up to 12 smaller equity investments in agribusiness, fisheries, construction, tourism, light manufacturing, and services SMEs. So far, the fund has invested in two start-up companies, a 100 percent acquisition of a manufacturing company, and a minority shareholding of a fisheries company. MIGA's actual gross exposure under the master contract was $8.6 million, about half of the expected coverage.

At the time of this report, MIGA coverage has been cancelled for all for subinvestments and all four investee companies have had considerable operational difficulties and financial losses. One of the start-up companies had no prospects for recovery and closed. Although the investment climate in Sierra Leone is difficult for any investor, the business model had inherent weaknesses that contributed to the financial losses and difficulties: three of the investments were vertically linked and interdependent for viability; the lack of authority to make decisions and enforce changes as a minority shareholder; and there were management problems.

SOURCES: MIGA project documents; IEG Sierra Leone case study.

of the investee company; financial failure of an investee company; and increased investor comfort with the investment without risk mitigation. Early cancellations compound the issue of cost effectiveness discussed earlier with respect to subsidized premium rates. And although MIGA charges a penalty for early cancellations, that fee is minimal compared to the lost premium income stream from the project, which has a typical tenor of 6–10 years. Generally insurers invest in underwriting up front with the expectation of sustained annual premium payments.

SIP projects have also experienced a number of disputes or pre-claims situations, although less so than MIGA's regular guarantees. MIGA helped resolve potential disputes between the SIP investor and the government. Although it potentially add value for MIGA, attending to requests by clients in settling disputes with the host government also has cost implications. Since FY06, MIGA helped resolve seven pre-claim situations and paid two claims under its war and civil disturbance coverage pertaining to SIP projects.[17] Reasons for the disputes underlying the SIP pre-claims include foreign investor's inexperience or lack of familiarity with host country conditions; small and medium investors' (SMIs') minimal resources and financial margin of projects; weak capacity of the investor to conduct rigorous due diligence and financial planning; and conditions in the host countries.

WORK QUALITY

As noted above, in spite of a streamlined process, SIP projects take MIGA as long to underwrite as mainstream SME projects. A review of the 41 operationally mature SIP projects supported during FY06–11 indicate that it takes 135 business days to approve a SIP project (from the receipt of the Definitive Application to signing of the SIP Underwriting Checklist by the MIGA Director of Operations) or 161 days, from the receipt of the Definitive Application to contract of guarantee signing. The actual processing takes about the same time as the five-month average underwriting period for SME projects with a regular MIGA guarantee.

Feedback from MIGA staff attributed the longer underwriting period for SIP projects to difficulties in obtaining required information and the significant time spent on providing guidance to MIGA SIP clients, especially small investors. SIP projects must still comply with MIGA's environmental, health, and safety requirements just like any regular guarantee project. In fact, SIP projects may require additional staff time to ensure that appropriate environmental, health, and safety measures are put in place, documented, and followed. In addition, MIGA client investors in SMEs typically do not have full environmental, health, and safety policies in place and encounter difficulties finding the resources to satisfy these requirements.

Verification of the internal rate of return threshold is not robust, which casts doubt on project viability. The SIP Checklist requires that real sector projects underwritten through SIP must have at least a 10 percent internal rate of return. IEG found insufficient assessment of the projects' business viability in 9 cases (out of 41 reviewed). MIGA relies mostly on investor warranties and representations, but weak record management makes verification of the soundness of SIP project business plans challenging and also reflects shortcomings in work quality.

The quality of the SIP Underwriting Checklist points to gaps in compliance with the SIP procedures. The Checklist serves as the formal project approval document for SIP projects in lieu of the Board report. It sets out the salient features of the proposed guarantee and records the due diligence procedures followed. IEG's review of MIGA's SIP work quality found the following:

• Missing signature by the MIGA Director of Operations or other underwriting team members in twelve of the 41 SIP projects reviewed. The Board approved in 2004 a waiver of the requirement (under MIGA's Operational Regulations Section 3.35) that MIGA projects must be circulated to the Board (under streamlined procedures) before the guarantee is issued. Internal approval of SIP projects was delegated to the MIGA Director of Operations, based on the recommendation from the SIP Review Committee. The final sign-off of the MIGOP Director in the SIP Checklist is consonant with the accountability function delegated by the Board when it approved the waiver. SME size indicators, for example, the actual number of employees, annual assets and/or revenues, are not presented in the SIP Underwriting Checklist.

- Poor record management in at least half of the 41 SIP projects reviewed by IEG. Internal World Bank electronic files lack one or more key underwriting documents, such as the SIP Underwriting Checklist, the Definitive Application, or the contract(s) of guarantee. Supporting documents such as business plans, feasibility studies, and financial projections could not be located in MIGA project files.

- For the nine SIP projects issued in FY11, five did not include the required Development Effectiveness Indicators System indicators attached as annex in the SIP contracts of guarantee.[18] The indicators system was set up to collect information once, three years after contract signing, from MIGA guarantee holders on DO results.

- Credit checks and consultations with IFC and World Bank field offices to guard against reputational risk appeared to be used only in half of the SIP projects reviewed (17 of the 41 projects) to verify information on project sponsors.

- E&S categorization may not reflect fully the environmental risks associated with projects under the SIP. A few projects may have been inappropriately categorized, such as a fisheries project categorized as Category B instead of a more appropriate category. One of MIGA's assumptions for SIP projects is that the financial sector and MAS projects carry a low environmental and social risks, hence can be approved in a streamlined manner. Disclosure requirements for SIP projects provide only that the Summary of Project Guarantee is disclosed for 15 days, which could add to reputational risks because of the shorter disclosure period compared to the 30 days for Category B projects underwritten under MIGA's regular guarantee. The sample of projects reviewed for this report indicates that not all approved SIP projects could be considered to have low E&S risks. Some SIP Category B projects have potentially significant E&S issues and have required (and will require) thorough due diligence and monitoring at a level consistent with a non-SIP Category B project. In these cases it is unclear that it can be cost-effective for MIGA, or why these projects should have a reduced disclosure period.

All SIP projects must meet MIGA's E&S requirements, but the extent of compliance for some projects is not known, despite increasing MIGA efforts to follow up on compliance with E&S standards. MIGA helps clients bring the project into compliance with its Performance Standards. After MIGA issues a contract of guarantee, under the terms of the E&S policy in effect since October 2007,[19] MIGA carries out a number of actions[20] to monitor project performance. MIGA does not typically require the guarantee holder to submit an Annual Monitoring Report containing information and data on the project's E&S performance. Instead, MIGA relies mainly on site monitoring visits to check this and to determine compliance with MIGA's E&S requirements. At appraisal MIGA may prepare an Environmental Action Plan detailing specific actions to be taken and a deadline for their completion and this is monitored through site visits. In projects that also involve IFC, MIGA relies on IFC's monitoring and supervision to ensure compliance with IFC and MIGA's E&S requirements, such as the hotel project in Burkina Faso.

For Category B projects it is understood that the aim is for the MIGA E&S team to visit these projects at least once every four years. Some higher-risk projects have received more intensive monitoring attention, whereas some of the other SIP projects have not yet been visited. For the SIP projects reviewed, in most cases, the MIGA E&S specialist's back-to-office report provides sufficient information to judge whether MIGA E&S requirements are being met. But an Annual Monitoring Report submitted by the client would provide more data regularly and this project reporting could indicate improvement trends over the years although this has to be managed carefully to ensure that key indicators are requested and that reporting is not onerous to the client.

Changes in the risk profile of the subborrower portfolio of SIP financial institution projects[21] may not be captured through one-off monitoring by MIGA. MIGA has not adopted a dynamic risk-based approach to monitoring these projects and changes in subloan portfolio risk may be overlooked because of limited client reporting. Relying on a monitoring mission to verify changes several years into the project may be insufficient to ensure that the guarantee holder and the project enterprise are meeting MIGA's requirements. It also presents a missed opportunity for MIGA to add value to the project and the sponsor.

PEFs investing in SMEs may not have the capacity to ensure compliance with MIGA's Performance Standards and manage E&S risks. One of the justifications for supporting PEFs that invest in SMEs is the potential to reduce E&S monitoring cost if the fund has in place a good E&S management system that meets MIGA requirements and the fund ensures that its investee companies meet Performance Standards and other MIGA requirements. Risks are higher, given that most SIP projects are in the target IDA and fragile and conflict-affected countries. IEG's visit to a PEF and its five investee companies revealed major lapses in environmental performance and limited in-house capacity to manage E&S issues.

Through its SIP, MIGA has facilitated investments in priority areas, such as Sub-Saharan Africa, IDA, and fragile and conflict-affected countries, and South-South investment. Although they are highly relevant to MIGA's priority areas, SIP project efficacy and efficiency and the program itself are uncertain. Work quality has major shortcomings.

SIP costs have been significantly higher than anticipated. Underwriting SIP projects does not involve significant gains in time or efficiency compared with underwriting regular guarantees, in spite of the streamlined procedures. Information gaps and significant facilitation efforts in assisting SMIs have resulted in actual processing times for SIPs of 161 days, instead of the 60 days target. Fifty-six percent of projects have been cancelled early.

Development outcomes of SIP projects are uncertain. Of the 41 projects reviewed, only 14 had information on project results available. Only two of these had established positive development outcomes. Nineteen projects did not have information on performance after the guarantee contract was issued, and seven projects had little information about project results and inconclusive.

MIGA had been supporting SMEs before the establishment of the SIP, and SIP has not significantly increased the deal flow to SMEs. SME deal flows mobilized through SIP amount to less than the value of MIGA's exposure to SME projects in the AMS, tourism, and financial sectors before SIP's implementation.

MIGA'S Regular Guarantee SME Projects

In contrast with the SIP, financial sector projects providing support to SMEs through wholesaling comprise the overwhelming bulk of MIGA's regular SME projects, representing 97 percent of the MIGA's gross exposure amount and 95 percent of the number of projects issued during the period FY06–12.

Regular guarantees targeting SMEs are highly concentrated by region, country classification and client. More than half (53 percent) of the SME projects covered by MIGA's regular guarantees are in IBRD (International Bank for Reconstruction and Development) countries, accounting for about four-fifths of MIGA's exposure. Projects in the Europe and Central Asia Region accounted for 66 percent of the number of SME projects and 89 percent of MIGA's gross exposure. Figure 3.9 presents the profile of MIGA projects targeting SMEs. Two repeat clients accounted for 68 percent of the number of regular SME projects covered by MIGA and absorbed nearly three-quarters of MIGA's gross exposure during the period FY06–12.

FIGURE 3.9 Profile of MIGA Mainstream SME Projects by Sector, Region, and IDA Status, FY06–12 (% and $ millions)

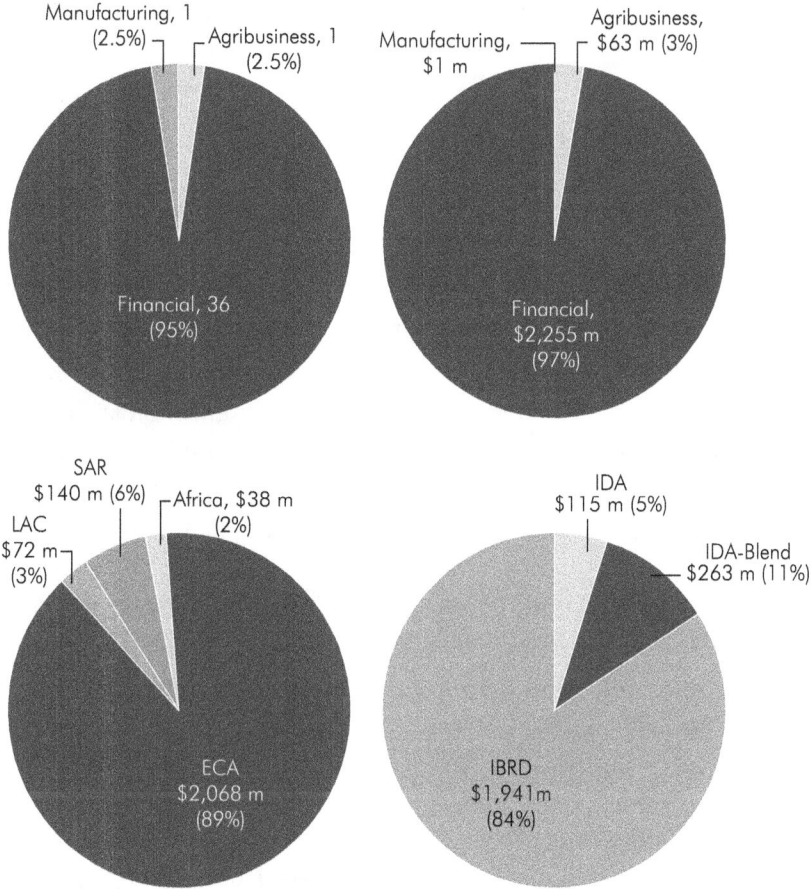

Manufacturing, 1 (2.5%)
Agribusiness, 1 (2.5%)
Financial, 36 (95%)

Manufacturing, $1 m
Agribusiness, $63 m (3%)
Financial, $2,255 m (97%)

SAR $140 m (6%)
LAC $72 m (3%)
Africa, $38 m (2%)
ECA $2,068 m (89%)

IDA $115 m (5%)
IDA-Blend $263 m (11%)
IBRD $1,941m (84%)

SOURCE: MIGA, IEG portfolio reviews.

NOTE: One manufacturing project reported in the graphs was issued as a non-SIP before the program was implemented. ECA = Europe and Central Asia; IBRD = International Bank for Reconstruction and Development; IDA = International Development Association; LAC = Latin America and the Caribbean; SAR = South Asia.

MIGA's business has benefitted both from the rapid credit expansion in several Europe and Central Asia countries prior to the financial crisis and from the regulatory treatment of MIGA-insured loans, especially by Austrian financial regulators. This has resulted in a significant degree of exposure concentration in the financial sector and in top clients in MIGA's overall guarantee exposure since 2003. To fund asset expansion, subsidiary banks relied substantially on shareholder loans, which were passed through as foreign currency loans to end borrowers, including SMEs. Four of these subsidiaries had repeat guarantees, with two or three guarantee contracts issued within the span of one year. In the aftermath of the new financial regulations imposed since the financial crisis, it is less likely that subsidiaries will rely on shareholder loans as the main source of funding for asset expansion. In 2011, Austrian financial regulators restricted the use of shareholder loans by parent banks to finance subsidiaries' operations. Subsidiaries of Austrian banks will have to increase their local deposit mobilization to fund lending activities.

RELEVANCE

Access to long-term finance and heightened liquidity and financial market risks[22] brought about by the global financial crisis were the two most frequently mentioned market gaps that the evaluated mainstream SME guarantees intended to address.[23] The lack of loans and leases with tenor over three years constrained the growth prospects of SMEs, especially those that have construction needs or are aiming to expand. Nearly all (8 of 10) of the regular SME projects mentioned lack of long-term financing as a market constraint. In addition, the adverse effects of the global financial crisis have led to a high incidence of bad loans and increased provisioning and inadequate capitalization that jeopardized the private foreign banks' liquidity, asset quality, and capital adequacy.

Currency transfer risk has also increased, especially in the crisis-hit countries in Europe and Central Asia Region. Support from the parent banks helped the financial institutions maintain their intermediation role and contain the impact of the crisis. This applies to five evaluated financial institution projects reviewed by IEG for this study.

In several country contexts, MIGA's support to foreign-owned banks has been important for the development of more competitive banking systems and opening access to previously underserved clients in the Europe and Central Asia Region. In this region, private foreign bank subsidiaries supported by MIGA operate in environments where state-owned banks and politically connected private banks limit other private banks' client pool for both loans and deposits.[24] Of the 16 financial institution projects reviewed by IEG, 7 banks started operations[25] during the 2000–08 period in transition economies where large state-owned banks had a substantial presence and where politically connected private banks provided loans mostly to related companies.

The SME sector was attractive to MIGA client banks because this was underserved and because of its potential to generate high margins via lending and cross-selling of other financial products. Only one commercial bank and a leasing company among the 16 financial institution projects reviewed focused on microenterprises and SMEs. The rest of the financial institutions supported by MIGA have universal bank licenses providing both banking and investment services. Their SME lending portfolio comprised 10–25 percent of total loans and the SME's share to total deposits is less than 10 percent.

MIGA's PRI is valued by parent banks that sought MIGA coverage to mitigate currency risks and since the global crisis, for capital enhancement. In nearly all of the 15 evaluated and rated mainstream SME projects, MIGA's role and contribution was rated satisfactory and above. In six of the seven rated mainstream TSME projects in the financial sector, MIGA's PRI was intended for capital enhancement (including Tier I or II capital increase and capital relief through exemptions from provisioning requirements) and outright liquidity support due to crisis. This particularly applies to projects insured under the Joint International Financial Institutions Action Plan in response to the global financial crisis.

Benefits of long-term MIGA PRI tenor were not passed on to end users. In all the mainstream projects reviewed for this study, MIGA cited the advantage of the long-term nature of its guarantees, which commercial insurers do not provide. This advantage was also mentioned in the MIGA client survey conducted by PricewaterhouseCoopers in 2009. In the report presented to the MIGA Board for seven of the mainstream SME projects reviewed for this study, MIGA also linked the lack of long-term PRI tenor with the scarcity in long-term SME financing. However, there is no evidence among the 16 financial sector projects reviewed for this study that the long-term tenor was passed on to end borrowers.

The typical tenor of SME loans among the mainstream SME financial institution projects with PERs is one year, mostly for working capital purposes and rarely for capital expansion. Even with the commercial bank that focused on MSMEs only, the typical loan tenor is six months. Only one evaluated mainstream SME financial institution project offered a three-year tenor but funds for this purpose came from a government scheme through a special rediscounting window by its central bank.

Finally, it is often difficult to discern MIGA's additionality in increasing SME access to finance, given the multiple sources of SME support available to project enterprises. Eight of the regular SME projects reviewed for this study also received funds from other international financial institutions for on-lending to SMEs. IFC, the European Bank for Reconstruction and Development, the European Investment Bank, Proparco, the Netherlands Development Finance Company, and the Inter-American Development Bank are among the donors that have provided loans to MIGA-insured subsidiaries for SME on-lending. IFC and the Netherlands Development Finance Company have also provided much-needed technical assistance to the subsidiary banks to set up and develop the banks' SME business lines, implying the possibility of complementarity. The use by foreign private banks of loans by international finance institutions for SME on-lending points to the high risk profile of the segment.

Development Outcome Results: Evidence from Project Reviews

MIGA often justified its support for regular TSME financial sector projects based on their stronger development impact through support of SMEs; however, financial sector projects that did not target SMEs as a project objective had higher DO ratings.[26] Eleven of the fourteen projects with PERs reviewed by IEG had satisfactory and higher DO ratings. All regular non-TSME financial institution projects (7) achieved satisfactory and higher DO ratings, compared to 71 percent (five of seven projects) with high DO ratings among the evaluated regular TSME financial sector projects. This finding is consistent with IEG's 2011 evaluation of MIGA's financial sector guarantees (IEG 2011, pp. 37–38). In the evaluation, IEG found that all of the developmentally successful financial projects had clearly focused and defined business segment based on the banks' competitiveness.

TSME financial institution projects supported by regular guarantees underperformed the other evaluated financial sector projects in three indicators of DO. Other evaluated financial sector projects have outperformed regular SME projects in terms of Business Performance, Economic Sustainability, and Contribution to private sector development (Figure 3.11), except in E&S effects.

FIGURE 3.10 Comparing Development Outcome Ratings: Mainstream SME Projects and Comparable Non-SME Group of Projects

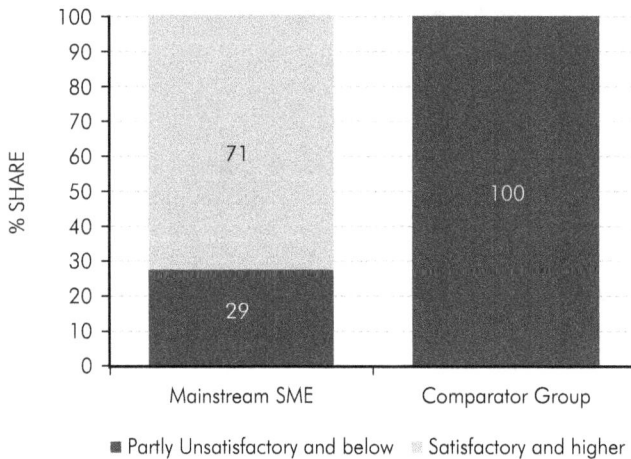

■ Partly Unsatisfactory and below   Satisfactory and higher

SOURCE: IEG portfolio review.

FIGURE 3.11 Comparison of Development Outcome Indicator Ratings: Mainstream SME Projects and Comparator Group

Ratings of Development Outcome Indicators of Mainstream SME Projects

Ratings of Development Outcome Indicators of Projects in the Comparator Group

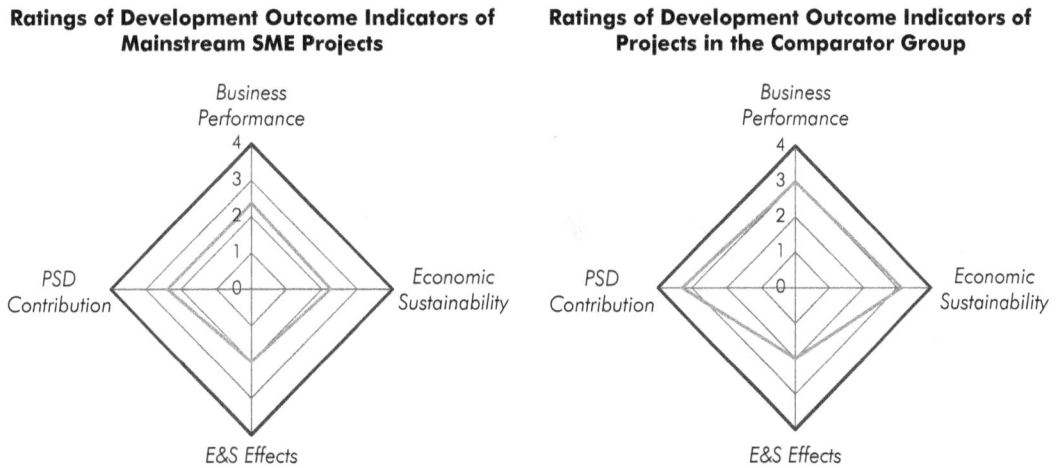

SOURCE: IEG portfolio review.

NOTE: E&S = environmental and social; PSD = private sector development.

The global financial crisis heightened vulnerabilities of the targeted SME projects but was not the only reason for weak business performance. Business performance of seven regular guarantee TSME financial institution projects with ratings had mixed results. Four were financially viable and provided sufficient returns to investors; the other three struggled with low returns.[27] The institutions were hit hard by the global financial crisis, but there are also internal reasons for weak business performance, among them (i) the inability to control costs, (ii) high incidence of loan default because of credit expansion before the global economic crisis, (iii) the consequences of a bank's real estate investments, and (iv) a low utilization of an SME credit line caused by the failure to attract qualified SME clients to borrow in foreign currency.

Among the universal banks, there is no evidence that lending to SMEs has been profitable because there is a lack of information on the spreads and margins earned by the evaluated financial institutions on their SME loan segment compared to their large corporate and consumer/retail portfolio. Interest rates on SME foreign currency-denominated loans, ranging from 28 percent to 60 percent annually, reflect the risk premium and the cost of administering small loans. High interest rates may also cause the high incidence of nonperforming loans in the banks' SME portfolio, if few borrowers were able to generate sufficient revenues to service the loans. Bank loans in foreign currency in the Europe and Central Asia Region had lower interest rates than local currency lending and the foreign exchange risk was passed on to borrowers.

An MSME bank and a leasing company focused on SMEs experienced losses as a consequence of a mass movement in the country to default on bank loans. It took the bank five years to clean up its loan books and return to profitability. As a consequence of the politically sanctioned default, the bank decided that microfinance and very small businesses are not profitable segments (see Box 3.3). The leasing company set up to help SMEs decided to close its operations in the same country as a consequence of the mass default. Regulatory

---

BOX 3.3 The Challenge of Banking with MSMEs in Central America

Operating an MSME bank in an uncertain political and regulatory environment and where the financial system is underdeveloped requires expert knowledge of the business segment, willingness and ability to offer financial advice to its MSME clients, and a strong, well-capitalized sponsor. Funding support from international financial institutions also helps in terms of accessing longer-term capital and, in some cases, cheaper sources of funds.

MSMEs' access to finance in Nicaragua has long been stifled by a highly concentrated banking system, where competition among banks is relatively weak, banks depend on short-term local deposits for funding, and there is little product differentiation among the large banks. Sustained lending to MSMEs suffered a further blow inflicted by a politically motivated mass movement that advocated for an across-the-board loan default (*Movimiento No Pago*) in 2008, which had a long-lasting negative effect on the financial system's profitability and willingness to lend to micro and small enterprises.

Against this backdrop MIGA insured a parent bank's $13.5 million shareholder loan to one of its Central American subsidiaries in 2010. To remain competitive, the bank adhered to a relationship-based lending strategy, which has proven to be effective to minimize bad loans and loan defaults. The bank has since reverted to in-sourcing its loan recoveries to forge closer ties with its customers.

It took nearly five years for the Nicaraguan subsidiary to recover from the effects of the *No Pago* movement. The bank experienced financial losses since 2009 but has now cleaned up its loan books through restructuring and write-offs, particularly for its microfinance loans. Loan recovery has been difficult because of legal constraints. The bank had also made a strategic retreat from providing very small loans (≤$2,000) because of high incidence of loan default in this segment, with little chance of recovery. The bank had also imposed a minimum deposit balance to reduce the cost of servicing deposits. As a result there has been a decline in the number of customers and depositors although its financial condition looks stronger.

SOURCE: IEG.

uncertainty caused by the absence of leasing law and difficulty in enforcing contracts was another factor in the leasing company's decision to exit the country.

There is no information on the welfare effects of MIGA's regular TSME projects on beneficiaries. MIGA does not collect general information from its clients on the volume and number of loans to SMEs, the quality of the loans to SMEs, or the effect of the MIGA guaranteed funds on SMEs' business, including the amount of investment, sales, and employment generated. Thus far, there is little evidence of increased employment, sales, additional investments made or increased productivity. Clearly, when a project fails to materialize, there are no welfare benefits, as was the case for a TSME project that would have benefitted SME construction suppliers.

Development results from projects reviewed reflect the financial institution's corporate performance[28] and not just the results of its SME portfolio. For most evaluated financial institution projects, SME loans represent a small percentage of the institutions' total loans. Only 1 bank and a leasing company had MSMEs as primary clients among the 16 mainstream financial institutions reviewed. Of the 7 mainstream TSME projects with PERs and ratings, SME loans represented 5 percent to 20 percent of the banks' total outstanding loans. Three among the four regular TSME financial institution projects that were rated satisfactory and higher were universal banks with a license to undertake commercial and investment banking operations and had the flexibility to shift focus, depending on the opportunity to make higher margins. This flexibility is essential to the banks' survival and ability to perform its intermediation function.

Although these four projects had good financial results, it is difficult to attribute their profitability to the SME loans guaranteed by MIGA or the contribution of the banks' SME portfolio to overall profitability. Although the banks focused or intended to focus on SMEs at the time of MIGA underwriting, their targeting of SMEs could shift. In one regular TSME financial institution project, MIGA stated in the President's Report that the bank would increase its SME lending from 30 percent to 45 percent, but the audited financial statements showed that its SME portfolio declined after the MIGA guarantee was issued.

Targeting of SMEs is often aspirational and not contractually binding. Providing access to finance to underserved SMEs is the frequently stated project objective in the President's Report. Beyond the aspirational statements, there is no mechanism for ensuring that the funds will be used for the purpose claimed in the Board document, the basis for the Board authorization for MIGA to provide guarantee to the project. Only two financial institution projects have explicit reference in MIGA's contract of guarantee (Clause 2a or 2b) that the guaranteed funds will be used for SME lending. The other six mainstream projects have no provision in the contract of guarantee that ties the funds guaranteed by MIGA for SME lending, even if stated as a project objective in the President's Report. And even in the two mainstream TSME financial institution projects that have Clause 2 reference, there is no provision in the contract of guarantee to ensure that the MIGA guaranteed funds will be used for SME lending. MIGA is also not requiring any reporting or tracking of the criteria used for lending to SMEs, number and volume of SME loans, number of SME borrowers, and the tenor and type of SME loans. Overall, it is difficult to ascertain if the SME loans insured by MIGA achieved their stated development objectives.

The aspirational approach to supporting SMEs is impractical. Evaluation findings of the financial sector projects reviewed indicate that private banks constantly shift their focus, strategies and decisions depending on their strategy and margin targets. This flexibility is also a key ingredient in maintaining a healthy, competitive banking system. Although the SME segment was a profitable niche for foreign banks investing in the Europe and Central Asia Region in 2004–05, the conditions started to change in 2006. In 14 of the 16 financial institution projects with PERs reviewed for this study, SME segments' margins narrowed, lending declined and there were early signs of repayment problems. In response, the banks shifted their focus from SME lending to consumer or to large corporate lending. In some cases, the banks increased their holdings of government securities with the onset of the global financial crisis.

EFFICIENCY OF REGULAR PORTFOLIO TARGETED SUPPORT TO SMES

IEG does not have information (actual or estimated) on the cost of underwriting and revenues from its regular guarantee projects. A review of MIGA's underwriting documents indicates an average period of five months[29] from the time the client files the Definitive Application, Board approval, to the signing of the contract of guarantee (Figure 3.12). Financial sector projects, including mainstream SME projects, have the advantage of supporting repeat clients familiar with MIGA processes and requirements and available information, unlike SIP projects. The quick turnaround time also allowed MIGA to issue two contracts of guarantee within one year for five evaluated projects. Although the premium rates are smaller—ranging from 0.45 percent to 0.75 percent—the guarantee amounts are larger, ranging from $10 million to $240 million.

FIGURE 3.12 Processing Time of Evaluated MIGA Financial Sector Projects Reviewed

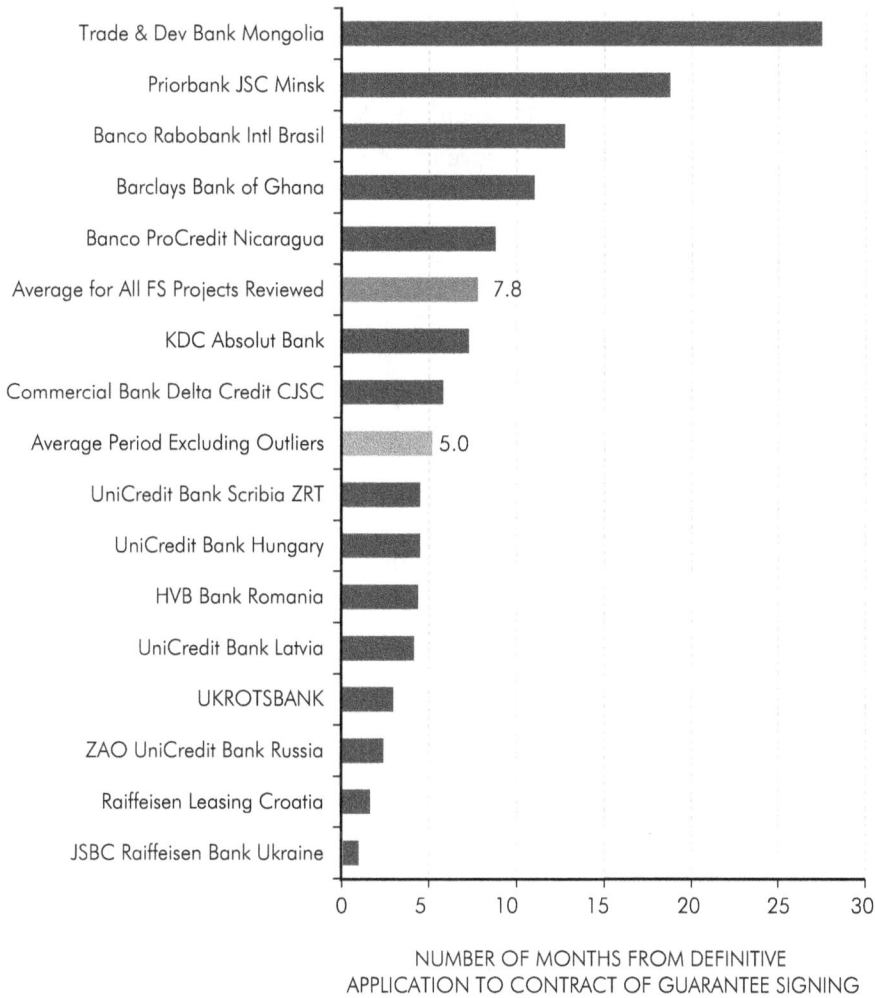

NUMBER OF MONTHS FROM DEFINITIVE
APPLICATION TO CONTRACT OF GUARANTEE SIGNING

SOURCE: IEG portfolio review.

Overall Conclusion

IEG's review of the SIP suggests that although it has high relevance, it is of doubtful efficacy and efficiency. MIGA's regular portfolio of TSME projects performs worse than other financial sector guarantees, and there is no evidence to determine their impact on SMEs. The viability and sustainability of SMEs investments, whether through SIP or the wholesale approach, could not be ascertained because of the lack of information on results and performance.

In terms of effectiveness, mainstream TSME financial institution projects had lower DO ratings than the group of comparable financial management guarantees but generally appear to be both more effective and efficient than SIP projects. It is also difficult to ascertain whether the MIGA-insured shareholder loans eased constraints faced by SMEs or if MIGA's support benefitted SMEs.

There is even less evidence about the development effectiveness of SIP projects, eight years into the program. Of the 14 projects that have information on development results, 12 have either failed or have serious financial and operational challenges that jeopardize the projects' viability and development outcomes. Cognizant of the challenges in investing into SMEs, only three Berne Union members have a special facility to provide PRI to investments in SMEs.

In terms of the relevance to the theories of change discussed in the first chapter, MIGA's strategy appears most related to the first set—facilitating financing of SMEs through direct investments and intermediaries as a way to create jobs or to enhance the degree to which financial systems sustainably help SMEs to create jobs. The problem in the former case is that the magnitude of SME financing mobilized through SIP and even through regular guarantees is extremely small compared to any financing gap. The question in the latter case is how much difference MIGA has made for financial systems in the long term through its guarantees. Certainly in the case of a Nicaraguan bank, it appeared that MIGA played a role in expanding financing of a key, long-term supplier of SME finance.

MIGA has also limited capability to target SMEs effectively using the wholesale approach because there is no enforceable provision or tracking mechanism to ensure that guaranteed funds benefitted SMEs. Lending criteria is not defined; there is no legal obligation—either in the MIGA contract of guarantee or loan covenants—to allocate the funds to SMEs. Also, reporting of SME loan portfolio and borrower performance is not required, and the volume, number, and SME loan beneficiaries are not tracked. Implications of the terms of the shareholder loans' pass through in the form of foreign currency loans to end borrowers are not assessed.

Supporting financial institutions still makes developmental and business sense for MIGA. Such projects have a higher DO rating than projects in other sectors. MIGA's support to them in the Europe and Central Asia Region facilitated the growth of a competitive banking system. Financial institution projects also take less time to underwrite and produce far larger guarantee amounts than SIP projects. As mentioned in the 2011 IEG report on MIGA's financial sector guarantees (IEG 2011, pp. 37–38), "support for SMEs is neither necessary nor sufficient for MIGA projects to have satisfactory development outcomes." A clearly focused and defined banking strategy based on the institutions' competitiveness is more important in the development of a viable and competitive banking system than targeting.

Notes

[1] MIGA had provided guarantees to cross-border investors in SMEs even before support to SMEs became one of its priority areas. Between 1991 (a year after MIGA issued its first guarantee) and 1999 MIGA issued more than 50 guarantee contracts to cross-border investors in SMEs in 26 countries, of which 17 are in IDA countries. These projects were underwritten as a regular or mainstream guarantee project. Twenty-six percent of MIGA's gross exposure amount during the period was below $2 million, the SME definition used by MIGA. (MIGA 2000, p. 52).

[2] Three MIGA strategies encompass the period covered by this evaluation: MIGA's Strategic Directions for FY05–FY08; MIGA Operational Directions FY09–11; and FY12–14 Strategy: Achieving Value-Driven Volume.

[3] MIGA's current strategy recognized that there will be projects outside its four operational priorities that would be highly suitable for support if compelling reasons arise. Such reasons may include responding to changing global economic conditions, in consideration of the project's/client's importance to MIGA's business, and finally, enhancing MIGA's ability to build and maintain a diverse portfolio. Specific examples mentioned in the FY12–14 strategy were supporting financial sector projects, particularly in crisis-affected areas, and cross-border investments in middle-income countries, but not support to SMEs.

[4] The two other insurers are AIG and ECIC, the export credit agency of South Africa.

[5] The Berne Union Investment Insurance Committee is comprised of 35 public and private investment insurers. It is committee within the Berne Union, a 78-member global organization of public and private companies in the export credit and investment insurance industry. These figures come from a report for the Investment Insurance Committee Spring Meeting. April 23, 2012.

[6] MIGA's Board approved the amendment to Section 3.35 of MIGA's Operational Regulations. Section 3.35(c) of the Operational Regulations required that a report on proposed guarantees be circulated to the Board prior to the approval of the guarantees by the President. Instead, the Board of Directors will be informed of the signed SIP projects through the EVP Quarterly Reports.

[7] Examples of SMIs include AMCO Fabrics of India, Cesur Packaging of Turkey, Tulbagh Holdings of the United States, and Prodenvasas Crown of Colombia.

[8] PEFs include the Africa Development Corporation and the Sierra/Manocap Investment Fund.

[9] Financial intermediaries include Corporacion Interfin of Costa Rica, Banco de la Microempresa of Peru, and Grupo ACP of Peru, Shorecap International Ltd.

[10] Large investors include ABN AMRO Bank, Whirlpool, SGS S.A., MTU Asia (a subsidiary of Daimler), Sojitz Corporation, Intertek International, DAGRIS/Geocoton, Geogas Trading S.A., Industrial Development Corporation of South Africa, and UniCredit Bank.

[11] IEG conducted a programmatic review of the SIP for this Report. The programmatic review used a combination of approaches/methods from document reviews, staff and stakeholder interviews, and site visits in connection with the country case studies. IEG triangulated information from Project Evaluation Reports/Validation Notes, review of literature, MIGA project documents, documents collected from the site visits, and interviews to arrive at the findings.

[12] The concession was later awarded to another company.

[13] The company was vertically integrated to a fisheries project, which was having financial difficulties and problems with the local partner. The company's business model was also unviable because of lack of customers that use the trucks for transporting goods back into the capital.

[14] Applies only to real sector projects. Financial rate of return is not used as metric for projects involving financial institutions (for example, banks and leasing).

[15] MIGA had already used the PEF structure in East Africa in the banking and information technology sectors.

[16] The credit enhancement advantage of a MIGA guarantee is that it helps fund managers raise risk capital to finance planned investments. For PEFs with multiple planned investments, MIGA developed a master contract of guarantee that would extend coverage to the PEF's entire portfolio without having to seek Board approval each time the fund makes an investment. But MIGA conducts due diligence on the fund, including its ability to meet MIGA's E&S standards, and reviews prospective investments proposed by the fund.

[17] The first claim pertains to damages incurred by a hotel project. MIGA paid the second claim related to property damage of a bank project.

[18] In 2010, MIGA began requiring developmental outcome reporting from MIGA guarantee holders, who must submit a completed form indicating a project's development effectiveness indicators at the end of year three of MIGA coverage. The Development Effectiveness Indicator System required that all MIGA contracts of guarantee include an appendix entitled "General Development Effectiveness Indicators and Definitions." The information will be provided by the guarantee holder and submitted to MIGA at the end of year three after contract execution.

[19] MIGA followed the Interim E&S Policies until the adoption of the Performance Standards in October 2007. SIP projects issued before then are not subject to Performance Standards.

[20] Require the project to submit periodic monitoring reports on its social and environmental performance as agreed with MIGA: Conduct site visits of certain projects with social and environmental risks and impacts; review project performance on the basis of the client's commitments in the action plan, as reported by the client's monitoring reports, and, where relevant, review with the client any performance improvement opportunities; if changed project circumstances would result in adverse social or environmental impacts, work with the client to address them; if the client fails to comply with its social and environmental commitments, as expressed in the action plan or legal agreement with MIGA, work with the client to bring it back into compliance to the extent feasible, and if the client fails to reestablish compliance, exercise remedies when appropriate; encourage the client to report publicly on its social, environmental, and other nonfinancial aspects of performance, in addition to reporting on the action plan as required by Performance Standard; and encourage the client to continue to meet the Performance Standards after the client has decided the MIGA guarantee is no longer necessary and has cancelled.

[21] Of the six financial services/banking sector projects reviewed, all were correctly categorized by MIGA in the ECM to Category C, with one Category FI, BRD, that is, lending to SMEs and investing in greenfield projects. However, this project is not active and there are no monitoring reports. One project was disclosed as a Category A project according to the MIGA SPG page, although the ECM clearly classified it as a Category C. Consequently, there were no lessons to be drawn from any of these projects. In Sierra Leone, MIGA entered into a master contract of guarantee with a private equity fund, covering the fund's $16.2 million investments in the country. Each of the investments was also reviewed by MIGA prior to approving coverage.

[22] These included lack of long-term financing for SMEs for five companies and stabilization/liquidity risks.

[23] IEG reviewed the findings, ratings and lessons from 15 Project Evaluation Reports plus findings from a site visit to a purposively sampled MSME bank project and a leasing company for a total of 17 projects reviewed. Of the 17 projects reviewed, 16 are financial projects and 1 is in the real sector. The 15 projects with Project Evaluation Reports were evaluated during FY06–13; IEG visited the MSME bank and leasing company in January 2013 as part of the Nicaragua country case study. These 17 projects comprised 26 percent of MIGA's gross exposure during the period. Nine of the 15 projects with evaluation reports and ratings involved projects that mentioned support to SMEs as a project development objective. Of these, eight were financial sector projects and one was a real sector project. Findings from the two purposively sampled projects are also included in the findings.

[24] Similar observations can be found in IEG's evaluation of MIGA's financial sector guarantees (IEG 2011, p. 36).

[25] Mostly through acquisitions.

[26] Only findings from FI projects with Project Evaluation Reports are included in the ratings count.

[27] Low business performance ratings: three banks; high business performance ratings: four banks.

[28] Because of the lack of information pertaining to the performance of the projects' SME portfolio, IEG usually evaluates the company's entire operations and not just the SME segment. IEG relies on the banks' audited financial statements and annual reports, which in most cases do not include information on their SME segment.

[29] Average processing time excluding two outliers.

References

IEG (Independent Evaluation Group). 2011. *MIGA's Financial Sector Guarantees in a Strategic Context*. Washington, DC: World Bank.

MIGA (Multilateral Investment Guarantee Agency). 2007. *Report on the MIGA Small Investment Program (SIP)*. Washington, DC: World Bank.

——. 2000. *MIGA Review 2000*. Washington, DC: World Bank.

4

The World Bank's Targeted Support for SMEs

CHAPTER HIGHLIGHTS

- The World Bank's portfolio of TSME projects represented about 7 percent of projects and 2 percent of commitment value. By product line, lines of credit, matching grants, and business development services projects dominate the lending portfolio.

- Although the Bank is more substantially engaged in low-income and fragile and conflict-affected countries, the relatively low level of commitments in IDA countries and the high level of commitments in upper-middle-income countries raise questions of relevance regarding reaching the frontier and building markets and market institutions where they are weakest.

- World Bank targeted support for SMEs is broader than suggested by its formal strategic focus on access to finance, and likely more driven by country and regional strategy and demand than by any central guidance.

- The great majority of closed projects achieved successful development outcomes. However, efforts to judge the efficacy and efficiency of World Bank TSME support are inhibited by the lack of serious quantitative evaluation of the development impact of its leading product lines.

- Some projects rated as successful in terms of their impact on beneficiaries provide little evidence on whether they have addressed underlying systemic obstacles.

- Work quality exhibits several strengths, including linkage to prior analytic work, a high rate of successful development outcomes, and a high rate of realism in self-evaluations. Weaknesses lie in overly complex designs, overly optimistic time frames for implementation, and the frequent need for delays, restructuring, and partial cancellation.

- Though TSME AAA is only a small fraction of the overall portfolio, AAA work is generally both relevant and important to SME challenges. It is delivered mainly to governments.

- Self-ratings indicate a high and rising level of success for TSME technical assistance. Technical assistance in the context of lines of credit appears effective at strengthening institutional performance and therefore in producing positive outcomes.

- Economic and sector work appears effective in some dimensions but had limited traction in influencing government policy.

Rationale

Although World Bank support for SMEs can be traced as far back as 1978,[1] over the past dozen years or so, the World Bank has taken a limited approach to SME support. This arises from a view, expressed by the leading author of its private sector development strategy, that:

> Establishing an equal playing field for all types of enterprises is often one of the most politically difficult parts of reform. Neither large nor small or medium-size firms should be favored. What should be favored are competition and the rule of law (Klein and Hadjmichael 2003).

A recent evaluation of World Bank SME support projects in Latin America noted that "the World Bank has advised developing country governments to focus instead on improving the investment climate for all enterprises, large and small, and on developing their financial markets and improving SME access to finance" (López-Acevedo and Tan 2011).[2] The World Bank's 2002 Private Sector Development Strategy makes reference to an SME strategy (for the now defunct joint IFC/World Bank SME Department) "to promote unsubsidized financial operations as well as market-based approaches to business development services." It calls for extending "the discipline of OP8.30"[3] to all on-lending operations, including rural and social development funds, granting IFC right of first refusal to any on-lending operation.

The Bank's 2007 Financial Sector Development strategy placed SME finance squarely on the agenda, suggesting that the Bank review cross-country developments in SME finance and "incorporate access issues into its policy-based and project lending operations" (World Bank 2007). It delegated to IFC "work to boost its advisory support to banks to upgrade their business models and risk management systems to better serve the SME sector" (World Bank 2002).

Consistent with this limited focus, only one of the new Finance and Private Sector Development practice areas—financial inclusion—explicitly supports SMEs, through its Micro and SME Finance unit. The financial inclusion practice website states that the World Bank Group takes a comprehensive approach toward financial inclusion, including "providing expert technical support and financing for policy initiatives, legal reforms and programs that support: micro and SME finance, trade finance, agricultural finance, innovative delivery mechanisms, alternative financial products and state and member-based financial institutions" (http://web.worldbank.org/WBSITE/EXTERNAL/TOPICS/EXTFINANCIALSECTOR /0,,contentMDK:23166935~pagePK:210058~piPK:210062~theSitePK:282885,00.html).

It does not explicitly embrace targeted support, nor does it assign these functions between World Bank, IFC, and/or MIGA.

Among other practice areas, the competitive industries practice intends to focus on better integrating and raising the productivity of SMEs in their role in global supply chains, providing inputs, components, and services. Still, there is little strategic guidance as to where targeted SME interventions fit in the Financial and Private Sector Development (FPD) strategy beyond access to finance. Some World Bank staff acknowledged this limited focus, although they suggested that future World Bank strategy may expand the scope for Bank SME support beyond finance, making more explicit the connection of size (or age and size) to the practices in competitive industries and innovation and entrepreneurship. However, the practice leaders in these areas did not identify activities undertaken with their engagement during the review period that constituted targeted support to SMEs, instead describing activities that generally have a non-size-delimited focus.

World Bank Lending Portfolio

Looking at the World Bank's lending portfolio, overall about 7 percent of projects representing 2 percent of commitment value were classified in the portfolio review as targeted SME.[4] In terms of commitment value, 27 lines of credit (14 financial intermediary loans, 9 specific investment loans, and 4 adaptable program loans) represented 51 percent of the commitment value in the TSME lending portfolio. The second greatest commitment value is associated with matching grants: 47 projects of smaller average value add up to 17 percent of portfolio value. Thirty-seven BDSs represent 2 percent of the projects in the Bank's lending portfolio, but at $741 million in total commitment value, this represents only 15 percent of the TSME lending portfolio value. Fifteen value chain linkage projects constitute an even smaller part of the total commitments—8 percent, with risk-sharing facilities, grants, and other access to finance projects accounting for the balance of lending (Figure 4.1).

Thus, in spite of the World Bank's limited strategic focus on SME, it is clear that a number of its operations and advisory activities addressed to SMEs do not concern the financial sector, and within the financial sector, a number do not follow the recipe suggested by the strategy (Box 4.1). This would suggest that in practice, World Bank support for SMEs is broader than suggested by its formal strategy and likely more driven by country and regional strategy and demand than by any central guidance. This could be interpreted as either "decentralized"

FIGURE 4.1 World Bank TSME Lending Portfolio FY06–12, by Commitment Value ($ millions)

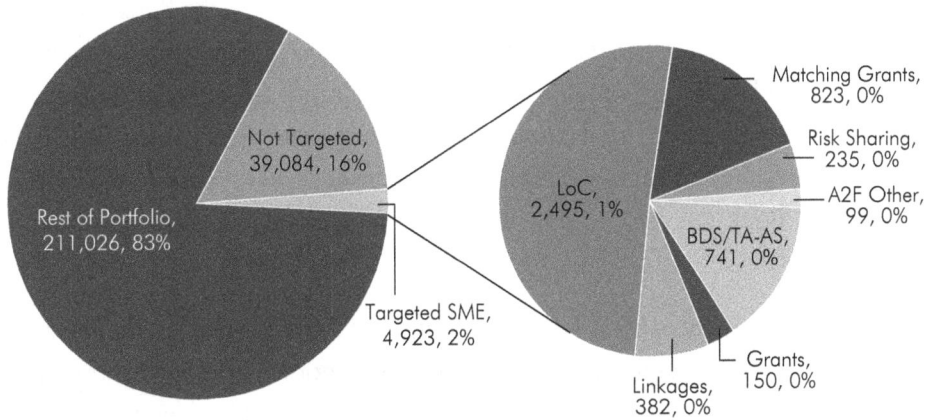

SOURCE: IEG portfolio review.

NOTES: A2F = access to finance; BDS = business development service; LoC = line of credit; TA-AS = technical assistance-advisory services.

and demand-responsive or lacking in strategic coherence. Either way, it imposes substantial challenges to evaluating the program against stated institutional objectives.

Although two-thirds of commitments were made by the FPD network, it is noteworthy that a large number reside with the Social Development Network and the Poverty Reduction and Economic Management Network. Regionally, a high percentage of portfolio value resides in Europe and Central Asia (31 percent), and more than two-thirds of TSME commitments were made in countries that were not among the poorest (non-IDA). One-third of commitments were in upper-middle-income countries alone. Eighty-five percent of the targeted SME

BOX 4.1 Identifying SME Projects: Incentives Matter

Although identifying the TSME portfolio in IFC generated a number of "false positives" consistent with the strong incentives in the institution to be proactive about SMEs, the World Bank's portfolio coding produced a lot of "false negatives"—projects that were targeted at SME development but had no MSME sector or thematic code. IEG found that only about 14 percent of projects coded as SME were not SME-specific, but 42 percent of the TSME portfolio eventually identified did not have an SME or MSME code. Instead, IEG had to use content searches and "manual" reviews of project documents to identify the full portfolio.

SOURCE: IEG portfolio review.

portfolio was in countries that are not categorized as either fragile and conflict-affected or transitional from that status. Part of this concentration was justified by the Bank's response to the global financial crisis, when it mobilized lines of credit to address perceived liquidity shortages in the banking systems of some middle income countries. However, looking at projects over time, there was a one-time surge in Financial Intermediary Loans in 2010. This suggests that there is now room to move toward the frontier of lower-income and more fragile economies where Bank interventions may contribute more to building financial sector capacity (Figure 4.2).

Over time, there is no notable trend in TSME activity, and there is a general decline in portfolio size in FY12. The commitment value of the TSME portfolio dropped sharply in 2011 but recovered subsequently. As a proportion of the total portfolio, TSME lending fell in the post-crisis period (2009–12), as the non-SME portfolio greatly expanded without a parallel increase in TSME spending.

Although the Bank is substantially engaged in low-income and fragile and conflict-affected countries, the relatively low level of commitments in the poorest (IDA) countries and the high level of commitments in upper-middle-income countries raise questions of relevance to reaching the frontier and building markets and market institutions where they are weakest. Clearly, absorptive capacity may be limited in some IDA and fragile and conflict-affected countries, and there may be underserved markets in middle-income countries—the question

FIGURE 4.2 World Bank Targeted SME Lending Portfolio FY06–12, by Total Commitments ($ millions)

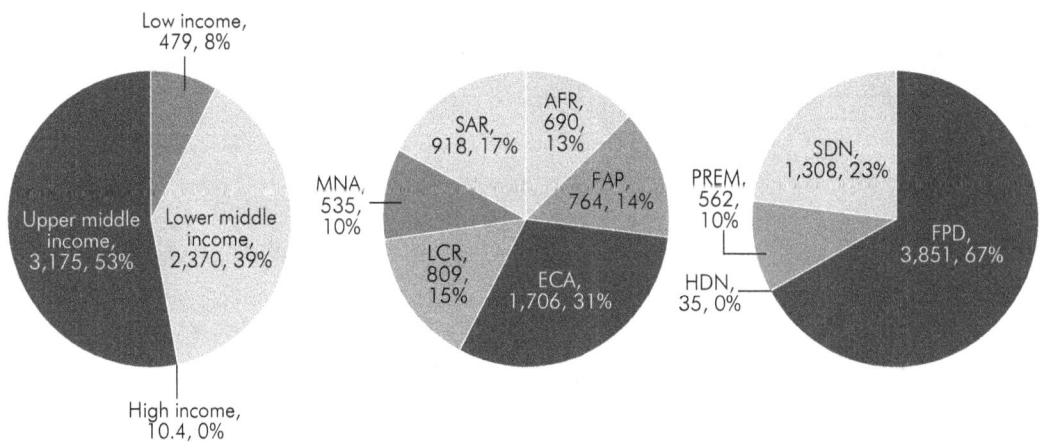

SOURCE: IEG portfolio review.
NOTE: **Sectors:** FPD = Financial and Private Sector Development Network; HDN = Human Development Network; PREM = Poverty Reduction and Economic Management Network; SDN = Sustainable Development Network. **Regions:** AFR = Africa; EAP = East Asia and Pacific; ECA = Europe and Central Asia; LCR = Latin America and the Caribbean; MNA = Middle East and North Africa; SAR = South Asia.

FIGURE 4.3 Trend in TSME and Overall Portfolio, FY06–12

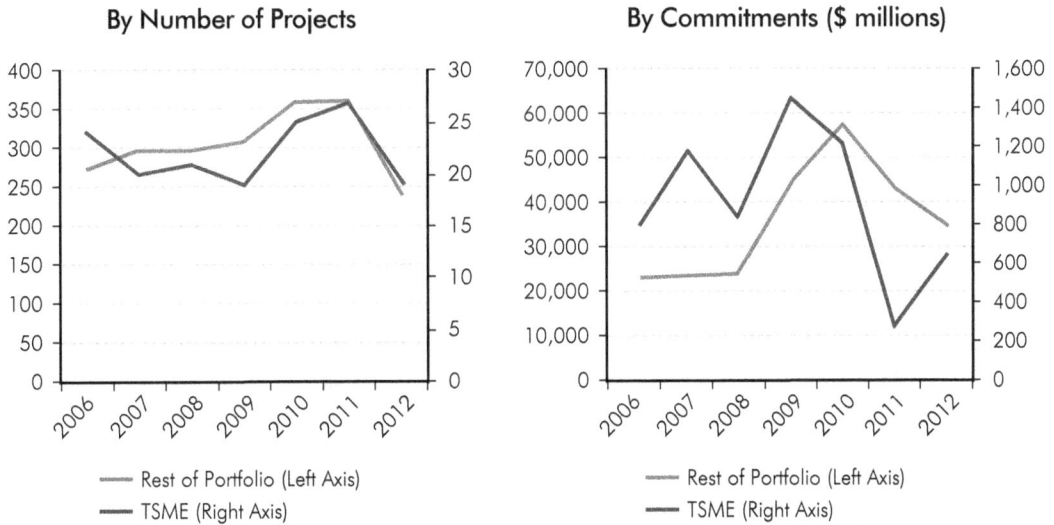

By Number of Projects

By Commitments ($ millions)

—— Rest of Portfolio (Left Axis)
—— TSME (Right Axis)

—— Rest of Portfolio (Left Axis)
—— TSME (Right Axis)

SOURCE: IEG portfolio review.

is one of portfolio priorities given constrained resources. IEG also found a number of cases where the emphasis seemed to be more on directly channeling financing to SMEs than on building institutions to deepen and broaden financial markets from the bottom up.

Lines of credit are the leading World Bank TSME product by value, accounting for just over half of the overall portfolio value during the review period (Figure 4.3).[5] In a line of credit, World Bank funds are channeled through a government agency, a state-owned bank, or with a government guarantee to financial intermediaries, who on-lend to SMEs. About $11 billion in lines of credit was approved between FY06 and FY12 through 49 projects, of which about $2.5 billion (26 projects) was in projects targeted at SMEs. This represents about 50 percent of targeted SME financing during the period. As Figure 4.4 makes clear, some $7 billion in financial intermediary loans was distributed across 40 projects approved between 2006 and 2012. They enjoyed a resurgence during the review period, peaking in 2010 at a level not seen since the early 1990s.

This can largely be explained by the Bank's response to the global financial crisis, with a series of loans reported to respond to a shortage of bank financing for SMEs through the banking system. In terms of the theory of change, the focus was more on assuring a flow of finance to SMEs, with a more subordinate role of developing the financial system through on-lending. The major institution building undertaken by the World Bank appears to have been raising partner banks' environmental standards and safeguards.

FIGURE 4.4 FILs in the World Bank Portfolio over Time—Number of Projects and Commitment Value ($ millions)

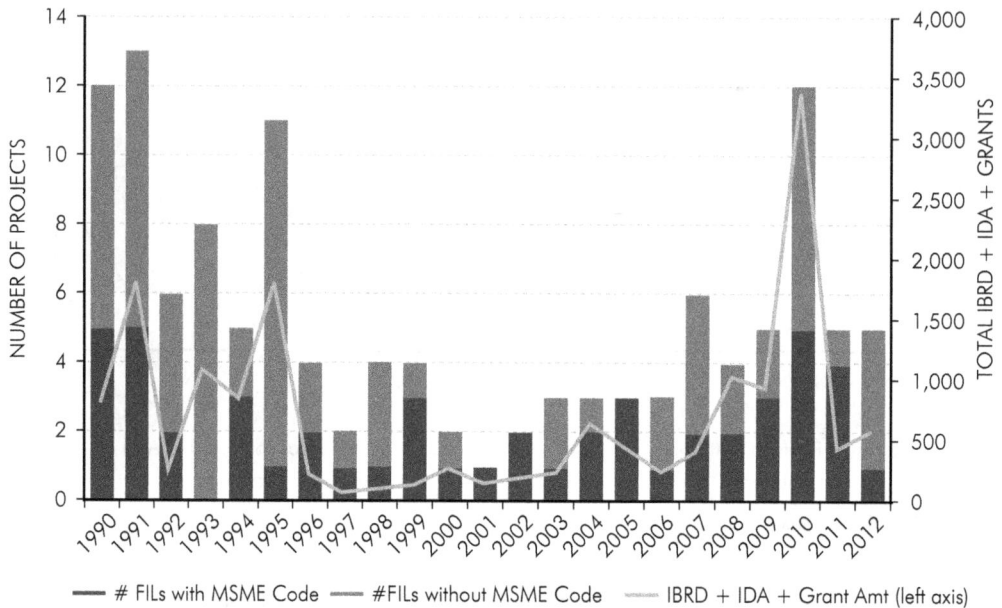

FILs with MSME Code   #FILs without MSME Code   IBRD + IDA + Grant Amt (left axis)

SOURCE: IEG portfolio review.
NOTE: FIL = financial intermediary loan; IBRD = International Bank for Reconstruction and Development; IDA = International Development Association; MSME = micro, small, and medium-size enterprises.

One example is the FY11 Sri Lanka SME Development Facility, which included a $28 million line of credit aimed to improve access for SMEs affected by the global financial crisis and a $13 million risk-sharing facility. The project also contained a $12 million policy and capacity enhancement component to strengthen banking capacity for SME lending and to undertake complementary diagnostic work. The project design explicitly builds on lessons of prior lines of credit as well as the recommendations of the IEG evaluation of lines of credit (IEG 2006), seeking, for example, to strengthen borrower accountability and management capacity, to clearly define indicators for monitoring the financial performance of intermediaries, and to effectively monitor overall project impact.

Matching grants were the most common form of TSME intervention—with 47 projects representing 30 percent of the projects identified during the review period. Matching grants grew in popularity over time as leading and secondary components of TSME and multipurpose projects, with a record level of projects (30) and commitments ($688 million) during 2009–12. Matching grants were especially popular in the Africa Region, where 30 of the 47 projects over the period took place. Because of their smaller average product size, they represent only 40 percent of the value of the portfolio.

By contrast, in Latin America and the Caribbean, 9 projects comprise 54 percent of commitment value (Figure 4.4). Matching grants have great appeal in part because of their seeming simplicity—once money is granted for an approved purpose, there is no need to seek repayment. Eligibility can be extremely simple or quite complex. Matching grants often appear as one component in a larger project, often bundling together support for policy reforms, enhanced business services, and financing into a single project. In a recent article on matching grants, Campos and others (2012) note that matching grants are an extremely popular means to try to "foster technological upgrading, innovation, exports, use of business development services and other activities leading to firm growth."

BDSs are components of many projects. Because this is seen as complementary to many other activities—for example, helping firms make better use of financing so they may gain access to financing through a project—it is often combined in multicomponent projects. For example, BDS training services are elements of 87 percent of the linkage projects reviewed (see Figure 4.5), 49 percent of the combined projects in BDS and technical advisory services to governments and financial intermediaries, 47 percent of matching grants projects, 41 percent of lines of credit, and 25 percent of risk sharing projects.

BDS training activities (including subcomponents of other projects) cover a diversity of topics. Almost half of BDS components provide general business development advice and support (Table 4.1). A significant percent offer skills and vocational training, technical upgrading, and science and technical center or incubator support. A smaller percent offer financial training, training on product quality, standards conformity, and product certification.

Partial credit guarantees and risk-sharing facilities constituted about 8 percent of projects and 5 percent of portfolio value. Some governments and donors came to favor this approach in

FIGURE 4.5 Projects by Primary TSME with BDS Training

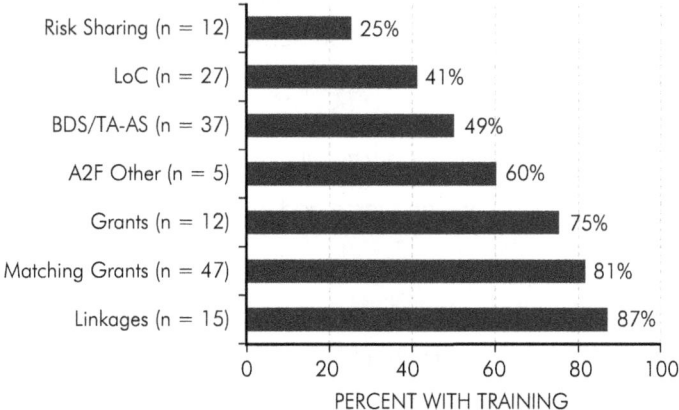

SOURCE: IEG portfolio review.
NOTE: Total projects = 155. A2F = access to finance; BDS/TA-AS = business development service/technical assistance-advisory service; LoC = line of credit; TSME = targeted small and medium-size enterprise.

TABLE 4.1 Focus of BDS Training Activities

Activities	Number of Projects	Percentage of Projects
General business dev. advice/support	48	51
Skill dev./vocational and sector specific training	16	17
Tech upgrading SMEs	14	15
Tech and science centers incubators	12	13
Financial training (bankable SMEs)	9	9
Improve prod quality/certification/standards	8	8
Entrepreneurial/managerial training	6	6
Improved facilities/infrastructure	6	6
BDS via tech solutions/services	5	5
IFC tools (Business Edge/SME Toolkit)	5	5
Training of trainers/BDS providers	4	4
CSR/E&S	4	4

SOURCE: IEG portfolio review.
NOTE: BDS = business development services; CSR = corporate social responsibility; E&S = environmental and social.

recent years to address the lack of collateral faced by many SMEs. IEG found five projects where risk-sharing facilities involved collaboration between the World Bank and IFC. For example, in Papua New Guinea, IFC covered 50 percent of the principal losses of a foreign bank, and IDA covered first losses of participating financial intermediaries through a financial intermediary loan, providing a credit of $11.67 million and technical assistance to financial intermediaries and to the Ministry of Commerce and Industry.

RELEVANCE OF THE WORLD BANK'S LENDING PORTFOLIO FOR TSME

For a TSME project to be relevant, there should be a clear, defining characteristic of the SMEs targeted relative to those not being targeted, to justify the focus of the inherent subsidy in the project. Given scarce resources, any justification for allocating resources to one size class of enterprises as opposed to another should be grounded in a clear definition of the class and a clear differentiation of the needs or contribution of that class of firms from firms of other size classes.

IEG's portfolio review found that 65 percent of Bank Group TSME lending projects failed to define the term SME in any way. Twenty-two percent used at least one enterprise size characteristic, namely, number of employees, value of annual sales, or value of assets, often drawing from national standards of the project country. Eight percent used some other enterprise characteristic, such as the legal form of the enterprise, its registration status, or the gender of its owner. A further 6 percent used the value of the support being offered (for example, in the form of a loan, grant, or guarantee) as the definition, presuming that only enterprises of SME characteristics would be interested.

World Bank staff preparing TSME lending clearly felt the need to identify market failures they were addressing. In 75 percent of TSME lending projects, IEG found a statement in the project document that there was a market failure being addressed by the project (Table 4.2). However, fewer than half of these projects identified what the market failure was, and of those, only a minority provided any evidence to substantiate the existence of the stated market failure

TABLE 4.2 Market Failure in World Bank TSME Lending Projects

Market Failure Claim, Definition, Evidence	Number of Projects	Percentage of Projects
Market failure claim	40	75
Market failure specified/defined	18	34
Market failure evidence	7	13
Market Failure Type		
Info asymmetry	29	55
Public goods	8	15
Non-comp markets	7	13
Externalities	3	6

SOURCE: IEG portfolio analysis and project documents.
NOTE: Number of projects with evaluations with ratings of = 53.

TABLE 4.3 Definition of SME in World Bank TSME Lending Portfolio

Criterion	Number of Projects	% of Projects
Not defined	100	65
At least one enterprise size distinction (employee, sales, assets)	34	22
Other criteria (type of organization, registered, women owned, and so forth)	12	8
Size of A2F support (loan, matching grant, guarantee, and so forth)	9	6
Total	155	100

SOURCE: IEG portfolio analysis and project documents.
NOTE: A2F = access to finance.

(Table 4.3). Where market failure was identified, information asymmetry was the market failure most often identified by far (in 29 projects) (see Box 4.2).

As shown in Chapter 1, it will always be possible to argue that SMEs get less finance than larger enterprise, as this is a feature of financial markets for all income levels, including high income. Establishing a market failure requires going beyond the observation of this feature and necessitates specifically identifying a condition that prevents a market from efficiently equilibrating supply and demand.[6] (For that matter, information asymmetries were first identified as a market failure affecting SMEs in seminal work characterizing U.S. financial markets, so merely identifying their existence does not necessarily justify a targeted intervention and may in fact call for a more systemic approach.) (See Box 4.3.)

TSME interventions may be referring to other factors than a narrowly defined market failure, and many do raise other justifications. It is necessary to have some analytic grounding that identifies a problem to which the project is the solution. Here, there are some questions on the depth and quality of analysis demonstrating the relevance of projects to an established need of firms.

IEG reviewed 53 projects with IEG evaluations that closed in FY06–12. Forty-eight of these linked the intervention to an identified constraint, often identified by prior Bank Group analytic work. Half of these 48 projects made general mention of access to finance constraints, with a smaller percentage narrowing this down to specific access constraints such as lack of capacity in financial intermediaries, lending terms, collateral requirements, or limited diversity of SME

IEG's portfolio review shows that market failure is a much-used term in project documentation, but only in the minority of cases found by IEG was it defined or specified in any economic sense of the word.

Market Failure Alluded To and Identified

However, there exist failures in the market for science, technology, and research and development. These market failures stem from certain characteristics of innovation such as (i) inappropriability of knowledge, (ii) partial intangibility of the assets involved in innovation, (iii) information failures, and (iv) network failures among researchers, institutions, and the private sector, meaning that individuals and institutions see a higher risk than benefit in collaborating, given the fungibility of knowledge. The document later cites literature quantifying the difference between social and private rates of return on R&D investments.

Market Failure Alluded To But Not Identified

The proposed project addresses the critical but temporary difficulties of firms that remain economically viable but face financially related problems brought about by the volatility of both the exchange rate and interest rates and a degree of market failure in the financial sector.

SOURCE: IEG portfolio analysis and project documents.

Turkey has a long history with World Bank lines of credit. The World Bank has provided 11 loans, worth $4 billion in commitments, to Turkish banks over the past 10 years, including two SME projects with $1.2 billion worth of credit lines (a third was recently approved). Despite Turkey's strong recovery from its 2001 financial crisis, in the early 2000s, lending to SMEs was relatively limited. Therefore, the SME loans intended to expand financing for SMEs. Initially, the SME loans were channeled primarily through the state-owned Halkbank and secondarily through the state-owned TSKB. The support through lines of credit fell under the growth and competitiveness pillar of the 2008–11 Turkey Country Partnership Strategy.

The project targets were satisfactorily reached, but no conclusions can yet be drawn about the impact of the credit lines on SMEs and on the financial system. (The Bank also invested significant resources to build capacity in the area of environmental safeguards midway through the project implementation.) The World Bank undertook an external evaluation of its entire credit line portfolio in 2011 that produced generally positive findings, but questioned additionality.

continued on page 130

The extent of lack of access to finance in Turkey is unclear. Although the 2008 enterprise survey identifies access to finance as the most important business environment obstacle, the same survey found that only 16.2 percent of small Turkish firms and 11.7 percent of medium-size firms identified access to finance as a major or severe constraint, placing it behind tax rates (identified as major or severe by 55.3 percent of small firms and 51 percent of medium firms), corruption (so identified by 46.8 and 38.8 percent of firms, respectively), licenses and permits (27.4 and 15.2 percent), tax administration (25.1 and 18.4 percent), electric power supply (20.5 and 33.3 percent), and education of workers (24 and 27 percent). In addition, results suggest that Turkish SMEs were more likely to get loans than those in Germany.

The contribution of World Bank lines of credit in Turkey varied over time. IEG's Country Partnership Strategy review finds that the Bank's lines of credit may have helped in the wake of the global financial crisis "until mid-2009" but after that may not have helped significantly (that is, IBRD's share in the loan market is small compared to the size of the credit market in Turkey) but contributed (a small share) to a troublesome credit bubble. In addition, the International Monetary Fund was concerned with the sharp increase in credit to the private sector financed by external inflows channeled through the banking system, and its link with the deterioration of the external current account. Between 2006 and 2012, both banks secured SME credit lines from other international financial institutions and HalkBank entered the Eurobond market.

What is the additionality of the World Bank lines of credit? The World Bank's self-evaluation of the Turkey Access to Finance for Small and Medium Enterprises Project and additional finance found that "the Bank is unable to tell whether it truly pushes out the supply curve for SME lending at market conditions" (World Bank 2011b). The loans were distributed to 801 private firms (745 HalkBank and 56 TSKB), although, given a high average loan size, in some cases their SME status can be questioned. Loans at TSKB averaged $2.5 million each (far exceeding IFC proxy threshold for SME loans) while at HalkBank they averaged $800 thousand each. The project uses a beneficiary survey that was subject to self-selection bias to find that the $600 million in financing led to gross creation of 8,250 jobs ($72,728 of financing per job created). Another additionality question was the role of TSKB. At the beginning it was intended to act as a wholesale lender in the project to reach other banks and leasing companies. However, the bank changed its role from wholesaler to a retailer bank and reached only 56 enterprises.

Monitoring and evaluation (M&E) of the lines of credit was weak. OP 8.30 guidance (replaced by OP 10 in April 2013) requires that lines of credit be used to finance investments in subprojects for increased production of goods and services. However,

continued on page 131

the project's impact on the ultimate beneficiaries (SMEs sales, profitability and employment data) was not systematically collected and reported throughout the life of the projects. Improving loan maturity for SME loans is critical for development impact, yet the M&E framework did not allow any conclusions to be drawn on whether the project "influenced the maturity structure of participating financial institution lending to SMEs over and above the bridge financing provided" (World Bank 2011b).

Are lines of credit the best product to enhance SME growth in Turkey going forward? With a growing private role in the financial sector and developed financial markets, it is not clear why the Bank continues to choose to work substantially through state banks and with lines of credit. A 2011 report on Turkish SMEs observed: "Policies enabling SME growth must take into account that SMEs tend to be associated with poorer economic outcomes than larger enterprises. Simply subsidizing SMEs would likely be counterproductive and lead to, for example, lower innovation, productivity, and wages. Reforming the business environment has been found to have a greater impact on the growth of SMEs relative to the impact on larger firms" (World Bank 2011b).

The World Bank and IFC presence in the SME market raises concerns over coordination. While the World Bank was pursuing SME finance through state-owned banks, IFC was actively pursuing projects with private sector banks, PEFs, and a leasing company aimed to improve SME access to finance. IFC's strategy "is to continue supporting banking sector development by working with individual institutions to broaden their reach and penetration in frontier regions and underserved sectors including SMEs, climate change, microfinance and agriculture." Although IFC claimed its project was in harmony with the Bank's strategy, its project document states that the project is responding to a problem of dominance of the financial sector by a few large banks, and its vehicle was the private banking sector.

SOURCES: World Bank 2011b; IFC project documents; IEG portfolio review.

financial products (Table 4.4). Twenty-three percent of projects suggested that problems on the part of SMEs justified intervention, ranging from limited capacity of management to limited workforce skills to limited ability to internalize technology and standards.

Nonetheless, the projects did not consistently establish that the constraint being addressed was a priority. For example, the product line review of financial intermediation loans suggests that several were proposed for countries where access to finance had not been identified by SMEs as a leading constraint in enterprise surveys, or where financial access by SMEs was far ahead of the norm. Even where access to finance was firmly established as an issue, the

TABLE 4.4 Constraints Identified in Program Documents Justifying TSME Projects, FY06–12

Constraints Identified by IEG	Number of Projects	% of Projects (over 48)
A2F constraints		
Limited A2F (general mention)	24	50
Lack of capacity to serve SMEs (staff skills, appraisal)	9	19
High interest/cost of financing/short tenor	8	17
Lack of collateral or stringent collateral requirements	7	15
Limited SME financial products/options	6	13
SMEs perceived as risky by fiscal intermediaries	5	10
Inadequate financial infrastructure[a]	3	6
Institutions serve large/corporate/government sectors	1	2
SME-side constraints		
Lack of capacity (financials/business skills/managerial)	11	23
Availability of quality/skilled workforce	10	21
Technology adoption/standards, information constraints	10	21
Limited training, BDS, Advisory Services opportunities	9	19
Cost, quality, and availability of inputs	2	4
Other general investment climate constraints		
Cumbersome business registration/regulation	9	19
Physical infra and logistics (including transport, electricity)	7	15
Taxes administration/costs	6	13
Inadequate legal system (including contracts, bankruptcy)	5	10

Constraints Identified by IEG	Number of Projects	% of Projects (over 48)
Corruption	4	8
Number of closed projects with constraints language	48	100
Number of closed projects with evaluation	53	N/A

SOURCE: IEG portfolio review.
NOTE: A2F = access to finance; BDS = business development services.
a. Includes inadequate credit information/reporting systems, payment systems, accounting systems.

justification of using a line of credit as the way to address it was often not accompanied by a careful consideration of alternatives. Thus, the relevance of the project to the problem was based on an incomplete logical connection.

The objectives in TSME support projects identified as project development objectives or in project component objectives were multiple and varied, but a few predominated. As seen in Table 4.5, objectives were recorded based on a review of 179 World Bank TSME lending projects. Eighty-six percent of the projects identified economic dynamism as an objective, 53 percent identified job creation as an objective, 47 percent economic growth, and 28 percent economic inclusion. Clearly, identifying an objective is an important precursor to connecting the specific choice of intervention(s) to a chain of events that will produce the desired result.

TABLE 4.5 World Bank Investment Project Objectives (projects committed FY06–12)

TSME	Number of Projects	% of Projects
Economic dynamism	154	86
Job creation	95	53
Economic growth	85	47
Inclusion	50	28

SOURCE: IEG portfolio analysis.

IEG's review of eight closed Bank TSME **lines of credit** found that they were primarily justified in terms of their direct benefits to recipient SMEs. It was not always clear or established in project documents that SMEs were relatively underserved in the country's financial system or that access to finance was a priority need of enterprises in the country (see Box 4.3). The project documentation did not always suggest long-term benefits that sustain banks' inclination to lend more to SMEs through enhanced capacity, information, and competition. For example, Mongolia had fundamental weaknesses in the regulatory and institutional framework for SME finance that negatively affected access to credit, yet the Bank began supporting reform of the regulatory and institutional environment through a Financial Sector Assessment Program development module in 2012, after the closure of the line of credit. IEG found no consistency in the definition or criteria used to identify SME beneficiaries. Five of eight offered some definition of SME, but not based on any consistent criteria across countries. Criteria ranged from firm characteristics to loan size to industry.

Matching grants are often justified in terms of market failures that lead firms to underinvestment in a variety of things seen as important to their success. Some are specifically geared to foster technological upgrading, to increase exports, and to foster use of business development services, whereas others aim to fill in financing where the formal financial system is not reaching.

BDS projects are geared to increase BDS consumption by SMEs. Under-consumption is often attributed to market failures, including information failure (businesses don't understand the value of BDS to their firm), externalities (businesses may experience benefits they can't fully capture, or lose staff who gain skills through BDS), and imperfect financial markets (businesses can't borrow to pay for services today that will yield profits tomorrow).

TSME projects are far more likely to be gender informed than are other FPD projects (Box 4.4). They are more likely to monitor gender dimensions of the assistance than are other FPD projects; IEG identified nine projects with specific gender components.

IEG evaluations suggest a generally successful record for TSME projects. Looking at 47 IEG-reviewed projects that closed in the 2006–12 period, 85 percent achieved successful development outcomes, a better result than the rest of the FPD SME-relevant portfolio and better than the Bank portfolio average (Figure 4.6). Over time, TSME performance has held fairly steady at a high level of performance. Unfortunately, there is not always clear evidence to suggest whether the project's impact was consistent with that promised by the underlying theory of change.

The importance of female ownership and entrepreneurship is reflected in the gender-informed nature of the World Bank TSME portfolio. A project database established by the World Bank in FY10–11 to monitor the gender content of Bank projects suggests that TSME projects are far more likely to be gender informed than other FPD projects (60 percent versus 33 percent), while roughly equal in this dimension to the rest of the World Bank portfolio (62 percent). According to the database, TSME projects are more likely than other projects to use M&E indicators that disaggregate by gender.

In the course of this evaluation, IEG reviewed nine Bank projects that had explicitly gender-oriented TSME components. All were active. Three projects had good progress to date in providing BDS for women entrepreneurs in Brazil, Cape Verde, and Grenada. There was also good progress on an access to finance projects in Egypt. Two projects are anticipated to be restructured because of unsatisfactory ratings during implementation—(i) an innovation grant for training and equipment for SMEs in the wood and tourism value chains in Cameroon, with competition rounds for women only, and (ii) a competitive fund for the development of new business plans for small and microenterprises run by women and youth in Costa Rica. A project in Togo is showing signs of delay mainly because of slow procurement processes, and projects in Jamaica and Papua New Guinea with BDS subcomponents for women entrepreneurs lack sufficient information to date to draw any conclusions in their implementation progress.

SOURCES: World Bank database; IEG portfolio analysis; http://bit.ly/18qde9a; database: http://bit.ly/17P6xOt.

FIGURE 4.6 Average Development Outcome, World Bank TSME Lending Portfolio

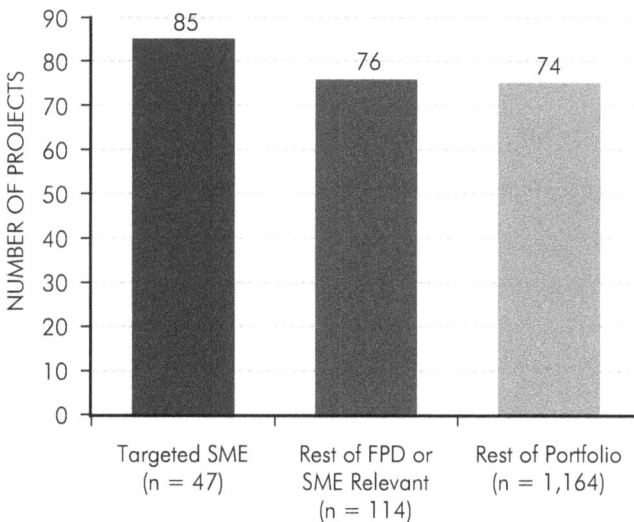

SOURCE: IEG portfolio review.
NOTE: FPD = Financial and Private Sector Development Network; TSME = targeted small and medium-size enterprise.

Efficacy of the World Bank's Lending Portfolio for TSME

Given that all the projects identified as TSME had multiple components, IEG separately reviewed the performance of the TSME components of the 47 projects. Sixty percent of projects had SME components with "positive" results (high, substantial, satisfactory, achieved, met, and so forth), 30 percent had "negative" results (modest, negligible, not achieved/met, and so on), and 6 percent had "mixed" results (there were multiple TSME components with mixed results or other components performed both better and worse than TSME). In one case, the SME component was dropped; in another case, the SME "component" was actually found to be financed separately by other donors. In 71 percent of the 28 projects whose TSME components had positive results, the assessment of the TSME component was the same as that of the overall project.

However, of the 14 projects whose TSME components were negatively evaluated, 57 percent performed worse than the overall projects. For example, the Philippines Rural Finance III Project had a component that was to benefit microenterprises and SMEs through a microfinance loan program. Loans were far smaller than anticipated, bringing into question whether a significant number of SMEs (as opposed to microenterprises) were being reached.

Efforts to judge the efficacy of World Bank TSME support are inhibited by the lack of serious quantitative (and sometimes qualitative) evaluation of the development impact of its leading product lines. Although the World Bank has a serious program of quantitative impact evaluation under way, it has only touched on the SME program to date. Specifically it has conveyed some lessons on entrepreneurial and skills training (pertaining to microenterprises more than SMEs) and lessons from the failure to be able to conduct an impact evaluation of matching grants. However, there have been no such efforts with regard to lines of credit that support SMEs. Partial credit guarantee schemes have been examined in the Middle East North Africa Region (Saadani, Arvai, and Rocha 2011) but not elsewhere with any rigor.

IEG's examination of closed project Implementation Completion and Results Reports suggests that even though projects are tracking indicators, many indicators are not obviously relevant to the project's impact, and often they stop at the level of project outputs. For example, two consecutive development policy loans in Indonesia supported the approval of a law, followed by an executive regulation, which put in place a system of warehouse receipts that was to expand SME finance. The outcome indicator it tracked was share of SME credit in total credit. However, interviews during the field visit suggested that the warehouse receipt system never became fully active because of the disinterest of banks, and informed observers said no SME was ever financed by it. Thus the indicators did not measure project outcomes.

TABLE 4.6 Characteristics of IEG-Reviewed TSME Investment Projects

Primary TSME Intervention	Number of Projects	Percent Successful	Percent with Restructure	Percent with Cancellation	Percent with Risk Flag	Average Extension (years)	Percent with Extension
BDS/TA-AS	19	84	0	26	74	0.9	5.3
Line of credit	10	90	10	50	80	0.9	60
Matching grants	10	70	50	50	90	2.0	90
A2F other	4	100	9	25	50	0.5	50
Risk sharing	3	100	0	33	33	0.8	33
Grants	1	100	0	0	0	0	0
Total	47	85	13	36	72	1.1	60

SOURCE: IEG portfolio review.
NOTE: A2F = access to finance; AS = advisory services; BDS = business development service; TA = technical assistance.

Other challenges faced in this area include indicators and evaluations that measure benefits to a limited group of SMEs but do not address the project impact on underlying market failures that the project claimed to be addressing; failure to identify SME beneficiaries; surveys of beneficiary satisfaction do not examine or weigh economic benefits and costs of a project; projects that report only gross benefits; and lack of evidence regarding beneficiary graduation or self-sufficiency.

Overall, nine of 10 **lines of credit** had successful development outcomes. In a product line review for this evaluation, IEG reviewed closing documents of eight lines of credit of which seven had reached their development objectives or project outcome indicators by the time of exit. China provides one good example (Box 4.5). In spite of this, it was difficult to quantify the additionality of some lines of credit. The question of whether they served to sustainably build the capacity of the financial system to serve SMEs often went unanswered. The product review also found that some appeared to be offering financial intermediaries better than market terms.

BOX 4.5 China Micro and Small Enterprise Credit Line

In the early to mid-2000s, the Chinese economy grew at more than 10 percent per year. Despite rapid financial sector growth in China, loans to micro and small enterprises were limited. According to recent enterprise survey results, 13.9 percent of small firms had a loan, bank finance accounted for only one percent of their investments, and collateral requirements averaged more than 200 percent of loan value, far exceeding norms for similar countries. The Bank Group identified constraints in financial markets and inability of financial intermediaries to assess MSEs as key reasons.

As part of broader efforts by the World Bank and IFC to expand MSME access to credit that included both systemic and targeted interventions, the World Bank used a 2007 financial intermediary loan of $100 million to support Chinese micro and small enterprises. The objective of the project was to expand credit flows to these enterprises through a mass market and on a commercially sustainable basis. It also aimed to help China Development Bank develop a new business line involving wholesaling of micro and small enterprise subsidiary loans and the provision of related technical support to participating financial institutions; and help the participating financial institutions build up a high-quality micro and small enterprise loan portfolio based on credit technologies.

The project had a clear definition for micro and small enterprise, based on firm size, and conditions for borrowing. The subloans were for long-term investments and working capital, and average loan size were around RMB100000.

At closure, more than 175,000 loans had been extended to micro and small enterprises (which exceeded the target by about 47 percent), and the portfolio quality was high. Cumulative lending to such organizations by the six participating financial institutions was 20 times the size of World Bank and KfW financing. Overachievement of the loans resulted from much larger than expected use of the six banks' own funds, indicating the profitability of utilizing new technology and mass marketing techniques for the participating financial institutions.

The project's success can be attributed in part to the timing of the project in the context of broader market-oriented reforms before and during the project period. These reforms included credit cooperative reforms, liberalization of lending rates, improved credit information, and opening of financial markets to greater competition among intermediaries. However, although it was originally planned to track both treatment and control groups to understand the project's impact, this approach was not implemented because of a lack of resources from the China Development Bank. Therefore, no conclusions can be drawn about the impact of credit lines on micro and small business performance (that is, job creation or profitability).

SOURCES: World Bank 2011b; IEG 2012.

In more developed financial markets, this increased the chance of crowding out private finance and distorting the pattern of financial sector growth. Five of eight had accompanying technical assistance to build capacity of the intermediaries. Project teams identified technical assistance to strengthen intermediaries' institutional capacity and skills in SME lending as critical for the success of the financial intermediary loans in Azerbaijan, China, Mongolia, and Vietnam. The cases indicated that the capacity of intermediaries was a key to success. Where strong or subsidized competition emerges, it hindered on-lending through a World Bank line of credit. In Armenia and Mongolia, competing donor-financed lines of credit on better terms reduced demand for the Bank-financed line of credit.

Seven of 10 **matching grant schemes** had a successful outcome, although many encountered difficulties in their implementation. A recent effort by the World Bank to evaluate African matching grant schemes found them unevaluable because of "continued project delays, politicians not willing to allow random assignment, and low program take up." The underlying causes included "political economy, overly stringent criteria that do not take account of where value added may be highest, a lack of attention to detail in 'last mile' issues, incentives facing project staff, and the way impact evaluations are funded" (Campos and others 2012).

BDS and other technical assistance projects had successful development outcomes in 84 percent of IEG evaluations from 2006 to 2012. Because BDS is often blended with other components, it is hard to evaluate the separate contribution of the product. As shown in Figure 4.5, BDSs are often elements of linkage projects and of technical advisory, matching grant, and line of credit projects.

Partial credit guarantee schemes and risk-sharing facilities were rarely evaluated, but the few that were show challenges in implementation. The IEG literature review notes challenges in appropriately structuring the pricing, funding, and institutional arrangements for partial credit guarantees. It finds a few single country studies with mixed results and concludes that more evidence is needed to gauge what characteristics constitute a successful credit guarantee scheme, exploiting the large variation in experiences across countries (Table 4.7). A World Bank review of schemes in the Middle East and North Africa Region found that guarantee schemes are not yet reaching smaller firms. Schemes were found to be financially sound with room to grow, but needed some key design and management improvements and "the introduction of systematic impact evaluation reviews."[7]

In IEG's case studies, the Nicaragua MSME project dropped a partial credit guarantee scheme that it could not implement. An Implementation Completion and Results Report from the Ethiopia Financial Sector Capacity Building Project states that its partial credit guarantee

TABLE 4.7 Subcomponents of World Bank TSME Lending Projects, by Project Type, Committed or Evaluated, FY06–12, for Projects with Required Documentation

Classification	Number of Projects	Avg. Number Components/ Subcomponents
A2F other	3	15
BDS/TA-AS	27	12
Grants	11	15
Linkages	13	10
Line of credit	32	6
Matching grants	56	11
Risk sharing	9	8
Total	151	11

SOURCE: IEG portfolio review.
NOTE: A2F = access to finance; BDS = business development service; TA-AS = technical assistance/advisory services.

facility had to be dropped because, in spite of the component's relevance, Ethiopia lacked necessary preconditions including Central Bank capacity to supervise and regulate the banking and insurance domains and "the functional financial infrastructure to allow for payments settlements and the transparent exchange of financial information."

Efficiency of the World Bank TSME Lending Portfolio

Without knowing more about the impact of World Bank lending projects, it is difficult to gauge efficiency. Logically, lines of credit should be highly efficient, as they move very large amounts of money for administrative costs of a single project. Packaging $11 billion in only 49 projects is extremely efficient compared to other business lines, from the point of view of minimizing processing and overhead costs. Furthermore, lines of credit are typically channeled through the existing financial system, and hence may not require administrative expenses of a separate system to channel resources to SMEs (although they may include technical assistance to strengthen capacity of existing financial entities).

However, weak targeting of lines of credit may introduce inefficiencies by diverting benefits to beneficiaries who were not suffering adversely from the conditions the line of credit sought to relieve. Line of credit targeting in effect was weak: some definitions were expansive and finance was channeled only to fairly large or fairly small firms. The definition used in Armenia covered about 98 percent of enterprises in the country. In Turkey and Ukraine, a number of large enterprises benefited (one bank in Turkey had an average loan size of $2.5 million), whereas in Vietnam benefits appeared to accrue primarily to microenterprises rather than SMEs.

Unlike what is possible with lines of credit, matching grant schemes usually require the establishment of a separate project management structure and may require intense oversight. The task team leader of one matching grant scheme estimated that administrative costs were equivalent to 30 percent of the grant value. In Nicaragua, establishing a system to oversee and administer matching grants took considerable time, as did setting up the selection process to insulate it from political interference. In Kenya, matching grants to value chain groups were slowed by an inefficient approval process, which required the sign-off of two consulting companies, a ministry, and the World Bank. BDS projects often have so many components that it is hard to judge the contribution of the BDS component to impact and weight that against component costs.

In spite of generally successful project outcomes, TSME projects are prone to cancellations, risk flags, and extensions. Although extension, cancellations, and restructuring may be the best response to particular events or situations, a high rate of them for any product line suggests something is wrong with the business model or the Bank's institutional ability to anticipate likely implementation conditions. Lines of credit were the most subject to cancellation (50 percent), 80 percent had risk flags, and 60 percent required extensions, again averaging almost a year. Matching grants were also subject to cancellation 50 percent of the time.

A number of projects are notably complex, adding elements that in retrospect did not add to the impact but did add to the difficulty and cost of administration. One indicator of complexity of design is the number of separate components and subcomponents a loan has—each one requiring oversight and coordination internally and with an often unique set of relevant counterparts and stakeholders. A count of components and subcomponents in World Bank TSME lending projects suggests that, averaged by product, the typical project has 11 moving parts. The product average ranges from 6 for lines of credit up to 15 for grants, with matching grants averaging 12 and BDS projects 11.

Projects in the Sustainable Development Network tend to have more subcomponents (12) than those in other networks, and Poverty Reduction and Economic Management Network projects average only 8. Regionally, projects in the Africa Region average 13 components,

TABLE 4.8 Characteristics of Complex TSME Investment Projects Closed FY06–12

TSME Portfolio with IEG Observed Problem	Number of Projects	Percent Successful	Average Extension (years)	Percent with Restructure	Percent with Cancellation	Percent with Risk Flag	Percent with Extension	Average Number Comp/Sub
Overly complex design	8	63	2.3	25	88	100	100	14
Rest of TSME	22	91	1/3	18	45	86	73	10
Total	30	83	1.6	20	57	90	80	11

SOURCE: IEG review of closed project evaluations.

compared to only 7 in East Asia and Pacific. Although counting components and activities may seem trivial, it relates directly to development outcomes.

A review of 30 closed investment projects suggests that projects identified by IEG microevaluations as overly complex in design have more components and are less successful (Table 4.8). They are more prone to restructuring, more likely to have elements cancelled, more likely to be extended, more likely to be flagged by management as risky, and more likely to have a longer average period of extension when they are inevitably extended.

Some projects appeared to be a kind of "to do list" of financial sector and private sector development reforms, rather than a tightly complementary set of actions aimed at a common purpose. In Kenya and Nicaragua, the IEG team saw projects with multiple components—an

TABLE 4.9 Lines of Credit—Projects Approved FY06–12

TSME Interventions	Number of Projects	Average of Extension (years)	Percent with Extension	Percent Restructured	Percent with Cancellation	Percent with Risk Flag
Lines of credit	27	0.8	33	11	15	48
Rest of TSME	128	0.5	27	9	12	66
Total	155	0.5	28	9	12	63

SOURCE: IEG portfolio review.

MSME competitiveness project and an MSME development project—that had been delayed and restructured, with elements cancelled, over their extended lives. Counterparts had changed on both the Bank side (task team leader and project team) and the counterpart side (deputy ministers, ministers, and whole governments) over the lives of the projects, sometimes multiple times. Overall, the IEG team was struck by the inefficiency embodied in the complexity of a number of projects. Committing funds, organizing activities, and then not implementing them do not appear efficient. Because complexity is a feature of project design, it also speaks to work quality (discussed in the next section).

Work Quality

Some aspects of work quality in World Bank projects excel, whereas others require further refinement. Areas of particular strength include the linkage of projects to prior analytic work (discussed under AAA) and the high level of "realism" in World Bank self-evaluations. The high rate of successful outcomes also suggests a high level of work quality. Where realism may fail is in the overambitious design of some projects, lack of economic evaluation of costs and benefits in project appraisals, overoptimistic time frames for implementing such projects (resulting in frequent delays), and the frequent need for restructuring and cancellation of components of some projects.

Other problems lie in highly specific but not necessarily justified definitions of SMEs, weak conceptual treatment of market failure, inconsistencies in linking project design to specific market failures, and the frequent lack of M&E that captures impact at the beneficiary level (Table 4.10). Beyond complexity, there appears to be a problem of continuity in case of staff changes—the case studies often found large, long-term projects that suffered in implementation and oversight when the task team leader changed. In the context of lines of credit, operation policy does not appear to be strictly regarded, and in fact, the guiding operation policy was recently abandoned. Finally, beyond frequent flaws in M&E, the fact that there has never been a serious quantitative evaluation of the development impact of whole product lines, such as lines of credit, is of particular concern.

A review of 48 closed TSME lending projects that were evaluable produces a list by which it is possible to see the frequency of the types of problems identified. In just over half the projects, either the M&E framework or the data collected through it were flawed. In just under half of projects, there were problems in the relationship of the project implementation unit with the World Bank staff. In 45 percent of projects, inadequate technical design was identified as a problem. Disruption by a crisis was identified as a problem in four of ten projects. Inadequate

TABLE 4.10 Problems Identified in IEG Evaluations—World Bank TSME Lending Projects

Problem Descriptions	Number of Projects	% of Projects (over 53)
Inadequate M&E framework, poor data quality	27	51
PIU experience with the World Bank	26	49
Inadequate technical design	24	45
Implementation disrupted by crisis	21	40
Inadequate supervision	14	26
Inadequate risk assessment	13	25
Overly complex design	12	23
Inadequate political or institutional analysis	9	17
Inadequate baseline data or unrealistic targets	9	17
Inadequate prior analytic work	9	17
Project restructured	9	17
Inadequate partner financing or coordination	8	15
At least one driver identified	48	91
Number of projects with evaluation	53	100

SOURCE: IEG.
NOTE: M&E = monitoring and evaluation, PIU = project implementation unit.

supervision affected 25 percent of projects, and overly complex design hampered 23 percent of the projects reviewed.

▶ Lines of Credit. The 10 IEG reviewed lines of credit projects had an average of 10 components. Sixty percent had to be extended (an average of 0.9 years), 10 percent restructured, and 50 percent cancelled. Eighty percent had a management risk flag

TABLE 4.11 Line of Credit Closed Project Characteristics

Primary TSME Intervention	Number of Projects	% Successful	Average Years Extended	% with Restructuring	% with Cancellation	% with Risk Flag	% with Extension	Average Number Com/Sub
Line of credit	10	90	0.9	10	50	80	60	6
Rest of portfolio	37	84	1.1	14	32	70	59	53
Total	**47**	**85**	**1.1**	**13**	**36**	**72**	**60**	**43**

SOURCE: IEG portfolio review.

(Table 4.11). These numbers place lines of credit near the norm for the TSME portfolio. However, a review of eight closed IEG-reviewed projects suggests further issues relating to work quality:

- Consideration of alternatives to lines of credit was inconsistent and incomplete. In countries with developed banking sector, other models of support may have better leveraged resources.

- All projects had M&E systems in place during the appraisal and identified indicators or measures to assess the outcome of targeted SME activities. However, these indicators focused on outputs, very few on outcomes, and only two of eight projects had indicators focused on subborrowers (Armenia and Vietnam). In no case was it possible to seriously examine counterfactuals or look at long-term impact on intermediaries. Where follow-up surveys were used, they were mostly consumer satisfaction, subject to response bias and entirely based on recall rather than baseline collection of data. The only planned serious quantitative impact evaluation of a fiscal intermediary loan was cancelled.

- Project documents reflected inconsistent reference to/observance of OP8.30 and BP 8.30, which applied to lines of credit throughout the evaluation period:

  - Several did not discuss why IFC was not playing "the lead Bank Group role in financial intermediary lending."

  - Some did not reflect the mandatory Bank/IFC coordination.

- Some did not appear to be justified in terms of "important sector and policy reform objectives that are included in the Bank's country dialogue."

- Some appeared to offer financial intermediaries terms better than those available in prevailing markets.

In late 2012, the World Bank's Financial Inclusion Practice, under contract with the G-20, issued an impact assessment framework for SME finance. It offers experimental and nonexperimental approaches to evaluating SME policy, program, and project interventions. The practice also reported working on a results and monitoring framework for MSME finance. IEG has not evaluated these.

▶ Matching Grants. Matching grant scheme projects have an average of 11 components. Although 75 percent of evaluated matching grant projects achieve a successful outcome, this was not without difficulty. Ninety-two percent are extended (versus 49 percent for the rest of the TSME investment portfolio), 42 percent restructured (versus 3 percent for the rest of the TSME portfolio), and 50 percent cancelled (see Table 4.12). Eighty-three percent had a risk flag in the system. Thus, an apparently straightforward product has proven in practice to be extremely difficult to implement.

▶ BDS. Looking at rated projects, the success of BDS services is just ahead of that of the overall Bank TSME investment portfolio. Seventy-six percent of BDS projects need to be extended, and they are extended for a much longer than average period (Table 4.13). As BDS projects have an average of 12 components and/or subcomponents, the opportunities for delay are abundant. BDS projects are about average for restructuring and cancellation.

TABLE 4.12 Performance of IEG-Evaluated World Bank Investment Matching Grant Projects

Targeted Classification	Number of Projects	% Successful	Average Years Extension	Extension (%)	Restructured (%)	Cancellation (%)	Risk Flag (%)
Matching grants	12	75	1.8	92	42	50	83
Rest of TSME	35	89	0.8	49	3	31	69
Total	47	85	1.1	60	13	36	72

SOURCE: IEG portfolio review.
NOTE: TSME = targeted small and medium-size enterprise.

TABLE 4.13 Performance of IEG-Evaluated World Bank Investment TSME BDS Training Projects

Primary TSME Intervention	Number of Projects	% Successful	Average Extension (yrs)	% with Restructure	% with Cancellation	% with Risk Flag	% with Extension
BDS training	17	88	1.5	12	35	76	76
Rest of TSME	30	83	0.8	13	37	70	50
Total	47	85	1.1	13	36	72	60

SOURCE: IEG portfolio review.
NOTE: BDS = business development service.

▶ Partial Credit Guarantees. IEG's portfolio review suggests that the small number of reviewed partial credit guarantee/risk sharing facility schemes have been successful. They have been less subject to extension than the average TSME operation, more subject to cancellation, and more subject to risk flags (Table 4.14). A deeper examination, however, suggests substantial implementation challenges.

The World Bank's own lending project database records provide a great deal of information on aspects of projects that may contribute to project success or failure. A number of "flags" identify a host of potential sources of problems. IEG econometrically tested a variety of

TABLE 4.14 Performance of IEG-Evaluated World Bank Investment TSME Partial Credit Guarantee Projects

Primary TSME Intervention	Number of Projects	% Successful	Average Extension (yrs)	% with Restructure	% with Cancellation	% with Risk Flag	% with Extension	Average Number Components/ Subcomponents
RSF/PCG	3	100	0.8	0	33	33	33	74
Rest of TSME	44	84	1.1	14	36	75	61	41
Total	47	85	1.1	13	36	72	60	43

SOURCE: IEG portfolio review.
NOTE: RSF/PCG = risk sharing facility/partial credit guarantee; TSME = targeted small and medium-size enterprise.

project characteristics and problems to see which appear to be significantly related to project outcomes. Three in particular proved significant.

First, once other factors had been controlled for, projects in lower-middle-income countries performed significantly worse in terms of development outcome than projects in other income levels of countries. (This was less the case for low-income countries.) Second, having a flag for project management was associated with a significantly worse development outcome. Third, and the factor with the largest regression coefficient, having an overly complex design was negatively associated with a lower development outcome. What did not significantly relate was also interesting—being in a low-income country, length and size (in dollars) of the project, the type of intervention, having a flag for M&E, and having a flag for inadequate risk assessment; none of these variables was significantly linked to poorer development outcomes. Perhaps most surprising was that having a flag for slow disbursement was significantly positively related to development outcome.

One relatively strong element of the TSME lending portfolio is the realism in self-evaluation (Table 4.15). The difference between the self-evaluation rating of development outcome success and that of IEG is 6 percent for TSME lending projects, compared to 7 percent for the rest of FPD and SME-relevant projects and 11 percent for the rest of the lending portfolio (Table 4.15). It would be good if that realistic approach extended better to project design—reflecting better what underlying problems are that merit a targeted approach, more carefully documenting a theory of change that maps project design onto those problems, more realistically planning actions that can be implemented within the project life cycle, and, finally, better capturing indicators that shed a bright light on the extent to which the project is solving those underlying problems.

TABLE 4.15 "Realism" in World Bank Self-Evaluation—TSME Lending Portfolio

Classification	Number of Projects	ICR DO % SU	IEG DO % SU	"Realism" (%)
TSME	47	91	85	–6
Rest of FPD or SME relevant	113	83	76	–7
Rest of portfolio	1,169	85	74	–11
Total	1,329	85	74	–11

SOURCE: IEG portfolio review.
NOTE: DO = Development Outcome; FPD = Financial and Private Sector Development Network; ICR = Implementation Completion and Results Report; SU = Successful.

World Bank Analytic and Advisory Work

RELEVANCE

Although AAA work is both relevant and important to the challenges faced by SMEs, only a small part of it can be categorized as TSME either by virtue of its exclusive focus on SMEs or its intended exclusive benefit to SMEs (or MSMEs). Furthermore, a great deal of AAA is subsumed in multicomponent investment projects, and further work is mobilized in parallel from sources other than the World Bank. Thus, although there is evidence of how strong AAA work can improve development and strengthen the impact of lending projects, the identified portfolio of 62 relevant projects, representing a collective expenditure of $11 million, is quite small.

Eighty-five percent of projects and 91 percent of project value for the World Bank TSME AAA portfolio consisted of technical assistance to governments, financial institutions, and others (Figures 4.7 and 4.8). In fact, 68 percent of the technical assistance projects identified in the TSME portfolio were aimed at governments or government agencies, 25 percent at financial institutions, 11 percent at private sector bodies, and the rest toward a variety of other stakeholders (Table 4.16).

The small role of economic and sector work in the TSME portfolio may be a result of SME issues that are often covered in such work with a broader focus that has important findings and recommendations pertaining to key constraints or market failures of critical concerns to SMEs. Thus, such nontargeted work as investment climate assessments (and the underlying enterprise surveys), value chain and competitiveness studies, and financial sector assessments, can be very important in guiding and shaping SME investments and/or follow-up AAA (Table 4.17).

FIGURE 4.7 World Bank TSME AAA Work FY06–12, by Number of Projects

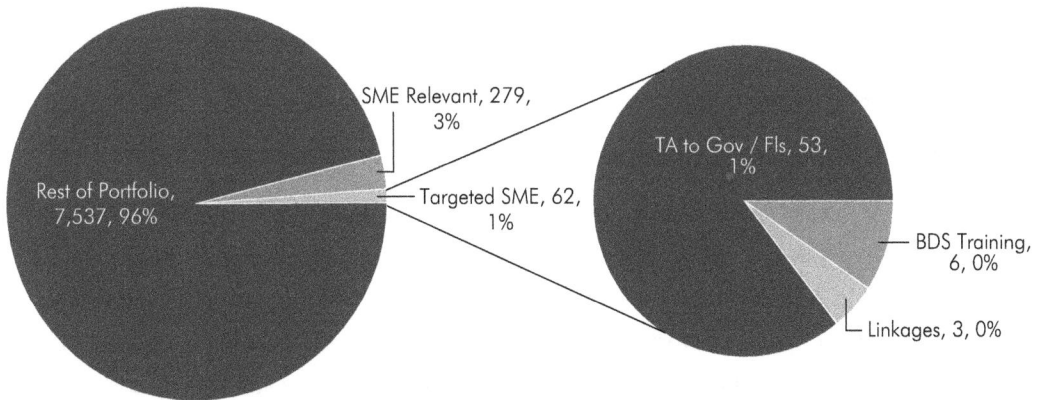

SOURCE: IEG portfolio review.

NOTE: AAA = analytic and advisory activity; BDS = business development service; FI = fiscal intermediary; TA = technical assistance.

FIGURE 4.8 World Bank TSME AAA Work FY06–12, by Commitment Value ($ millions)

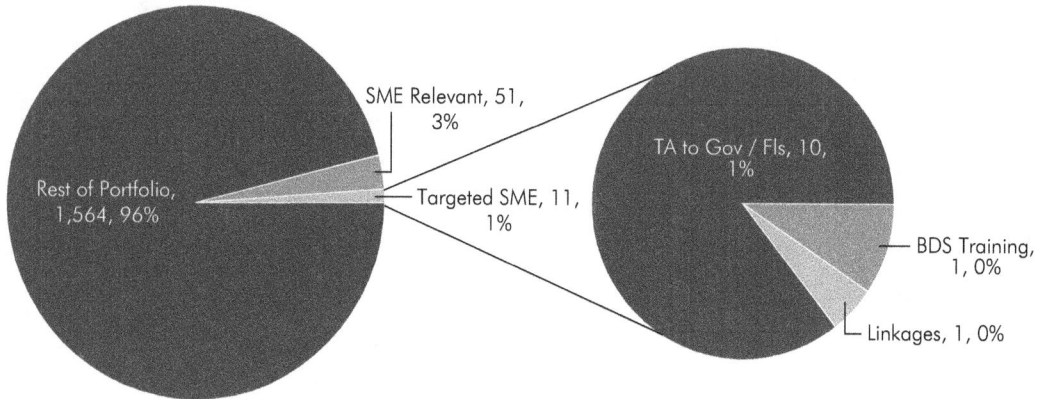

SOURCE: IEG portfolio review.
NOTE: AAA = analytic and advisory activity; BDS = business development service; FI = fiscal intermediary; TA = technical assistance.

TABLE 4.16 Stakeholder/Audience for World Bank Projects with Technical/Advisory Assistance

Stakeholders/Audience	Number of Projects	% of Projects
Government	38	68
Financial institution	14	25
Private sector	6	11
Donor community	3	5
Academia	2	4
Other	8	14
Projects with TA-AS	56	100

SOURCE: IEG portfolio review.
NOTE: TA-AS = technical assistance/advisory services.

Financial Sector Assessment Programs and Reports on the Observance of Standards and Codes each serve to inform policy dialogue, country strategy, and operations pertaining to SMEs. In fact, in its portfolio review of 98 projects mentioning analytic work, IEG identified the types of work mentioned. Investment climate assessments were the most commonly mentioned source, followed by Doing Business, enterprise surveys (which usually underpin the climate assessments), and then Financial Sector Assessment Programs, Reports on the Observance of Standards and Codes, and the Country Economic Memorandum.

TABLE 4.17 Analytical Work Mentioned in TSME Lending Projects

Analytical Work Mentioned	Number of Projects	% of Projects
ICA	48	51
Doing Business	42	44
Enterprise survey	19	20
FSAP	13	14
ROSC	10	11
CEM	8	8
Other	49	52
Number of projects	98	

SOURCE: IEG portfolio review.
NOTE: CEM = Country Economic Memorandum; FSAP = Financial Sector Assessment Program; ICA = Investment Climate Assessment; ROSC = Report on the Observance of Standards and Codes.

AAA EFFICACY AND WORK QUALITY

IEG did not evaluate AAA during the evaluation period, so World Bank self-evaluations (activity completion summaries as exported from an internal database) provide the sole guide of quality. The TSME portfolio was rated successful 86 percent of the time, whereas the rest of the FPD, SME, and World Bank AAA portfolio was rated successful 88 percent of the time, a very small difference (Table 4.18). The trend over time has been positive for TSME AAA—rising from 81 percent successful in the period 2006–09 to 90 percent successful in 2010–12 (Figure 4.9).

Technical assistance has been somewhat more successful than economic and sector work, according to the self-evaluations (Figure 4.9). Although TSME economic and sector work somewhat underperforms compared to the rest of that portfolio, TSME technical assistance performs at least as well as the broader portfolio. AAA work seems to be most successful in low-income countries, and least successful in high-income countries (Figure 4.10). This is much less true for the general AAA portfolio than for the TSME AAA portfolio, which suggests that technical assistance has the greatest traction where it is most needed, in low-income countries. There is a slight trend over time towards greater efficacy of the AAA portfolio

TABLE 4.18 Success of World Bank TSME AAA versus Rest of FPD/SME Relevant and Entire AAA Portfolios

Classification	Number of Projects	% Successful
TSME	56	86
Rest of FPD or SME relevant	1,476	88
Rest of portfolio	5,066	88
Total	6,598	88

SOURCE: IEG portfolio review.
NOTE: AAA = analytic and advisory activity; FPD = Financial and Private Sector Development; SME = small and medium-size enterprise; TSME = targeted small and medium-size enterprise.

FIGURE 4.9 World Bank Self-Evaluation of Success—ESW and Technical Assistance, TSME Portfolio, FY06–12

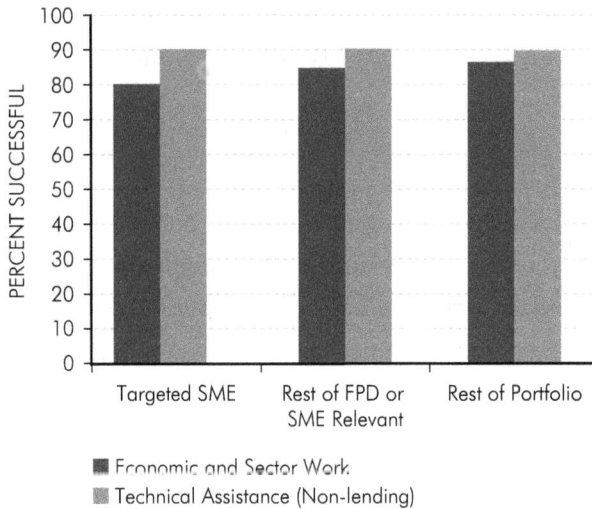

SOURCE: World Bank database.
NOTE: ESW = economic and sector work; FPD = Financial and Private Sector Development.

(Figure 4.11). Recent IEG work emphasized the importance of "how to" advice, long-term engagement, responsive customization and use of local expertise and knowledge as elements of success (Box 4.6).

World Bank self-evaluations suggest that AAA does not perform equally well at all tasks. Technical assistance is rated successful 96 percent of the time at "facilitating knowledge exchange," 88 percent of the time in assisting in client policy or program implementation,

FIGURE 4.10 Success Rate for TSME AAA Work, by Country Income Level

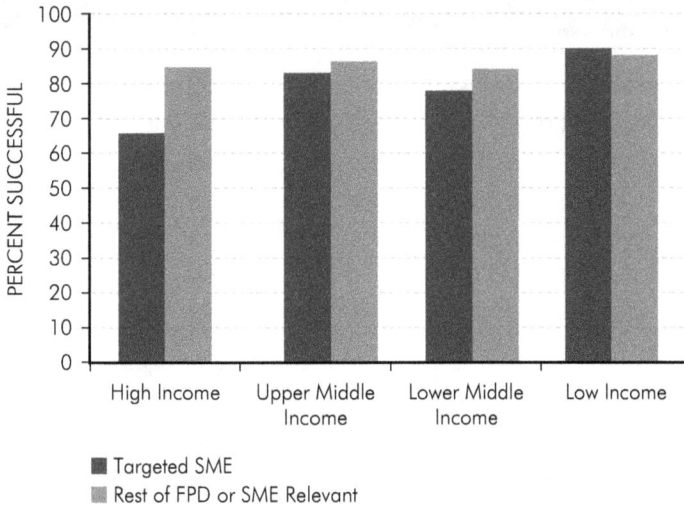

SOURCE: World Bank database.
NOTE: AAA = analytic and advisory activity; FPD = Financial and Private Sector Development; TSME = targeted small and medium-size enterprise.

FIGURE 4.11 World Bank TSME AAA Portfolio: Success over Time

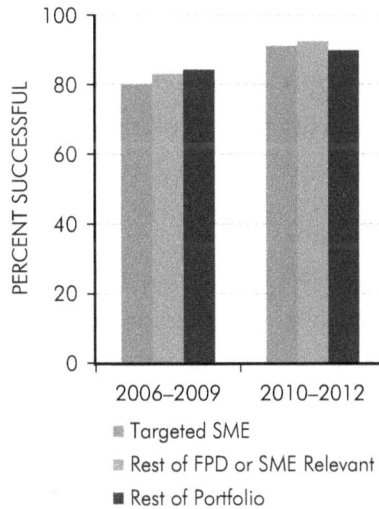

SOURCE: World Bank database.
NOTE: AAA = analytic and advisory activity; FPD = Financial and Private Sector Development; TSME = targeted small and medium-size enterprise.

and 79 percent of the time in developing or strengthening institutions. Compared to the rest of the private sector development/SME technical assistance portfolio and the general AAA portfolio, it appears that technical assistance is roughly at the norm in facilitating knowledge exchange, well above the norm in assisting in client policy or program implementation, and just under the norm in promoting institutional development and strengthening (see Kazakhstan

IEG's recent evaluation of knowledge-based country programs finds "the Bank Group was more effective when it worked on specific sectors rather than broad topics, designed tasks to address specific client concerns, customized international best practice to local conditions, generated data to support policy making, and formulated actionable recommendations that fit local administrative and political economy constraints" (IEG 2013, p. xi). It stresses

> a need to emphasize "how to" options rather than diagnostics and "what to do" recommendations; stay engaged and responsive through implementation phases of advisory activities (using programmatic approaches, for example); use local expertise to enhance the impact of advisory activities; design advisory projects with relevant responses to client concerns; and remain engaged in areas that are relevant to a client country's medium-term development agenda to maintain its capacity to see the big picture and provide multi-sectoral development solutions.

SOURCE: IEG 2013.

example, Box 4.7). IEG's field visits showed the potential for technical assistance components to strengthen implementation, including for a highly motivated and well-trained counterpart group within a key ministry in Nicaragua. As noted, complementary technical assistance can improve project performance by building institutional capacity to implement project elements.

Economic and sector work self-evaluations provide multiple dimensions by which to measure performance, and the success rate varies dramatically between them (Figure 4.12). Self-evaluations suggest that this work is most effective at building client analytic capacity—indeed, far more successful than is the rest of the portfolio. In other dimensions, it appears to underperform the rest of the portfolio, showing a 72 percent success rate at informing and stimulating public debate, a 70 percent success rate at informing lending (versus an institutional norm of 78 percent), only a 44 percent success rate at informing government policy (the norm for FPD/SME is 71 percent), and a success rate of 40 percent in influencing the development community (compared to 71 percent for the rest of FPD/SME).

Although there are benefits from informing debate, it is worth asking whether economic and sector work should influence government policy only a minority of the time. At its best, it can guide government policy and World Bank (and IFC and MIGA) strategy and projects. For example, a well-timed and well-focused 2005 value chain study identified the potential

Targeted Technical Assistance in Kazakhstan

Kazakhstan's ambitious Joint Economic Research Program of policy advice for economic and social development reform yielded dozens of AAA activities for the Bank, many of which focused on the business enabling environment. Three activities were identified as targeted SME. Two dealt with the introduction and implementation of international financial reporting standards for SMEs, to support the government's strategy for expanding non-oil sector exports and employment.

According to the FY12–17 Country Partnership Strategy, the standards component is meant to support the government's strategy. Both were rated fully successful at developing and strengthening institutions and facilitating knowledge exchange, and the one focusing on SME training also fully succeeded (according to self-evaluation) at "assisting in client's policy/program implementation." A third technical assistance project focused on SME taxation, succeeding in developing institutions and facilitating knowledge exchange, but rated "not applicable" in assisting policy/program implementation.

SOURCES: IEG case study; World Bank 2012a, 2012b, 2011a.
See also http://www.worldbank.org/en/news/feature/2002/04/06/kazakhstan-joint-economic-research-program.

FIGURE 4.12 World Bank Self-Evaluations of TSME Economic and Sector Work Portfolio (FY06–12)—Dimensions of Success

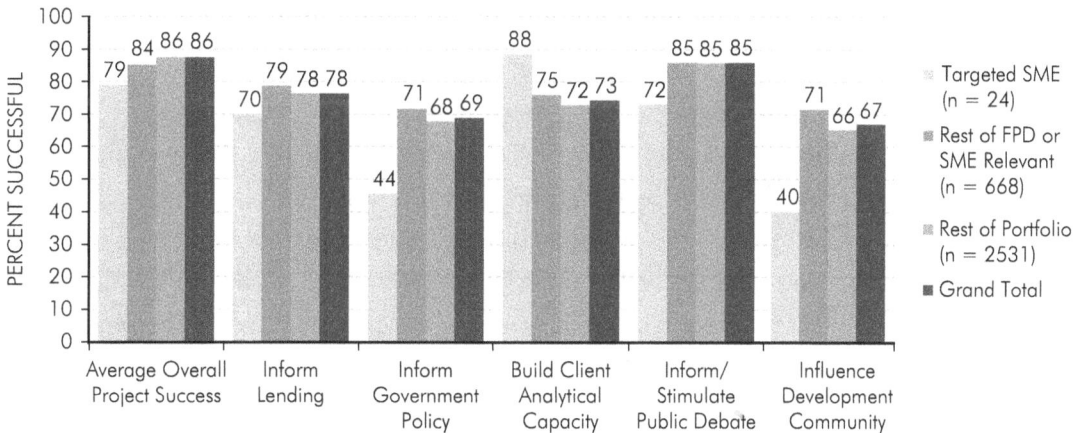

SOURCE: World Bank database.
NOTE: FPD = Financial and Private Sector Development; TSME = targeted small and medium-size enterprise.

of several sectors that became the focal point of the Kenya MSME competitiveness project (http://siteresources.worldbank.org/EXTAFRSUMAFTPS/Resources/note_8_screen.pdf). The FY12 Tunisia MSME Development Project references World Bank SME AAA in identifying both the key constraints to SMEs and the key obstacles to Tunisian banks in extending credit to SMEs.

Although more generic economic and sector work can provide broad strategic guidance, it often lacks the specificity to shape components of Bank projects or the detailed design of government reforms. And the low traction with the broader development community suggests either a weakness in relevance or a weakness in disseminating to relevant audiences. This coincides with the finding of the recent IEG evaluation of World Bank knowledge-based country programs (IEG 2013) that customization and specificity are key elements of success, and lack of relevance and follow-up are sources of ineffectiveness (Box 4.6). The limited traction at the government policy level suggests that a great deal of economic and sector work may not be achieving its potential impact.

SPECIAL TOPIC: LESSONS FROM SIX COUNTRY CASE STUDIES ON SEQUENCING, COMPLEMENTARITY, THE RELATIONSHIP OF SYSTEMIC TO TARGETED REFORM, AND WORLD BANK GROUP COORDINATION

In general, a solid base of analytic work both helped to tailor the design of interventions and to build World Bank Group credibility on reforms. For example, the World Bank's analytic work in Indonesia informed an ongoing policy dialogue that underpinned a long series of development policy loans. This work ranged from broader studies, such as investment climate assessments and Financial Sector Assessment Program, to more specific works of policy, sectoral or program analysis, such as the evaluative assessment of the government's partial credit guarantee scheme. In Kenya, sectoral competitiveness work was repeatedly cited by World Bank and counterpart officials as having provided specific guidance to value chain work that followed. Where analytic work was insufficient or local sectoral specifics (including political economy) were not understood (such as in the case of Indonesia's warehouse receipts financing scheme) implementation could be frustrated. In Sri Lanka, IFC had led a banking survey of the SME market in Sri Lanka in 2006–07, which identified key constraints faced by SMEs and specific problems constraining bank financing of SMEs, many of which were subsequently addressed through World Bank Group interventions.

Often policy, legal, and regulatory frameworks need to be in place for targeted investments to succeed. For example, a series of legal reforms in Kenya, supported by an earlier World Bank financial and legal technical assistance project, were credited with improving the environment for MSME credit, amplifying the effect of sectoral investments. Where systemic reform has not yet been achieved, this may need to precede targeted interventions. Counterexamples are numerous, such as a partial credit risk guarantee scheme in Nicaragua that had to be abandoned because neither the legal nor institutional framework was in place. In Nicaragua, efforts to catalyze growth in leasing through strategic investment and guarantee fell prey to the lack of a legal and regulatory framework for leasing, while MSME finance suffered a major policy reversal (the *no pago* movement) during the evaluation period.

In Kenya, work in the Pyrethrum sector was substantially delayed (and ultimately unsuccessful) because the sector remained dominated by an unreformed commodity board, an aspect of the institutional and regulatory environment which needed to be addressed before productive value chain investments could be made. In Ukraine, IFC spent over half a million dollars studying and piloting mediation before concluding that the legal environment did not support it.

Nonetheless, perfection of the policy, legal, and regulatory was not a precondition to targeted interventions where the state had reasonable credibility with investors and the direction of reform was understood. Countries like Indonesia had relatively poor Doing Business rankings, suggesting a long agenda of reforms yet to make, yet IFC was able to successfully pursue TSME investments in part because of the strong record and clear direction of reforms in the period prior to and during evaluation, and because conditions were sufficient for banks and SMEs to operate profitably. In Ukraine, IFC advisory work first supported improved tax provisions for leasing and the establishment of a national leasing organization, then pursued investments in two leasing companies, one of which performed well. Sometimes systemic and targeted reforms can complement each other to catalyze development of new markets.

Each institution should play to its strengths. IFC proved adept at certain areas of technical assistance, including a string of regulatory reform successes in Kenya during a reformist period. Yet high-level policy dialogue remained in the comparative advantage of the World Bank Group in several countries. Where the Bank did not assume a strong place in advocating tax, legal, and regulatory reforms through its policy dialogue, important systemic reforms could be neglected. This appeared to be the case in Sierra Leone, where the Bank did not have a broad-based private sector development project in the country and left the work on investment climate entirely to IFC. IFC, while technically proficient and able to coordinate with other donor work, could not effectively advocate the public administration needed to effectively implement reforms, and had to package its efforts in projects of limited duration and funding.

In Kenya, work on businesses' identified leading constraint—high corporate taxation—remained largely unaddressed in World Bank Group dialogue with the government, apparently because IFC felt the issue was too high level for its technical advisory relationship with the government and the World Bank had, in effect, delegated tax and regulatory reform to IFC.

Conversely, a strong policy dialogue in Indonesia and, in recent years, in Sri Lanka, appeared to have assisted a series of reforms that enhanced the prospects of targeted investments. MIGA guarantees appeared helpful in mobilizing foreign investors in the financial sector, such as a leading MSME bank in Nicaragua, which also benefited from IFC finance.

Coordination and communication strengthen performance where there are shared objectives. The background case studies suggested that where IFC and the World Bank were in habitual dialogue, they were often able to act in a complementary fashion even without joint activities. Often, the institutions appear to do better by dividing responsibility according to comparative advantage, rather than trying to act jointly.

In field visits, IEG found varying degrees of coordination between the Bank and IFC. In the more successful cases, although the institutions were not working jointly, staff working in related areas consulted each other on relevant topics and invited each other to relevant meetings. The Africa MSME program (Box 4.8) represented a major coordinative initiative that achieved moderate success. However, it became clear that for most activities, there was a division and assignment of responsibilities, rather than integration. The risk capital component proved an exception, benefitting from fairly close coordination in its early stages—a Bank-funded subcomponent supporting the initiation of a risk capital fund that drew on an IFC SME risk finance model and technical assistance, as well as an initial pipeline of eligible SMEs identified by IFC's SME Solutions Center. Each partner maintained its own operating procedures, timing and projects. Outside the case studies, the Bank's India SME Financing and Development Additional Finance project appraisal document elaborates IFC's role in participating in the project's risk-sharing facility by covering second loss. The Bank and IFC have collaborated on a number of TSME risk-sharing facilities (IEG found five in its portfolio review), with widely varying degrees of success.

In Sri Lanka's recent Country Partnership Strategy, the roles of the Bank and IFC in promoting finance are clearly delineated and separate, with each institution focusing on different strategic priorities, except for one collaborative activity in an underserved region. More broadly, in less successful cases of IFC-Bank collaboration, coordination was limited to structured meetings on the Country Partnership Strategy and meetings at infrequent intervals, without evident day-to-day cooperation. In some country offices visited, colocation did not overcome the barriers to coordination. MIGA has benefited from business leads provided by IFC, whereas IFC sometimes invested in projects benefiting from MIGA guarantees,

BOX 4.8 IFC and World Bank Collaboration: The Africa MSME Program

In December 2003, a joint pilot program for Africa was launched between the Bank and IFC. The objective was to reduce poverty though employment generation in MSMEs by supporting their growth through an integrated package of financial support, BDS, and investment climate reforms. Between 2003 and 2005, projects in seven countries were approved under the pilot program—in Ghana, Kenya, Madagascar, Mali, Nigeria, Tanzania, and Uganda.

By combining Bank and IFC expertise, it was believed that the project could better support the national governments in their efforts to foster private-public sector dialogue and more effective donor coordination in private sector investment. However, several of the project appraisal documents also noted the inherent risks of potential conflicts of interest, or the perception thereof, as a result of the joint activities. Accordingly, the Bank and IFC have established a framework that includes the creation of separate teams; a rule stating that no confidential information will be shared among teams; and transparent eligibility criteria for the selection of beneficiaries.

Overall, implementation was slower than originally anticipated, with five of the seven projects being restructured, four having partial cancellation of funds, all having risk flags, and all extending their original closing dates. Among the most common risk flags were slow disbursement (six projects), M&E (five), and project management (five). Overall results were moderately satisfactory.

In Kenya, the second MSME pilot project became effective in December 2004. Like some other projects, it had three subcomponents focused on access to finance, BDS, and the business environment. Part of the access to finance component for the project was supported by an IFC project aimed at raising risk capital for SMEs. IFC contributed $3 million to the $15 million Risk Capital Fund, which was approved in June 2004, signed in August 2012, and completed in the first half of 2013. The Bank committed $6.5 million to finance a portion of the fund's operational expenses as well as to create a separate technical assistance fund. To date, 40 SMEs have received advisory assistance, amounting to $500,000 through these funds.

Meanwhile, a second component, Strengthening Enterprise Skills and Market Linkages, included a business plan competition, tools for business schools to better train managers, and a value-chain-based subsector matching grant fund. It was deemed highly successful. However, the business environment component was unsuccessful and ultimately dropped during a project restructuring in 2009. Earlier implementation efforts suffered from long delays in the selection of a suitable consultant, and the performance of the consultant turned out to be unsatisfactory. The restructuring reallocated the Bank credit proceeds to other components and extended the original project closing date for two and one-half years.

SOURCE: IEG portfolio review.

although advance coordination was not always evident. Unfortunately, some efforts to act jointly confronted problems of overall project complexities, different time frames of the two institutions, and different standard operating procedures.

At the same time, too little coordination can lead to at least four problems:

• **Missed opportunities for leverage**—There were cases where IFC had clear views about the need for investment climate or sectoral reforms that were not part of the Bank's policy dialogue. If technical advisory work on policy reforms produces sound technical proposals without follow-up reforms (as in the case of the Nicaraguan draft leasing law), could the technical ideas be brought into the policy dialogue?

• **Issues that fall between the cracks**—In Kenya, the leading constraint to businesses was high tax rates. World Bank and IFC staff agreed that corporate taxation followed the "high rates, many exceptions" format. Yet the World Bank had ceded the lead on regulatory and tax reforms to a well-funded IFC team, which felt it did not have the authority to address tax policy, only administrative simplification.

• **Duplication of efforts**—In at least one case, IEG found IFC "reinventing the wheel" by creating a project as advisory work for a single company on backward linkages that followed almost precisely the template of recent, sectorwide value chain work by the World Bank. The task manager was completely unaware of the history of World Bank work in the sector.

• **Contradiction of efforts**—IEG noted in some countries that the Bank was supporting SMEs through financing channeled through the public sector at the same time that IFC was working on projects designed to activate private sector SME finance. The potential for "crowding out" was there, given the Bank's lending terms, and the lack of a common perspective was evident from some informal complaints IFC staff made about the Bank's role.

Counterpart/client capacity is key. A key frustration in Sierra Leone was limited counterpart capacity, which clearly undermined both government-facing and private sector-facing interventions. Some MIGA guarantees fell victim to weaknesses in both the guarantee holder's and the project companies' management capability. In Ukraine, the poor choice of a public institution through which to channel a line of credit factored into that effort's poor performance. In Nicaragua, limited government administrative capacity required a simple design of interventions. The case study found that for the Bank's MSME competitiveness project, both the number of responses bundled into its components and the nature of some of them in practice proved to exceed counterpart implementation capacity or political will.

Where the project found traction—for example, in its matching grant scheme—the Bank had taken pains to build counterpart capacity throughout the project life. IFC's Business Edge program succeeded best in Sri Lanka with a local Chamber of Commerce that had unusually good leadership, motivation, and capacity.

Notes

[1] IFC's Roadmap recalls "a paper in 1978 . . . laying out the case for supporting SMEs, mainly on the basis of their potential for employment creation in developing countries." The paper itself calls for a focus on "handicaps, stemming from governmental and institutional policies," financial sector development, lending in local currencies, greater flexibility in the provision of working capital finance, simplification of procedures for project evaluation, subsidized interest rates, and experimentation with different arrangements with intermediaries (World Bank 1978).

[2] The authors continue: "The Bank has been largely disengaged from developing country efforts over the past decade to support SMEs, including ongoing reforms in many countries to introduce market principles into service delivery."

[3] OP 8.30, governing Financial Intermediary Lending from 1998 until its replacement in 2013, establishes the policy on how the Bank may finance lines of credit through financial intermediaries. This includes consultation of IFC, removal of interest rate distortions, a bias against directed credit, transparent and fiscally sustainable subsidies (if any), working through viable and autonomous financial intermediaries, pricing competitive to the existing market, and effective monitoring and evaluation.

[4] As with the entire portfolio review, this was based on identification of language in project/program documents specifically identifying SMEs as the intended beneficiaries, and excluding larger firms. In cases where microenterprises were included as beneficiaries but larger firms were excluded, the project was regarded as targeted. See Appendix A for the detailed methodology of the portfolio review, which included identification by coding, by programmed content search of project documents, and by extensive "manual" review of project documents.

[5] There are four main options used by the World Bank in the design of a financial intermediary loan: (i) a wholesale banking operation to be carried out by an apex bank or government agency; (ii) several predetermined participating banks, each of which receives a line of credit for on-lending to clients; (iii) a preselected government bank to retail the credit to clients or targeted groups; and (iv) a combination of the first and the third of the above.

[6] Market failure is an economic term referring to a set of conditions where markets do not efficiently allocate resources. Some of the most common forms are information asymmetries, noncompetitive markets (or monopoly), principal-agent problems, externalities, and public goods.

[7] Saadani, Arvai; Roberto (2011). Among the improvements needed: "Some schemes should consider tightening their eligibility criteria to improve targeting (for example, reducing the ceiling on firm and loan size), while other schemes may need to build an additional margin of flexibility. . . . Some schemes should consider reducing slightly their coverage ratios to levels closer to international standards. Most schemes should consider linking both coverage ratios and fees more closely to risk. . . . In some [Middle East and North Africa] countries guarantee schemes could play a more proactive role in capacity building . . . improving risk management practices of domestic banks."

References

Campos, Francisco, Aidan Coville, Ana Maria Fernandes, Markus Goldstein, and David McKenzie. 2012. "Learning from the Experiments that Never Happened: Lessons from Trying to Conduct Randomized Evaluations of Matching Grant Programs in Africa." World Bank Policy Research Working Paper 6296, Washington, DC.

IEG (Independent Evaluation Group). 2013. *Knowledge-Based Country Programs: An Evaluation of the World Bank Group Experience.* Washington, DC: World Bank.

———. 2012. "Evaluation of the World Bank Group's Support for Investment Climate Reforms." Approach paper, World Bank, Washington, DC.

———. 2006. *Lending for Lines of Credit: An IEG Evaluation.* Washington, DC: World Bank.

Klein, Michael U., and Bita Hadjmichael. 2003. *The Private Sector in Development.* Washington, DC: World Bank.

López-Acevedo, Gladys, and Hong W. Tan, eds. 2011. *Impact Evaluation of Small and Medium Enterprise Programs in Latin America and the Caribbean.* Washington, DC: World Bank.

Saadani, Youssef, Zsofia Arvai, and Roberto Rocha. 2011. "A Review of Credit Guarantee Schemes in the Middle East and North Africa Region." World Bank Region Background Paper, Washington, DC.

World Bank. 2012a. "International Bank for Reconstruction and Development and the International Finance Corporation—Country Partnership Strategy for the Republic of Kazakhstan for the Period FY12–FY17." Report No. 67876-KZ, World Bank, Washington, DC.

———. 2012b. "JERP: Enhancing SME Financial Reporting and the Relationship with Tax Reporting in Kazakhstan." World Bank, Washington, DC.

———. 2011a. "JERP: Financing Reporting by Small and Medium Enterprises in Kazakhstan: Current Status and Policy Options." World Bank, Washington, DC.

———. 2011b. "Turkey Improving Conditions for SME Growth Finance and Innovation." Washington, DC. World Bank Report No. 54961-TR. https://openknowledge.worldbank.org/handle/10986/12211.

———. 2007. *Financial Sector Strategy for the World Bank Group.* Washington, DC: World Bank.

———. 2002. *Private Sector Development Strategy—Directions for the World Bank Group.* Washington, DC: World Bank.

———. 1978. "Employment and Development of Small Enterprises." Sector Policy Paper 11025, Washington, DC.

5 Conclusions and Recommendations

Motivation

A thriving SME sector is strongly associated with rapidly growing economies that have lifted citizens out of poverty. The World Bank Group promotes growth through both systemic and targeted interventions. TSME support has often been justified by the special contributions of SMEs in developing economies to growth, jobs productivity, or investment; or by the special challenges confronting SMEs that do not apply to other sizes of firms and the proposition that the delivery of targeted benefits to SMEs addresses and contributes to the resolution of systemic constraints.

The evidence on the first justification is not conclusive—it appears that firms of multiple sizes contribute to employment growth and that size may not be the most important factor. Enlarging the SME sector does not cause growth but may well accompany it. The second justification is consistent with notions of just and inclusive growth and a "level playing field," but it relies on evidence that targeted approaches contribute to the sustained elimination of the special SME challenges—that is, that targeted growth eliminates systemic constraints. The objective is not to benefit SMEs as an end in itself, but to create economies that can employ more people and create more opportunity.

If projects differentiate SMEs as a group in need of special support because of their special needs or disadvantages or their special contribution to the economy, then it matters a great deal that they are accurately distinguished from other firms. How SMEs are defined establishes their relevance to World Bank Group development objectives of poverty alleviation and inclusion. For SMEs to be a meaningful category of enterprises, it should be a group of firms that is specifically differentiated from others by the way that it experiences particular policy, institutional, or market failures or the way it benefits the economy or the poor.

However, the definition that IFC and MIGA use is not adapted to the conditions of specific countries; the World Bank's definition appears to accept local definitions without always determining if they relate to the underlying problems being addressed by their SME strategy. Both the upper and lower limits of IFC/MIGA's definition look too high for some countries.

From a financing perspective, setting an appropriate line between microfinance and SME finance is important. Selectivity is required for both efficacy of targeting—to ensure both benefits reach those in need and efficiency of targeting—to avoid the high cost of supporting those that don't need it. Looking at enterprise survey data suggests that how firms are constrained depends not only on firm size, but on the interaction of size with country conditions, especially income level. Therefore, not only is an appropriate definition of SMEs contingent on but which size classes of firms to target is contingent on country conditions. One size classification does not fit all.

It is important to remember that that priority SME needs include many systemic challenges, including providing a reliable electric power supply, an honest and transparent public sector, moderate taxes, political stability, fair rules of the game so that informal firms cannot compete unfairly, and an educated workforce. It is also critical to ensure that the legal, regulatory, and institutional environment supports the growth of a deep, competitive, and stable financial sector, where banks seek SMEs as part of their client base. Reforms to establish the essential infrastructure underpinning well-functioning product and factor markets are central to the growth of the SME sector, but many are not be targeted—they can benefit microenterprises and large enterprises as well. Finding the right combination of systemic and targeted interventions to address these constraints is central to addressing these challenges.

The Logic of Targeted Support for SMEs

SMEs exist and operate in the same environment as other firms, although they may experience it differently. For financing, IFC's rough estimate of the magnitude of the "financing gap" for SMEs is large enough that the World Bank Group's annual expenditures for on-lending are substantially less than one half of one percent. Therefore, it is simply not credible to argue that the Bank Group can play a significant global role just by channeling finance through intermediaries or directly to SMEs. This means that, except in special circumstances, such as response to a crisis or in extremely small economies, the only credible argument for channeling finance to SMEs is to build the capacity and sustained activity of the financial sector to supply SME credit demand. Financing projects, therefore, that form the bulk of the targeted SME portfolios, needs to demonstrate not only that they are meaningfully targeted but that they are strategically designed to fix market failures—whether by building capacity, creating a demonstration effect, or stimulating competition.

This also implies that the agenda is strongest where the financial sector is weakest—where the financial sector is developed and serving the SME sector, the Bank Group should be less active. Additionally, M&E needs to capture not only how SMEs benefited but how the financial system benefited. With regard to the other four theories of change, when providing advisory services to financial intermediaries and government bodies, the Bank Group should clearly show how it will remediate institutional or government failures constraining SMEs and collect evidence of those changes.

Similarly, BDS, like financing, cannot be credibly justified unless a sustainable market for services is promoted through the activities. Otherwise, the scope of existing interventions is too tiny to make a global difference. Therefore, for BDS projects, the Bank Group needs to provide clear evidence not only of benefits to direct beneficiaries but of benefits to the market. Finally, value chain interventions should similarly create new dynamics within the sectors in which they are working that can be sustained beyond the project's life.

Thus, the objective of this evaluation has been to determine how well the World Bank Group has promoted inclusive growth through targeted support to SMEs, which in turn requires addressing the market, institutional, and policy failures underpinning their constraints. To do this, IEG explored the relevance, efficacy, efficiency, and work quality of each institution's TSME work, to develop an understanding of how the World Bank Group is doing and where experience can be applied to have a greater development impact. The limits to information to answer these questions form part of IEG's findings—and have implications for how to proceed.

IFC and Targeted Support to SMEs

IFC regards SME support as a strategic objective based on these firms' job creation potential. A nuanced analysis of the literature on job creation suggests that job creation is likely more evenly shared between SMEs and large firms and that factors other than size may be important to consider. The lack of strong evidence for favoring SMEs over other size classes of firms means that new evidence is needed to support a key rationale typically offered for TSME support.

IFC's TSME portfolio is significant in its overall size. As TSME support is mainly provided through financial intermediaries, these projects are concentrated in the financial markets industry group. Most SME investment projects do not define SMEs, which brings into question the precision of targeting; nor do they specify that benefits be directed to SMEs. Most projects also do not clearly connect the SME support provided to the correction of an established market failure or as an appropriate response to an established SME constraint.

As seen in Chapter 1, IFC's strongest contribution to SMEs takes place by developing markets and institutions that can then operate sustainably on their own. Given that most TSME support is through the financial sector, the most credible theory of change underpinning much of it lies in its contribution to developing sustainable private markets for SME finance, rather than the direct benefits it delivers to firms.

This means that IFC's relevance is greatest where the financial sector (or other service markets) is weakest in serving SMEs. It is greater when it operates at or near the frontier, in countries where the financial sector has not yet developed to serve SMEs, regions within countries where SMEs are not served, and specific intermediaries without a firmly established SME practice. This is especially relevant in low-income and fragile and conflict-affected situations. To stay near the frontier would require IFC to enter some new markets earlier and exit some established ones earlier as well.

IFC's TSME investment projects generally did not perform as well as the overall portfolio and the rest of the financial markets portfolio. However, TSME projects improved their performance over time after 2006. IFC often refers to the reach of its SME banking portfolio, but its reach data raise questions about the relative effectiveness of their targeted SME projects in growing the SME portfolio compared to projects in the general portfolio. Not only does this raise questions about the efficacy of the current model for service delivery, but it also points to IFC's broader lack of sufficient M&E information on its TSME projects, which would enhance understanding of their development impact.

By contrast, IFC's TSME advisory services, overall, have performed better than the rest of the advisory portfolio, except in low-income countries. Nearly half of IFC's targeted advisory services portfolio took the form of technical assistance to financial institutions and governments. In general, advisory dollars were focused largely on poorer countries (IDA and IDA blend), and 40 percent of expenditures took place in Africa. Many advisory projects were linked with complementary investment projects. Where TSME investment projects were delivered in tandem with advisory services, IFC achieved superior development outcomes in its investment projects.

MIGA and Targeted Support for SMEs

MIGA's support to SMEs takes two approaches: directly to foreign investors making small investments in SMEs or indirectly to foreign financial intermediaries for their investments in subsidiaries to on-lend to SMEs. MIGA's support for SME projects has been substantial during FY06–12, comprising 50 percent of projects and 30 percent of MIGA's gross exposure. Of these, 57 percent of projects were underwritten under MIGA's SIP, but these account for less than 8 percent of gross exposure in support of SMEs and 2 percent of overall gross exposure.

Small Investment Program

Although SIP has extended MIGA's engagement in low-income and fragile countries and with types of investors it has not traditionally supported, the program has fallen short in meeting objectives of offering streamlined and efficient underwriting of SME projects, it has also had weak development outcomes and suffered from inconsistent work quality. As one of only three political risk insurers offering a special facility and underwriting procedures that support SME investments in developing countries, MIGA occupies a special place in the market. However, the extent of unmet demand for PRI from SME investors remains unclear. SIP projects are collectively relevant to three of MIGA's operational priorities: (i) supporting investments in IDA countries; (ii) supporting investment in conflict-afflicted and/or fragile environments; and (iii) supporting South-South investments.

However, the viability of SIP projects is challenging because of the location of most SIP projects in high-risk countries. SIP projects have a high rate of early cancellation and experience a number of pre-claim situations. Further, IEG found indications that some projects raised questions about E&S standards. SIP's streamlined processing of guarantees has not produced efficiency gains in terms of reduced processing time. Feedback from MIGA staff also indicates little savings in underwriting resources compared to regular guarantees, especially in light of new streamlined procedures for "plain vanilla" mainstream guarantees.

REGULAR GUARANTEES

MIGA's regular guarantees offer a wholesale means to channel a large amount of political risk coverage to benefit SMEs. In theory, this could offer an efficient way to serve the needs of SMEs, analogous to IFC work with financial intermediaries. However, at present, there is no mechanism for targeting benefits to SMEs to ensure that funds will be used for the purpose stated in the Board document. The wholesale guarantees that target SMEs are highly concentrated with a few clients driven by regulatory provisions in their home countries.

Wholesale guarantees that target SMEs underperformed relative to a comparable group of financial market guarantees in terms of business performance, economic sustainability, and contribution to private sector development. In addition, there is no evidence that the long-term tenor was passed on to end borrowers. Overall, the lack of systematic tracking of project performance makes it difficult to determine project results or whether the expected project objectives were achieved.

The World Bank and Targeted Support for SMEs

LENDING PORTFOLIO

World Bank targeted support for SMEs is broader than suggested by its formal strategic focus on access to finance; it also likely is more driven by country and regional strategies and demand than by any central guidance. By product line, lines of credit (financial intermediation loans), matching grants, and BDS projects dominate the lending portfolio. Although the Bank is substantially engaged in low-income and fragile and conflict-affected countries, the relatively low level of commitments in IDA countries and the high level of commitments in upper-middle-income countries—partly influenced by the response to the global financial crisis—raise questions looking to the future of the relevance of this portfolio to reaching the frontier and building markets and market institutions where they are weakest.

Another relevance concern arises from the 65 percent of Bank Group TSME lending projects that failed to define the term SME in any way. Further, although 75 percent of TSME lending projects state that they address market failure, only 34 percent say what it is and only 13 percent provide any evidence. Limited SME access to finance is by far the leading justification for intervention, yet as noted in Chapter 1, this is a universal feature of financial markets. It is often a symptom of market failure, but not a market failure in itself. Economic dynamism is the leading objective identified for projects, followed by job creation, economic growth, and economic inclusion. However, it is often difficult to trace the connection among the problem identified, the intervention selected, and the dynamism aimed for through a clear theory of change or logical framework. It is even more difficult to find good measures to validate these connections.

IEG evaluations of completed World Bank investment projects find the great majority achieved successful development outcomes, achieving a result better than the rest of the FPD SME-relevant portfolio and better than the World Bank portfolio average. However, efforts to judge the efficacy and efficiency of World Bank TSME support are inhibited by the lack of quantitative evaluation of the development impact of its leading product lines. Even though projects track indicators, not all are relevant to a project's theory of change, and few include a serious quantitative assessment of what the project changed in the performance of beneficiary SMEs or the performance of the markets they were trying to enhance or create. Finally, even projects that appear to be efficient from the point of view of administrative costs can be inefficient because of poor targeting.

TSME lending projects identified by IEG as having a more complex design have, on average, four more components or subcomponents than others. Projects with more elements are more prone to delays, cancellations, and restructuring and also to longer delays.

Work quality exhibits several strengths, including linkage to prior analytic work, a high rate of successful development outcomes, and a high rate of realism in self-evaluations. Weaknesses lie in overly complex designs, overly optimistic time frames for implementation, and the frequent need for delays, restructuring, and partial cancellation.

ANALYTIC WORK

Although only a small fraction of the analytic work underpinning TSME projects is itself targeted, AAA work is both relevant and important to SME challenges. Most AAA projects consisted of technical assistance, mainly to governments but also to financial institutions. Self-ratings (not validated by IEG) indicate a high and rising level of success for TSME technical assistance. Technical assistance in the context of lines of credit appears effective at strengthening institutional performance and therefore in producing positive outcomes. However, although economic and sector work appears effective in some dimensions, it has limited traction in influencing government policy. If it is yielding reforms through some other path, that is not documented, which raises important questions about efficacy and efficiency, as well as the lack of M&E.

Conclusions and Recommendations

In spite of its many achievements, the current portfolio does not consistently reflect a clear and strategic view of which firms should be targeted, why, and for which services, or of how serving them promotes market development to sustainably meet their demand. Targeted support for SMEs needs to be more firmly rooted in a clear, evidence-based understanding of what distinguishes an SME and how the proposed support will sustainably remove the problems that constrain the ability of SMEs to contribute to employment, growth, and economic opportunity in developing economies.

The lack of relevant information on portfolio performance makes it difficult to learn from experience or even to establish the existence of additionality of World Bank Group interventions. As noted in Chapter 4, current inconsistencies across institutions result in missed opportunities for institutions to leverage each other's strengths. The lack of institutional consensus on what constitutes an SME, when it is appropriate to support them, and how success is defined seems especially inappropriate as the Bank moves toward global practices that cross traditional institutional barriers. As One World Bank Group, the need for a common perspective has never been stronger. As a solutions Bank, it is vital that World Bank Group approaches be informed by the best evidence and learning, as well as well-tailored strategies that take full account of local conditions.

As the World Bank Group continues supporting SMEs, to help them realize their potential contribution to developing economies (based on portfolio and case study reviews, data analysis, field visits, and extensive literature review), IEG concludes that, to make TSME support more effective, the World Bank Group needs to do several things.

Recommendation 1: Clarify the Approach to Targeted Support to SMEs

IFC, MIGA, and the World Bank should harmonize their SME approaches to make clear the objectives and analytic justification for TSME support, how it relates to systemic reform, where it is appropriate, what main forms it will take and how it will be monitored and evaluated.

For countries where SME development is a priority, any targeted support should be firmly grounded in the Country Partnership Framework/Strategy, in the relevant parts of the Systematic Country Diagnostic based on country analytic work, and in other instruments that provide an analytic and strategic framework that identifies the sequence and mix of systemic and targeted interventions that will address systemic challenges to SMEs, building markets and access to services. The specification of the target for TSME projects should relate to country-specific conditions and in some cases address small and medium firms differently based on how they experience existing country conditions. Shared country strategies that leverage and sequence the expertise and comparative advantages of the World Bank Group institutions should ensure complementarity, maximize impact, and reduce the potential for redundancies and inconsistencies, despite the different institutions' business models. Targeted support for SMEs needs to be firmly rooted in a clear, evidence-based understanding of how the proposed support will sustainably remove the problems that constrain SMEs' ability to contribute to employment, growth, and economic opportunity.

The M&E framework should be designed to capture the effect of project interventions in these dimensions—at the beneficiary, client, and broader market level. At all levels, information is needed to understand the counterfactual—what would have happened without the project, that is, where possible, a rigorous, fact-based approach that generates information on the baseline, the post-project period, and control group. A longer-term time frame may be required to collect data to evaluate sustainability of impact.

Recommendation 2: Enhance Relevance and Additionality

World Bank Group management should refine its SME approaches to shift benefits from better-served firms and markets to states with underdeveloped financial systems, especially low-income and fragile and conflict-affected states, frontier regions, and underserved segments.

A key indicator of whether such a shift is occurring would be the evolution of the distribution of the TSME portfolio as well as the composition of beneficiary institutions and firms. This also implies including in the M&E of targeted projects indicators of the impact of the project on the targeted population of firms as well as the impact on financial intermediaries.[1]

Recommendation 3: Institute a Tailored Research Agenda

World Bank Group management should institute a tailored research agenda to support and assist these clarifications and refinements of its SME support approach. Utilizing the best qualified researchers (for example, a great deal of qualified expertise focused on this agenda resides in the Development Economics Vice Presidency), this should produce more policy- and contextually relevant distinctions of the definition of SME; a better understanding of the dynamic contributions of SMEs to economic growth, employment, and poverty alleviation; deeper knowledge about how the design of interventions should vary contingent on country conditions; a project-relevant definition of the frontier; a clearer view of the correct sequencing and combinations of systemic and targeted; and more rigorous analysis of the actual performance and impact of key types, combinations and sequences of World Bank Group and other donor interventions. Enterprise surveys should be refined to better identify market failures and unmet demand for financial and other services; and to generate more panel data that better account for firm dynamics and allows more confident relating of explanatory factors to firm growth and employment.

Recommendation 4: Strengthen Guidance and Quality Control

Relevant World Bank Group management should provide guidance and quality control so that any project documents for Bank Group projects targeting SMEs will:

i.   Define the group of firms to benefit by measurable criteria such as number of employees and annual revenues.

ii. Justify the definition of the beneficiary group targeted (which could be a subset of SMEs) based on country-specific evidence that this group suffers from size-specific market failures or constraints.

iii. Specify and wherever appropriate embed in legal provisions the mechanism to reach the targeted group.

iv. Include in its results framework and M&E framework indicators of the impact of the project on the targeted group and on the constraints or market failures justifying the project.

All projects that describe themselves as targeting benefits to SMEs should reflect this approach. In addition, these projects should be coded accurately with regard to whether or not their benefits are in fact predominantly or exclusively available to SMEs. Coding systems and practices should be reviewed and modified to assure that targeted SME projects are correctly coded, to reduce "false positives" and "false negatives."

Recommendation 5: Reform MIGA's Small Investment Program

MIGA should radically rethink its approach to providing guarantees for investments in SMEs through the SIP program, considering either a merger with its regular program or a fundamental redesign to improve performance.

If MIGA decides to eliminate SIP as a separate window, it can maintain its relevance to the frontier and continue to guarantee small investments under its regular procedures, processing qualifying projects under its expedited "no objection" procedure where eligible. MIGA could maintain its SIP brand by establishing an SIP trust fund or a MIGA-funded, SIP-branded transparent subsidy mechanism to reduce the cost for the premium and underwriting for high value-added SME projects that reflect highly additional new investments into small companies in frontier regions or markets.

If SIP is to be retained as a separate window, then the current weaknesses need to be squarely addressed, including through improved selectivity and screening, greater quality control of the preparation process, better targeting to SMEs rather than small investments, and improved M&E. Cost and revenue accounting should be improved to permit informed management decisions about SIP program resources in the context of overall MIGA strategic priorities.

To strengthen capacity of less-experienced SME guarantee holders, MIGA should provide stronger capacity-building and technical assistance to implement and manage E&S requirements for small projects.

Note

[1] A program of more rigorous quantitative impact evaluation of a defined sample of projects (to limit cost) would allow a far clearer view of the impact of projects on intended beneficiaries. Evaluation methods should include collection of baseline data and the use of control groups for comparison so that the counterfactual can be understood. To the extent that historical or retrospective information can be collected to understand prior trends and that follow-up monitoring is possible to better understand longer-term effects of interventions, this will add to management's learning from experience. In addition, there is a need to collect sufficient quantitative information on the intermediaries (clients) and on the markets in which the intermediaries operate Sampling projects for more detailed and rigorous evaluation can limit costs and burden on clients.

Appendix A
Portfolio Review Methodology

The Independent Evaluation Group's (IEG) literature review and interviews with key staff knowledgeable on the World Bank Group's support to small and medium-size enterprises (SMEs) revealed the main issues to be considered by the evaluation. These were discussed in the evaluation's Approach Paper as the theory of change for SME support. These models guided IEG to develop questionnaire templates for both the portfolio review and country-based analysis. With these tools, IEG reviewed the targeted SME (TSME) portfolios for each of the Bank Group institutions. Throughout the portfolio identification process, however, IEG identified a series of challenges with regard to project classification and coding in the Bank Group's database systems. These challenges provided misleading results, given the number of false negative and false positive observations (see Tables A.1 and A.2).

WORLD BANK: Projects may contain up to five sector or five thematic codes. IEG isolated projects that contained either the sector code "SME Finance" or the theme code "Micro, Small and Medium Enterprise (MSME) Support," which produced a preliminary list of 134 MSME-coded projects. However, of these 134, only 67 percent were TSMEs. In addition, 42 percent of TSME projects were identified using other methods.

IFC INVESTMENT: IEG identified 484 self-standing projects and 152 trade finance transactions that were coded in IFC's database system as either small or medium, totaling 635 projects, of which 384 were TSMEs. In addition, IEG's review revealed that less than half of the 384 targeted projects' legal agreements defined SMEs, specified eligible subborrowers as SMEs, or mentioned SMEs in the loan provision.

Example of not targeted:

- "The project is to provide a loan of up to $15 million and equity of up to $10 million equivalent for up to 10 percent of Absolut Bank ("Absolut" or the "Bank"). IFC's loan will be used to expand the Bank's residential mortgage lending program in Russia where the mortgage market is quite large and underserved."

TABLE A.1 World Bank Lending

MSME Code	Number of Projects	% Projects	Method	Targeted SME Number of Projects	% Projects
Targeted SME	90	67	FIL lending instrument	2	1
SME relevant	25	19	Development Policy Actions database	9	6
Not targeted	19	14	FPD network	15	10
Total	134	100	Atlas.ti	39	25
			MSME code	90	58

SOURCE: IEG.
NOTE: FIL = Financial Intermediary Loan; FPD = Financial and Private Sector Development Network; MSME = micro, small, and medium-size enterprise.

TABLE A.2 IFC Investment

Project Type	Number of Projects	% Projects
GTFP	152	24
Not targeted	99	16
Targeted SME	384	60
Total	635	100

SOURCE: IEG.
NOTE: GTFP = Global Trade and Finance Program.

- "United Water, established in 2003, has built a portfolio of five water supply and wastewater treatment projects with a total contracted capacity of 640,000 tons per day serving a population of around 2 million across an area of 500 km². The Company is currently planning to invest about $27 million in the expansion of its water plants (the Project) . . ."

MIGA: The institution does not have a coding mechanism or strategy with regards to SME support and thus it was a challenge to identify projects that aimed to support this segment. IEG relied on the project descriptions as available on MIGA's website and appraisal documents. For example, the guarantee issued under Raiffeisenbank Serbia will cover a non-shareholder loan that will be used to "expand its medium-term lending to Serbia's corporate sector, which is dominated by small and medium-size enterprises (SMEs) . . . The project also reflects MIGA's efforts to rebuild post-conflict nations, and to support small and medium-size business growth through improved access to finance."

Evaluation Project Database: World Bank Lending TSME Portfolio

For the purpose of this evaluation, IEG identified 155 TSME Bank lending projects and 62 TSME analytic and advisory activities (AAA) approved between FY06 and FY12.

For both these portfolios, the identification of these projects was as follows:

IEG downloaded a list of all IBRD/IDA projects and activities approved between FY06 and FY12 from an internal Bank database. Given that projects may contain up to five sectors and up to five theme codes, IEG developed a preliminary list of TSME projects by isolating those which contained either the sector code "SME Finance" or the theme code "Micro, Small and Medium Enterprise Support." This produced a preliminary list of 134 MSME-coded projects.

For each of these projects, IEG systematically reviewed the Project Appraisal Document or other available appraisal documents such as Program Document or Project Paper to identify language regarding the project's intention to directly support or contribute to SME development. Projects were coded as being fully targeted or containing a targeted component. In the latter case, projects may have also supported firms of other sizes or characteristics, but the targeted component focused on supporting SMEs while excluding firms of other sizes. Projects containing SME indicators were also classified as providing targeted support to SMEs. Of the 134 projects only 90 (67 percent) were targeted.

Projects (and project components) that included both SMEs and MSMEs were included if they excluded large enterprises from their support; however, projects that included only microenterprises were not included.

In addition, IEG reviewed all remaining Bank lending projects under the Financial and Private Sector Development Network (79 projects), those that utilized financial intermediary loans (11 projects), and those in another database that contained SME prior actions or benchmarks

(388) following the methodology described above. An additional 26 TSME projects were identified in this manner.

Finally, IEG screened all remaining projects with Atlas.ti, a qualitative data analysis software application, using a series of keywords as described below. Projects that contained more than one "hit" (59 projects) were manually reviewed as described above. An additional 39 targeted projects were identified in this manner.

SME SEARCH STRING

SME Mention:= SME|SMEs|MSME*|medium enter*|MSE|micro and small enter*|small enter*|medium and large enter*|small and medium enter*|medium business*|small business*|small firm*|medium firm*|

Examples of TSME language:

- "The project development objective is to stimulate the growth of micro, small, and medium enterprises (MSMEs) in selected value chains."

- DPL Prior Action: "(i) Set up machinery for Empowerment Programme to spend Rs5 billion over 5 years on social protection, retraining and SME support; (ii) Design measures to facilitate growth of formal SME sector through access to finance, technical assistance and capacity building and consultancy services."

- "Component 2: Support to the development of entrepreneurial capacities ($4.0 million). This component targets the micro and small enterprises (MSEs)—the primary source of job creation in Togo and aims at developing the entrepreneurial capacities of MSEs through targeted and practical business training, coupled with matching grants, as well as mentoring for informal (also referred to as 'traditional') businesses."

Evaluation Project Database: IFC Investment and Advisory Services TSME Portfolio

For the purpose of this evaluation, IEG identified 384 TSME IFC Investments approved between FY06 and FY12.

The identification of these operations was a multistep process that involved the following steps.

Using a Management Information System extract, IEG filtered projects by commitment dates FY06–12. IEG also used the "SME Type" flag to isolate those projects which were coded as small enterprise or medium enterprise in the system. This resulted in a list containing 703 investment projects. IEG screened these and filtered out rights issues, sectorwide approaches, B-loans, and so on (68). Similarly, trade finance transactions (152) were filtered out as they would be reviewed programmatically given that the program seeks to reach SMEs through selection of participating banks and does not have specific targeting mechanisms at the transaction level. Thus, the preliminary list included 484 self-standing projects coded as either small or medium.

For each of the remaining 484 projects, IEG systematically reviewed the Board Report (as well as other project cycle documents) to identify language regarding the project's intention to directly support or contribute to SME development. Projects were coded as being fully targeted or containing a targeted component. In the latter, projects may have also supported firms of other sizes or characteristics but targeted components focused on supporting SMEs while excluding firms of other sizes. Projects containing SME indicators were also classified as providing targeted support to SMEs. Of the 484 projects, 384 (72 percent) were targeted projects.

Projects (and project components) that included both SMEs and MSMEs were included if they excluded large enterprises from their support; however, projects that included only microenterprises were not included.

Examples of TSME language include:

- "The purpose of the project is to provide the Bank with the necessary long-term funds for on-lending to small and medium-size private Russian companies (SMEs)."

- "The objective of the Fund is to establish a local vehicle in Kenya capable of delivering finance and technical assistance to local SMEs in a commercially sustainable manner."

- "The project entails a $3.0 million senior loan to Azerigzbank (AGB or the 'Bank'), a privately owned medium-size local bank providing services primarily to small and medium enterprises (SMEs), local entrepreneurs and individuals in Azerbaijan. The project would help AGB, an existing IFC client, to expand its lending and leasing activities in the SME sector."

For the purpose of this evaluation, IEG identified 273 TSME Advisory Service projects approved between FY06 and FY12.

The identification of these operations was a multistep process that involved several steps.

The evaluation's literature and document reviews, together with interviews with IFC Advisory Services strategy staff, revealed the following product lines as most likely to provide targeted SME support: SME Banking, Trade Finance, GEM Access to Finance, Farmer and SME Training, and Strategic Community Investment. Given that projects are coded by product line (often containing more than one product line per project), the evaluation's preliminary review categorized as TSME any project that contained at least one of these product lines and where either the client or beneficiary was specified as being a SME in the Advisory Services database.

IEG also reviewed the remaining projects to identify any additional TSME projects. In order to streamline this process, IEG extracted project memo fields (project development objective, project description, strategic relevance, and market failure) from the Cognos Viewer ASID Dashboard Memo Listing and performed a series of keyword-based searches. Keywords used include SME, Small and Medium Enterprise (or firm, business, company, and other variations), Small Enterprise, Medium Enterprise, Micro and Small Enterprise, Medium and Large Enterprise, and so forth. Projects containing these keywords were added to the preliminary list of TSME projects.

The original list of projects contained 1,661 projects. Following the steps above, the preliminary list of TSME projects revealed a total of 668 projects to be analyzed manually, following the methodology described above. IEG systematically reviewed project documents to identify language regarding the project's intention to directly support or contribute to SME development. Projects were coded as being fully targeted or containing a targeted component. In the latter case, projects may have also supported firms of other sizes or characteristics but targeted components focused on supporting SMEs while excluding firms of other sizes. Projects containing SME indicators were also classified as providing targeted support to SMEs. However, it should be noted that a parallel investment climate evaluation will be examining many legal and regulatory reforms, some of which disproportionally benefit SMEs, but few of which would exclusively benefit SMEs. However, in country case studies, these projects were considered as relevant to SME strategy. Of the 668 projects, 273 were identified as TSME (41 percent).

Projects (and project components) that included both SMEs and MSMEs were included if they excluded large enterprises from their support; however, projects that included only microenterprises were not included.

Examples of TSME language include:

- ". . . the technical assistance program will focus on the following areas: Developing Access Bank's capacity to outreach to the SME segment through exposure to best practice institutions/initiatives . . ."

- "The project aims to enhance the performance of a group of SMEs in the olive oil cluster in West Bank and Gaza strip in terms of product quality and export growth."

- "The goal of the proposed Project is to improve the business enabling environment for Georgian SMEs."

Evaluation Project Database: MIGA SIP and TSME (Non-SIP)

For this evaluation, IEG identified 37 TSME (non-SIP) and 50 SIP projects issued between FY06 and FY12.

The identification of these operations was a multistep process:

Collecting the list of all MIGA SIP and non-SIP projects for the period FY06–12 using the advanced search function in MIGA's website available at "http://www.miga.org/projects" as well as the "guarantees issued" Excel spreadsheet from MIGA.

DEFINING A PROJECT

Although projects may be composed of one or more contracts of guarantee that may be issued over time, IEG defines projects as the collection of contracts of guarantee under one project identification, catalogued by the original fiscal year of issuance. Thus, projects with multiple guarantees count as one project in the database, and project amounts reflect the sum of all guaranteed amounts for each project.

For the purposes of this evaluation, this includes projects that received MIGA support for the first time between FY06 and FY12 or projects that received MIGA support for the first time during the evaluation's FY06–12 scope (this includes those projects that had received MIGA support in the years prior to the evaluation's scope).

EXCEPTION: Although ProCredit subprojects were covered under two master contracts (each with a unique project identification), these subprojects were recorded as a single project for each host country. In cases where the host country had more than one guarantee, the collection of guarantees for that host country counted as one project (Georgia, Serbia, and Ukraine).

DEFINING TSME PROJECTS IN MIGA'S PORTFOLIO (SIP AND NON-SIP)

SIP PROJECTS: Given the SIP's objectives, SIP projects were considered as targeted support to SMEs and were analyzed as such by IEG. The program aims to support investments in companies that qualify as SME based on MIGA's SME definition, which mirrors that of IFC and is based on whether companies fulfill two of the three criteria related to employment, assets, and sales (see Board paper for definition).

NON-SIP PROJECTS: To determine whether non-SIP projects were TSME, IEG began by reviewing each project's description via the Project Brief, available on MIGA's website. IEG identified projects with language within these project briefs that described whether supporting the project enterprise would contribute to SME development and the expansion of the SME sector. Keywords used to identify such support include SME, Small and Medium Enterprise (or business, firm, and other varieties), local businesses, and so forth.

After identifying the preliminary list of TSME projects via the project brief, IEG reviewed each project's President's Report for additional language regarding the project's intention to directly support or contribute to SME development. Projects were coded as being fully targeted or containing a targeted component. In the latter case, projects may have also supported firms of other sizes or characteristics but the targeted component focused on supporting SMEs while excluding firms of other sizes.

Projects (and project components) that included both SMEs and MSMEs were included if they excluded large enterprises from their support; however, projects that included only microenterprises were not included.

IEG excluded projects that did not mention direct support to or contribution to the development of SMEs.

Examples of TSME language include:

• "[the bank] will concentrate mainly on trade finance activities, in particular for small- and medium-size companies. It will also finance real estate and industrial activities, but on a smaller scale."

• "The funds will be utilized to finance various Ghanaian SME projects, mostly in the agribusiness, manufacturing, services, tourism and transportation sectors."

Appendix B
Methodology and Finding of Statistical and Econometric Analysis of Enterprise Survey and Portfolio Data

Part 1: SME Constraints, Financial Access, and Employment Growth—Evidence from World Bank Enterprise Surveys

This appendix uses recent World Bank enterprise surveys to provide empirical evidence on the leading constraints of SMEs and the factors that influence firms' access to finance and employment growth, two key themes in SME assistance. This part consists of three sections: leading constraints to SMEs, factors influencing enterprise-level employment growth, and factors influencing access to finance, specifically, bank financing.

I. LEADING CONSTRAINTS TO SMES

Top Five Constraints Facing Firms

In this first part, major constraints that firms face are identified, in particular, those identified by SMEs. The perceptions that firm owners and senior managers hold about the constraints they are facing provide a good indication of their serious bottlenecks and can provide policy guidance, when private perspectives are carefully balanced with other evidence.

WHAT ARE THE MAJOR OR SEVERE CONSTRAINTS FACING FIRMS? To answer this question, we used the World Bank Group's enterprise survey data, and analyzed responses of 46,396 enterprises in 108 developing countries. These firm-level surveys were carried out by the World Bank during 2006–11 in six regions. The survey asks the firm's manager to rate the degree of severity of 15 elements of the business environment faced by his or her establishment, on a parallel rating basis. Scores range from 0 to 4, with 0 representing no problem, 1 representing a minor problem, 2 representing a moderate problem, 3 representing a major problem, and 4 representing a severe problem. The list of these obstacles, along with the global average of responses, is shown in Figure B.1. The figure represents the percentage of firms finding the constraint "major" or "severe," to distinguish more serious from less serious constraints.

Taking the sample as a whole (and it is a sample where the great majority of firms are what the survey defines as "SMEs"), access to electricity tops the list of constraints, with 40 percent of firms

Percent of Firms Facing Major or Severe Constraints

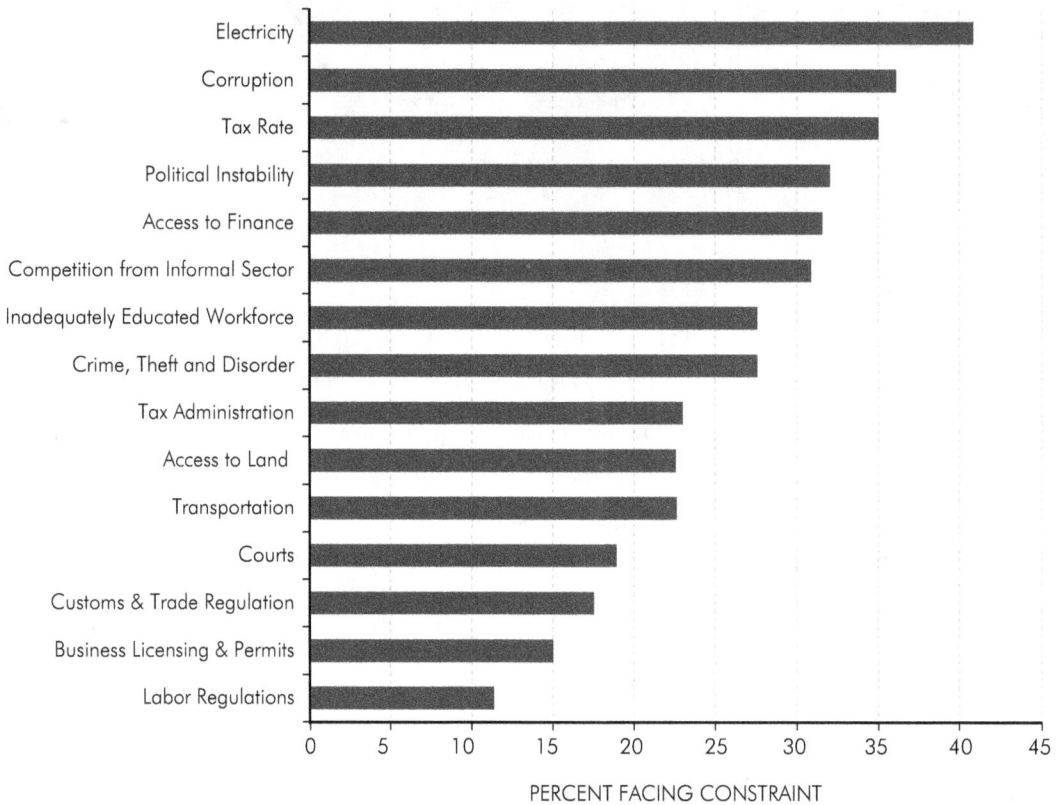

Electricity
Corruption
Tax Rate
Political Instability
Access to Finance
Competition from Informal Sector
Inadequately Educated Workforce
Crime, Theft and Disorder
Tax Administration
Access to Land
Transportation
Courts
Customs & Trade Regulation
Business Licensing & Permits
Labor Regulations

PERCENT FACING CONSTRAINT

SOURCE: Global Enterprise surveys.
NOTE: 108 countries.

expressing it as a major or severe constraint. Concern over corruption ranks second, with 37 percent of firms listing it as their major or severe constraint, followed by tax rate (35 percent), political instability and access to finance. Of least concern are the issues relating to the labor regulations, business licensing and permits, and custom and trade regulation; these are at the low tail of distribution, with an average of 15 percent of firms expressing each of these concerns. This indicates that although these may be important for some firms, they are not the biggest priority.

CONSTRAINTS FACING MSMES. Disaggregating by firm size (in terms of number of employees), the international findings of the enterprise surveys indicate that access to electricity is the top constraint for firms of all size. Corruption is the second leading constraint for firms of up to 99 employees; however, tax rates are the second leading constraint for firms with 100–299 employees (those within IFC's definition of SME but not Enterprise Surveys), and firms with over 300 employees identify skills of workforce as their second leading constraint. In third place for firms with up to 99 employees is tax rates; corruption ranks third for firms with 100 or more employees. In this sense firms with 5–99 employees are somewhat similar to each other, and somewhat different from larger firms. Access to finance is listed among the top five constraints only for firms with 5–9 employees (defined by IFC as microenterprises.) For firms with 10–300+ employees, access to finance is not among the top five constraints. Instead, political instability and informal competition round out the top five for firms with 10–99 employees, and worker skills ranks fifth for enterprises with 100–299 employees.

Constraints by Country Income Group

However, if we look at the ranking of the top five by country income groups (Tables B.1 and B.2), in low-income countries, electric power supply remains the leading constraint, but access to finance rises to the second leading rank. Access to finance is among the top five constraints in lower-middle-income or upper-middle-income countries. Access to power is also one of the five leading constraints in all country income groups. Tax rates are a top five constraint in all groups except lower-middle-income countries. In low-income countries, tax rates ranks third, followed by corruption and political instability. In lower-middle-income countries, corruption is the leading constraint, and crime enters the top five in place of taxes. For upper-middle-income countries, taxes and corruptions are top concerns, but worker skills are one of the top five constraints. For high-income countries, corruption is not among the top five constraints.

TABLE B.1 Top Five Major or Severe Constraints Facing Firms by Firm Size

	Number of Employees				
	5–9	10–19	20–99	100–299	300+
1st obstacle	Power (38.92%)	Power (42.52%)	Power (41.13%)	Power (43.94%)	Power (43.91%)
2nd obstacle	Corruption (35.07%)	Corruption (37.95%)	Corruption (37.48%)	Tax rate (35.74%)	Worker skills (35.63%)
3rd obstacle	Tax rate (34.87%)	Tax rate (35.24%)	Tax rate (35.48%)	Corruption (34.87%)	Corruption (33.03%)
4th obstacle	Finance (33.75%)	Political instability (32.80%)	Political instability (32.23%)	Political instability (33.32%)	Transportation (32.11%)
5th obstacle	Political instability (31.16%)	Informality (32.39%)	Informality (31.01%)	Worker skills (33.28%)	Tax rate (32.06%)

SOURCE: IEG portfolio review.
NOTE: Micro firm = 5–9 employees; small firm = 10–19 employees; medium firm = 20–99 employees; large firm = 100–299 employees; extreme large firm = 300 or more employees.

TABLE B.2 Top Five Major or Severe Constraints Facing Firms by Country Income Group

	Income Level			
	Low	Low Middle	Upper Middle	High
1st obstacle	Power (54.59%)	Corruption (41.04%)	Tax rate (37.76%)	Tax rate (36.15%)
2nd obstacle	Finance (43.77%)	Power (35.44%)	Corruption (36.27%)	Worker skills (29.64%)
3rd obstacle	Tax rate (38.94%)	Political instability (35.24%)	Power (34.09%)	Power (29.42%)
4th obstacle	Corruption (37.94%)	Crime, theft, disorder (33.00%)	Worker skills (33.90%)	Political instability (23.70%)
5th obstacle	Political instability (34.84%)	Informality (30.76%)	Informality (30.47%)	Finance (20.48%)

SOURCE: IEG.

Constraints from a Regional Perspective

Ranking of constraints also differ by region (Table B.3). In Sub-Saharan Africa, just over half of firms identify access to power as a major or very severe obstacle, whereas firms in other regions consider other obstacles to be their top constraint. In East Asia and Pacific, Latin America and the Caribbean, and the Middle East and North Africa Regions, firms are most likely to rank corruption as a major or severe constraint. In Europe and Central Asia, tax rates tops their concerns. In the South Asia Region, political instability was the leading concern, identified as serious by more than half of firms, while electric power supply was close behind, identified by 53 percent of firms as a major or severe constraint. These findings are consistent with Hallward-Driemeier and Stewart (2004) and Gelb and others (2007). Finance is the second leading constraint in Sub-Saharan Africa and ranks fourth in South Asia.

In conclusion, the leading constraints vary by country groups and enterprise groups—both country income level and firm size matter. Looking at regional variation (which may in part reflect the size and income composition of economies within each region) brings further nuance. Regarding finance, it is of relatively greater concern to the smallest firms (up to 20 employees), the poorest countries (low income), and the Africa and South Asia Regions.

TABLE B.3 Top Five Major or Severe Constraints Facing Firms by Region

	Region					
	AFR	EAP	ECA	LAC	MNA	SAR
1st obstacle	Power (50.79%)	Corruption (26.37%)	Tax rate (40.29%)	Corruption (41.75%)	Corruption (65.70%)	Political instability (55.13%)
2nd obstacle	Finance (44.64%)	Power (24.99%)	Political instability (36.07%)	Skills (37.15%)	Political instability (61.10%)	Power (53.00%)
3rd obstacle	Informality (37.72%)	Skills (23.08%)	Power (34.90%)	Power (35.56%)	Land (57.49%)	Corruption (27.35%)
4th obstacle	Corruption (37.60%)	Political instability (20.47%)	Corruption (33.31%)	Tax rate (34.65%)	Electricity (53.64%)	Finance (26/36%)
5th obstacle	Tax rate (36.23%)	Tax rate (20.22%)	Worker skills (29.77%)	Political instability (33.40%)	Informality (31.02%)	Land (21.00%)

SOURCE: IEG.
NOTE: AFR = Africa Region; EAP = East Asia and Pacific Region; ECA = Europe and Central Asia Region; LAC = Latin America and the Caribbean Region; MNA = Middle East and North Africa Region; SAR = South Asia Region.

Part 2: Access to Finance Facing SMEs

COMPOSITION OF BANK FINANCING SOURCES

The global enterprise surveys collected data regarding the proportion of investment and working capital financed from six main sources.[1] IEG's analysis of survey data shows that internal funds was the main source used for MSMEs' working capital and for investment (65–66 percent), whereas the share from Bank financing has been relatively small—under 20 percent for investment purposes and about 12 percent for day-to-day operations. Other sources of finance are trade credit and advance payments from customers (5 percent),[2] equity (4.6 percent), borrowing from moneylenders, friends, relatives, and so forth (2.9 percent), and borrowing from other financial institutions (2.2 percent).

Figure B.2 breaks down bank financing for fixed (investment) capital and working capital by firm size. It shows that microenterprises and SMEs have a lower proportion of their fixed

FIGURE B.2 Bank Financing for Fixed Assets and Working Capital, by Firm Size

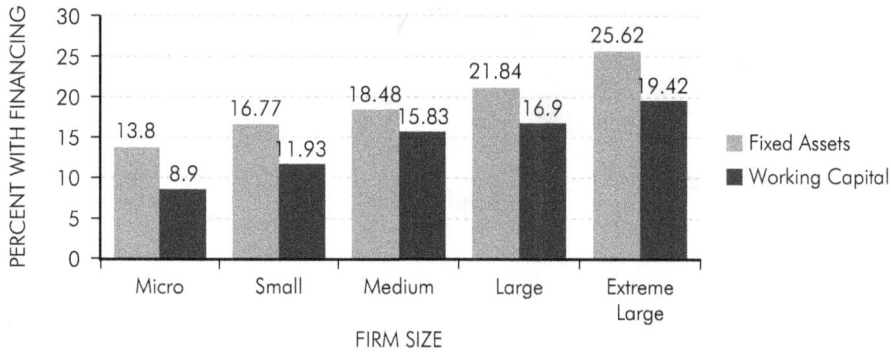

SOURCE: IEG portfolio review.
NOTE: Micro firm = 5–9 employees; small firm = 10–19 employees; medium firm = 20–99 employees; large firm = 100–299 employees; extreme large firm = 300 or more employees.

assets financed through commercial bank loans than large firms: MSMEs' bank loans account for 13–18 percent of their sources versus 22–26 percent for large and very large firms. For working capital, firm size differentials also persist. Bank financing for working capital amounts to 9–16 percent for microenterprises and SMEs and 17–19 for large and extremely large ones. These findings are consistent with the literature, which states that SMEs are usually in a less favorable position to access bank loans than the large ones (Ayagari, Demirgüç-Kunt, and Maksimovic and others 2008; Beck and others 2006).

The regression model of Table B.1 shows that access to bank loans or lines of credit is significantly and positively associated with higher employment growth. The relevant policy-oriented question is whether the banking system in developing countries provides a broad-based access to financial services or a more narrow access.

With this concern, we further look at the determinants of the likelihood of having a bank loan or line of credit from a financial institution by running a logistic regression model where the dependent variable is a binary variable predicting the likelihood of a firm having a bank loan or line of credit.

Model Specification

Likelihood of access to bank loan $= a + e^{X+Z+Ym+Im}$,

where X is firm size captured by a series of dummies: micro, small, medium, large, and extremely large (with extremely large firms omitted). As stated before, the particular interest is in the firm size differentials in access to a bank loan.

The model also controls for other firm characteristics, Z, for example, by using age and sector dummies. In addition, the model includes an indicator of country-level financial development: credit to private sector as percent of gross domestic product. In light of the literature showing the connection of finance and growth, the model also controls for country level, the regulatory environment captured by two variables—legal rights of creditors indicator ranging from 1 to 10, with 10 being the best legal right situation, and depth of credit information ranging from 0 to 6, with 6 being the best. These two variables are also taken from Doing Business database and refer to the situation in 2006.

An additional firm-level investment climate and regulatory variable is also introduced in the model, captured by a series of dummies: moderate regulatory burden (manager spent 5–15 percent of time per week in dealing with government regulation) and heavy regulatory burden (manager spent over 15 percent of time per week in dealing with government regulation). The omitted category is light regulatory burden (with less than 5 percent of manager time in dealing with regulation). To ease the concern of "omitted variable" bias which might have acted both on a firm's likelihood of accessing a bank loan or line of credit and firm size, a firm productivity variable is also introduced at the base year, captured by sales per employee at $-i$. Finally, year dummies (Ym) and country income group dummies (Im) are also included.

KEY FINDINGS

A logistic regression was carried out to do estimations, and coefficients were transformed into odds ratios and are presented in Table B.4. Findings from the logistic regression confirm that microenterprises and SMEs were less likely to have access to a bank loan than the extremely large firms. The odds ratio for a micro firm is 0.212 (exp −1.553), which means that the micro firm only has a 21 percent chance of getting a bank loan or line of credit, compared with extremely large firms (reference group in the model). For small and medium firms, the odds ratio is 0.31 (exp −1.188) and 0.48 (exp −0.732), respectively. In other words, a small firm has only a 30 percent chance of getting a bank loan of that of extreme large ones, and for a medium firm the chance is only 48 percent. This firm size differential in access to bank loan is robust when a country-fixed effect model is used, which is not shown in the table.

Country financial development also benefits firms' access to bank loans. The odds ratio of 1.489 (exp 0.398) means that an increase of one unit (one percent) in the ratio of private credit over gross domestic product could increase an average firm's chance of getting a bank loan by almost 50 percent. Legal rights of creditors and depth of credit information are also positively correlated with the chance of obtaining the bank loan. Surprisingly, companies whose management spent more time dealing with government regulations were more likely to have a bank loan or line of credit.

TABLE B.4 Logistic Regression of Accessing Bank Loan or Line of Credit on Firm Size and Financial Development (main effect model)

Predictor	Coefficient	Odds Ratio
(Standard error in parenthesis)		
Constant	−0.911*** (0.201)	
Labor productivity at base year	−0.198*** (0.010)	
Size of firm[a]		
Micro	−1.553*** (0.064)	(0.212)
Small	−1.188*** (0.063)	(0.305)
Medium	−0.732*** (0.059)	(0.481)
Large	−0.418*** (0.065)	(0.658)
Regulatory burden[b]		
Moderate (5–15 % manager time in dealing with govt regulations)	0.318*** (0.034)	(1.374)
Heavy (>15 % manager time in dealing with govt regulations)	0.209*** (0.034)	(1.232)
Finance development at country level		
Credit to private sector as % of GDP	0.398*** (0.055)	(1.489)
Doing business indicator at country level		
Legal right index	0.017** (0.007)	(1.017)

Predictor	Coefficient	Odds Ratio
Depth of information on credit	0.049*** (0.009)	(1.050)
Controls for		
Age of firms	Yes	
Sector dummies	Yes	
Country income group dummies	Yes	
Year dummies	Yes	
−log likelihood	15,770	
Likelihood ratio chi-square	5,639	
Df	31	
Pseudo R-squared	0.152	
N	27,009	

SOURCE: Global Enterprise Surveys, 108 countries.
a. Omitted group is extreme large firm.
b. Omitted group is light regulatory burden (with less than 5% manager time in dealing with government regulations).
***$p < 0.01$, **$p < 0.05$.

ACCESS TO FINANCE: GOING BEHIND FIRM SIZE

Access to finance has been listed as a top constraint among firms in low-income countries. Do firm size differentials vary across country income group? The World Bank Group may need to take into account the interaction of country income level and firm size in designing interventions to assist those firms that are differentially constrained.

Empirical Implementation

The desired empirical test is whether the variation of access to finance by firm size is contingent on country income group. In other words, instead of having one slope for small firms, for example, it can vary across three country income groups. Here is the simple model specification:

$$\text{Prob (Having bank loan access or not)} = a + bZ + cW + vY + e \qquad (1)$$

$$\text{Prob (Having bank loan access or not)} = a + bZ + cW + vY + uWY + e, \qquad (2)$$

where W is a series of dummies denoting firm size, Y is a series of dummies denoting country income level, and Z is a vector of firm characteristics such as the firm's age—young, middle-aged, and old; firm's labor productivity captured by sale per worker at the prior years; firm's sector composition; and year dummies.

WY is the interaction term between firm size and country income level. As these two models are hierarchical, the reduction of likelihood between the two models (main-effect model, which is model 1, and interaction term model, which is model 2) relative to the change in degrees of freedom is indicative if the interaction model improves statistically upon the main-effect model.

KEY FINDINGS

The findings reported in Table B.5 show that a change of likelihood of 21 units (18,145 − 18,124 = 21) relative to the change of 8 degrees of freedom warrants a rejection of null hypothesis that the firm size differentials in access to finance do not vary across income group at $p < 0.01$ level. Thus the firm size differentials in access to finance are significantly contingent on country income level.

The odds ratios of interaction terms (firm size and income levels) further suggest that SMEs in low-income countries are significantly different in their likelihood of getting a loan, whereas SMEs in middle-income countries are not significantly different from large firms in their likelihood of getting a loan once the interaction effect of income and size is controlled for. SMEs in low-income countries are further limited in their access to bank loans, as shown by the significance of the interaction terms in the second model. The odds ratio of 0.457 for interaction term (small*low income) means that the difference in the likelihood of access to bank credit between small and extremely large firms (the omitted group) in low-income countries could be twice that compared to their difference (small versus extremely large) in high-income countries. So it is particularly relevant to address the issue of access to finance in low-income countries. Two other interesting aspects of the model: once interactions are accounted for, large firms (which IFC/MIGA definitions count as medium size) are not differentially constrained from extremely large firms with more than 300 employees. This suggests that in middle-income countries, policy attention regarding access to finance should be focused on firms with fewer than 100 employees.

TABLE B.5 Logistic Regression of Having Bank Loan or Lines of Credit: Role of Firm Size and Income (access to bank loan or lines of credit)

	Model			
	Main Effect Model		Interaction Model	
Predictor	Coefficient ratio	Odds	Coefficient	Odds ratio
Size of firm[a]				
Micro (5–9 employees)	−1.676***	(0.187)	−0.945***	(0.389)
Small (10–19 employees)	−1.284***	(0.277)	−0.909***	(0.403)
Medium (20–99 employees)	−0.781***	(0.458)	−0.573***	(0.564)
Large (100–299 employees)	−0.450***	(0.637)	−0.322	(0.725)
Income level[b]				
Low	−1.017***	(0.362)	−0.382*	(0.683)
Middle	−0.353	(0.702)	−0.047	(0.954)
Interaction terms				
Micro*low income			−1.087***	(0.337)
Micro*middle income			−0.761***	(0.467)
Small*low income			−0.783***	(0.457)
Small*middle income			−0.354	(0.702)
Medium*low income			−0.566**	(0.568)
Medium*middle income			−0.183	(0.833)
Large*low income			−0.202	(0.817)
Large*middle income			−0.132	(0.876)

continued on page 192

Predictor	Main Effect Model		Interaction Model	
	Coefficient ratio	Odds	Coefficient	Odds ratio
Controls for				
Sale per capita at base year	Yes	Yes		
Firm age	Yes	Yes		
Sector dummies	Yes	Yes		
Year dummies	Yes	Yes		
-log likelihood		18,145	18,124	
Df		25	33	
N		30,742	30,742	

SOURCE: World Bank global enterprise surveys.
a. Omitted group is extreme large firm with at least 300 employees.
b. Omitted group is high income country.
***p <= 0.01, **p <= 0.05, *p <= 0.10.

Part 3: Factors and Firm Characteristics Association with Employment Growth

In this section, we examine how potential explanatory factors relate to employment growth (Aterido, Hallward-Driemeier, and Pages 2007; Hinh, Mavridis, and Nguyen 2010). As we are working from cross-sectional data, it is difficult to conclude more than an association between variables that prove significantly related.

MODEL SPECIFICATION

To address empirically the issue of how the sound investment climate and regulatory environment could possibly contribute to employment growth, we incorporate investment climate and regulatory environment into the conventional growth model, which has the following model specification:

Employment growth $t - i$ and $t = a + bE\,t - i + cZ + dX + Cm + Ym + e$

The dependent variable is the annualized employment growth between base year of $t - i$ ($I = 2$ or 3, depending on country) and current year at t. The annual rate of employment growth has been around 6 percent for the sample as a whole. It is estimated by taking the log difference in permanent full-time workers of firms over a period of two or three years, depending on the country, and further annualizing it by dividing it by 2 or 3, depending, on the countries where base year could be two or three years ago. As a growth model, we include a variable of total employment at the base year captured by a series of dummies of its firm size at $t - i$.

The key predictors are "Z"—the investment climate and regulatory variables. For Z, we are using three sets of objective measurements on investment climate and regulatory interventions, which are supposed to have an impact on employment growth:

• Access to finance captured by whether firm had bank loan or line of credit

• Access to power captured by a variable whether firm had or shared a power generator

• Regulatory environment captured by a series of dummies: (i) moderate regulatory burden and heavy regulatory burden (omitted group is light regulatory burden).

The models control for other predictors, X, which include a firm's other characteristics such as age, sector composition, whether firm offers formal training to its employees, and a firm's use of IT captured by whether firm has interacted with clients by email or through a website. Country dummies (Cm) and year dummies (Ym) are also included.

ISSUE OF CAUSALITY

Ideally these investment climate and regulatory variables are to be measured in the years preceding the dependent variable. Using cross-sectional data, both the dependent variable and investment climate and regulatory variables are concurrent. However, when managers responded to survey questions pertaining to their investment climate and business regulation environment, it could reflect recent years in their memory, not necessarily the year when the survey was administrated. Assuming that investment climate and business regulatory situation do not change over a short time span (Griliches and Hausman 1986), the concern of causality may be reduced. To ease somewhat this concern, we include a predictor of firm's productivity (sale per employees) at base year ($t - i$) to be a proxy for the possible "missing variable."

It is also noticed that in using enterprise survey data, we are also subject to the issues of survival bias. Many SME firms exited before the surveys were conducted because of poor performance. The survey only captures those firms that were able to survive at the time when the survey was conducted. The group of survivors will have grown more than an average that includes exited firms, and may have different characteristics than the cohort of all firms (survivors and non-survivors) at entry. Many microenterprises and SMEs that exited could have faced severe constraints such as obstacles in licensing and permits, tax rate, and so forth.

KEY FINDINGS (FROM TABLE B.6)

In general, the regression indicates that a better investment climate regulatory environment and better access to finance is associated with employment growth.

- More specifically, better access to power (through the presence of generator), a healthier business regulatory environment (reduction of regulatory burden), and better access to finance (have bank loan or line of credit) all are positively associated with employment growth.

- Compared to extremely large firms, MSMEs registered faster employment growth, with a larger coefficient the smaller the firm.

- These findings are robust where a country-fixed effect model is used (model 2).

TABLE B.6 OLS Regression of Employment Growth on Firm Size and Investment Climate and Regulatory Environment (main effect model)

Predictor	Model 1	Model 2
Constant	−0.264*** (0.023)	−0.271*** (0.245)
Labor productivity at base year	0.022*** (0.001)	0.026*** (0.001)
Size of firm[a]		
Micro (5–9 employees)	0.207*** (0.006)	0.208*** (0.006)
Small (10–19 employees)	0.097*** (0.006)	0.099*** (0.006)
Medium (20–99 employees)	0.067*** (0.005)	0.068*** (0.006)

Predictor	Model 1	Model 2
Large (100–299 employees)	0.030*** (0.006)	0.030*** (0.006)
Regulatory burden[b]		
Moderate (5–15% manager time dealing with regulations)	−0.006* (0.003)	−0.007** (0.003)
Heavy (>15% manager time dealing with regulations)	−0.001 (0.003)	0.003 (0.003)
Access to bank loan	0.024*** (0.003)	0.024*** (0.003)
Had email to contract with clients	0.009** (0.004)	0.014*** (0.004)
Had own website	0.017*** (0.003)	0.020*** (0.003)
Offered training to employees	0.035*** (0.003)	0.036*** (0.003)
Had or shared generator	0.015*** (0.003)	0.012*** (0.003)
Controls for		
Age of firm	Yes	Yes
Sector dummies	Yes	Yes
Country income group dummies	Yes	No
Year dummies	Yes	Yes
Country dummies	No	Yes
R-squared	0.144	0.174

continued on page 196

CONTINUED TABLE B.6 OLS Regression of Employment Growth on Firm Size and Investment Climate and Regulatory Environment (main effect model)

Predictor	Model 1	Model 2
Adjusted R-squared	0.143	0.168
n	18,438	18,438

SOURCE: World Bank global enterprise surveys.

NOTE: Standard error in parentheses. OLS = ordinary least squares.

a. Omitted group is extreme large firm (300+ employees).

b. Omitted group is light regulatory burden (with less than 5% manager time in dealing with government regulations).

***$p < 0.01$; **$p < 0.05$; *$p < 0.10$.

Notes

[1] These six sources are internal finds or retained earnings; equity shares; private and state-owned commercial banks; other financial institutions; purchases on credit from suppliers and advances from customers; and money lenders, friends, and relatives.

[2] Medium-size and large firms had a higher share of trade credit compared to small firms. Firms in Latin America and the Caribbean had nearly 15 percent of financing from trade credit, whereas this credit type was not common in the East Asia and Pacific, and Sub-Saharan Africa Regions. Therefore, business culture within regions might have played a role in regional differentials for trade credit acquisition. Its use also varies across industries; firms in the metal industry used it the most (16 percent), but it was less used by firms in the chemical industry (4 percent).

References

Aterido, Reyes, Mary Hallward-Dreimeier, and Carmen Pages. 2007. "Investment Climate and Employment Growth: The Impact of Access to Finance, Corruption and Regulations across Firms." IZA DP No. 3138.

Ayyagari, Meghana, Asli Demirgüç-Kunt, and Vojislav Maksimovic. 2008. "How Important Are Financing Constraints? The Role of Finance in the Business Environment." *World Bank Economic Review,* 22(3): 483–516.

Beck, Thorsten, Asli Demirgüç-Kunt, Luc Laeven, and Vojislav Maksimovic. 2006. "The Determinants of Financing Obstacles." *Journal of International Money and Finance,* 25(6): 932–52.

Gelb, Alan, Vijaya Ramachandran, Manju Kedia Shah, and Ginger Turner. 2007. "What Matters to African Firms? The Relevance of Perceptions Data." World Bank Policy Research Working Paper No.4446, Washington, DC.

Griliches, Zvi, and Hausman, Jerry A. 1986. "Errors in Variables in Panel Data" *Journal of Econometrics,* 31(1): 93–118.

Hallward-Driemeier, Mary, and David Stewart. 2004. "How Do Investment Climate Conditions Vary Across Countries, Regions and Types of Firms?" Background paper for the World Development Report 2005, World Bank, Washington, DC.

Hinh, Dinh T., Dimitrics A. Mavridis, and Hoa B. Nguyen. 2010. "The Binding Constraint on Firms' Growth in Developing Countries." World Bank Policy Research Working Paper No. 5485, Washington, DC.

Appendix C
Econometric Analyses of IFC and World Bank SME Lending Projects: "Drivers" of Successful Development Outcomes

IFC Investments

RESEARCH QUESTIONS

• Do project characteristics matter in the development outcome?

• Does the product line of the intervention have an impact on the development outcome?

DATA

To address these two questions, IFC project-level data were used. Documents were pooled and projects rated across a number of indicators. In the end, a total of 103 SME targeted projects were rated and subject to analysis.

VARIABLES CONSTRUCTION AND ESTIMATED STRATEGY

To address these issues discussed at the beginning, we mainly consider the variation of projects' development outcome (DO) as a function of two types of variables:

• Country-level condition under which SME projects are implemented, including income level

• Project-level conditions, which involves supervision, risk management, monitoring and supervision of loans, as well as duration, sector, product line and loan size (Kilby 2000).

Accordingly, the following model specification is to be estimated.

Development outcome $= a + bX + kW + hP + iZ + e,$

where X is the country-level variable, W is the control for project characteristics such as sector, length of project, and size of project, P is the product line/intervention type, and Z is a vector of the project-level variables. The e is the random error term, normally distributed.

The DO is captured by an IEG rating scheme, which has value from 1 to 6, with 6 being highly satisfactory. As noted above, the main predictors in the model are the project characteristics and project-specific characteristics.

Aggregate country level variable, X, is captured by the country income level variable, presented as a series of dummies. The product line/intervention, P, is also captured by a series of dummy variables: funds, investment in SME, leasing, on-lending, and others, with others as the omitted group in the model.

There are four main project characteristics, Z, brought into analysis:

• SUP supervision, a constructed variable

• Inadequate technical design, which is presented as binary variable (yes or no)

• Inadequate risk management, which is also presented as a binary variable

• Number of problems observed by IEG in the project.

The means and standard deviation (plus min and max value) of each of these variables are shown in the Table C.1.

Two ordinary least squares regression models are presented. First, the IEG DO variable is regressed on X (country-level income variable), W (basic project information such as length and size of project and industry composition), and P (product line/intervention). In the second model, other project characteristics are included. This two-step estimation strategy with increment of R squared will give some insight as the role of project characteristics on the IEG rating.

Findings

Descriptive statistics (Table C.1) show that among the IFC TSME sample of 103 projects, the majority of them were in the financial management industry, accounting for 89 percent. Projects from manufacturing, agriculture, and services industry and infrastructure industry account for 7 percent and 4 percent, respectively.

The duration of projects averaged 4.5 years.

Most projects were in the lower-middle-income, upper-middle-income, and high-income countries, accounting for 34, 38, and 20 percent, respectively. Only 8 percent of projects were in low-income counties.

By product line, on-lending accounts for 59 percent of projects. The second most popular product line was funds, which accounted for 16 percent.

In terms of project characteristics, the IEG rating scheme suggests that 26 percent of projects were identified as having an inadequate design; 23 percent were identified as having inadequate risk management. (Note: The whole list of problems identified by IEG

TABLE C.1 Means and Standard Deviations of Variables in the Analysis

Variables	Mean	Standard	Minimum	Maximum
(n=103)				
IEG rating	3.70	1.22	1	6
Duration	4.53	0.65	3	7
Loan size (in log)	9.20	1.80	0	12.52
Product line/intervention				
Funds	0.16	0.36	0	1
Investment in SME	0.08	0.27	0	1
Leasing	0.10	0.30	0	1
On-lending	0.59	0.49	0	1
Other	0.07	0.27	0	1
Sector				
FM industry	0.89	0.31	0	1
Infra industry	0.04	0.19	0	1
MAS industry	0.07	0.25	0	1
Country income level				
Low income	0.08	0.27	0	1
Lower middle	0.34	0.48	0	1
Upper middle	0.38	0.49	0	1
High income	0.20	0.40	0	1

continued on page 200

Means and Standard Deviations of Variables in the Analysis

Variables	Mean	Standard	Minimum	Maximum
Project characteristics				
SUP Supervision	2.85	0.56	2	4
Inadequate design (yes)	0.26	0.44	0	1
Inadequate risk mgmnt (yes)	0.23	0.42	0	1
Number of problems flagged	1.88	1.46	0	6

SOURCE: IFC.

NOTE: FM = financial management; MAS = manufacturing, agriculture, and services.

included inadequate risk assessment, inadequate technical design, inadequate supervision, inadequate political or institutional analysis, inadequate baseline data or unrealistic targets, inadequate M&E framework, poor data quality, inadequate partner financing or coordination, implementation disrupted by a crisis, and project restructuring.) The average score for supervision is 2.85, which is close to satisfactory (3 in the rating system). The average rating for DO is 3.7, which is between moderately unsatisfactory and moderately satisfactory.

The main findings of the analysis are presented in Table C.2. In the baseline model three findings emerge:

• Projects in upper-middle-income countries generally have higher DO ratings than projects in high-income countries; however, projects in low-income and lower-middle-income countries are not significantly different from high-income countries, other things equal.

• Length of project from initiation to maturity seems to be positively related to the DO rating.

• Among product lines, investment In SME seems to have significantly positive association with IEG rating at the 10 percent levels; however, this difference becomes insignificant in model 2, which controls for project-relevant characteristics.

Model 2 (column 2) includes project-relevant characteristics. One obvious finding is the significant increase of R-square value from 0.271 (model 1) to 0.468 (model 2). This clearly suggests that relevant project characteristics are important predictors of the IEG rating. This finding is consistent with recent findings that "a striking feature of the data is that the success of individual development projects varies much more within countries than it does between countries" (Denizer, Kaufmann and Kraay 2011).

TABLE C.2 OLS Regression of IEG Outcome Rating: Role of Project's Characteristics

Predictor	Model Specifications		
	1	2	3
Constant	−0.613	0.020	−0.321
Length of project in year	0.499***	0.408**	0.420**
Loan size in dollars (in log)	0.028	0.002	0.072
Product line/Intervention[a]			
Funds	0.142	0.311	0.028
Investment in SME	1.105*	0.133	0.232
Leasing	0.433	0.361	0.618
On-lending	0.799	0.672	0.917*
Sector[b]			
FM industry	1.098*	0.219	0.118
Infra industry	0.175	0.301	−0.132
Country income level[c]			
Low income	0.183	0.432	0.172
Lower middle	0.156	0.162	0.128
Upper middle	0.617**	0.584**	0.653**
Project characteristics			
Supervision	---	0.497***	0.384*
Inadequate technical design (yes)	---	−0.679***	---
Inadequate risk assessment (yes)	---	−1.005***	---

continued on page 202

OLS Regression of IEG Outcome Rating: Role of Project's Characteristics

Predictor	Model Specifications		
	1	2	3
Number of problems flagged out	---	---	−0.318***
R squared	0.271	0.468	0.422
N	94	94	94

SOURCE: IFC projects data.
NOTE: Dependent variable is the IEG rating, which ranges from 1 to 6, with 6 being the highly satisfactory. Supervision ranges from 1 to 4, with 4 as excellent. FM = financial markets; OLS = ordinary least squares; --- = not applicable.
a. The omitted group is other category.
b. The omitted group is MAS industry.
c. The omitted group is high income countries.
***$p < 0.01$; **$p < 0.05$; *$p < 0.10$.

More specifically, model 2 suggests that project supervision quality is positively correlated with IEG's DO rating. One unit increase in the rating of supervision is associated with a half of unit increase in IEG's rating.

In addition, a project that has a problem of inadequate risk assessment is associated with one unit lower IEG DO rating as compared to a project without the problem. A project identified as having an inadequate design is associated with a two-thirds of a point lower IEG DO rating.

Model three (in column 3) is an extension of model 2, where two specific project problem variables are replaced by one variable, the number of problems observed. The results further suggest that one problem observed is associated with one-third unit lower IEG DO rating. Finally, the results indicate that controlling for these additional factors, on-lending is associated with significantly better development outcomes than other product lines.

World Bank Investments

The main questions to be addressed are threefold:

In seeking to understand the project-relevant factors that are associated with successful development outcomes, the team sought to answer three questions:

• How does the type and characteristics of TSME intervention relate to DO ratings?

• How does country income level relate to DO ratings?

- How do measured design, oversight, and evaluative variables relate to DO ratings?

EMPIRICAL IMPLEMENTATION

To address these three issues, the variation of projects' development outcome as a function of country income where the project was implemented and project-specific characteristics. In terms of country conditions, a strong institutional setting could ensure a better and efficient implementation, leading to better development outcomes (Khwaja 2009; Kraay 2010; Rajan and Subramanian 2008). Project-specific characteristics include the type of project (product line), length (in years), and size (in dollars), and variables related to design, implementation (and/or supervision) and monitoring and evaluation (Kilby 2000). In light of three questions raised in the evaluation, the following model specification is to be estimated.

Development outcome $= a + b\mathbf{X} + i\mathbf{Z} + k\mathbf{W} + e,$

where X is the country-level variable, Z is a victor of the project-level variables, and W is the controls for particular loan characteristics. The e is the random error term, normally distributed.

The DO is measured by IEG outcome rating, ranging from 1 (highly unsatisfactory) to 6 (highly satisfactory). Ordinary least squares regression will be used for estimation.[1]

The main predictors in the model are the intervention type, which is captured by a series of dummies, and whether loans are business development services/technical assistance, matching grants, line of credit, or "other."

Another set of predictors is project characteristics, captured by four variables: (i) number of risks for a project's monitoring and evaluation (M&E); (ii) number of risk flags for project management; (iii) number of risk flags for slowness of disbursement; and (iv) whether the project was identified as having an overly complex design.[2] Country income level is represented in four categories: low, lower middle, upper middle, and high. An alternative World Bank classification variable was tried and dropped.

MAIN FINDINGS

Descriptive statistics are presented in Tables C.3–C.5.

Table C.3 contains the analytical findings, with two model specification to answer the three policy questions.

TABLE C.3 Frequency Distribution of Intervention Type

Intervention Type	Number	%
BDS/TA	24	51.06
Line of Credit	12	25.53
Matching grant	7	14.89
Other	4	8.51
Total	47	100

SOURCE: World Bank lending project.
NOTE: BDS = business development service; TA = technical assistance.

TABLE C.4 Mean of Variables

Variable	Mean	Standard
Overly complex design	4.23	0.89
Flag M&E	0.17	0.48
Flag project management	0.26	0.61
Flag slow disbursement	0.60	1.35
Length of project (years)	4.26	3.05
Size of loan ($ millions)	178	214

SOURCE: World Bank lending project.
NOTE: n = 47. M&E = monitoring and evaluation.

Model 1 of Table C.4

- The analysis does not show a significant association between intervention type and IEG outcome rating.

- TSME interventions in lower-middle-income countries are less effective in IEG outcome rating than loans that go to upper-middle-income countries, other things being equal. The loans to SMEs in low-income countries are not significantly different in outcome.[3]

TABLE C.5 Means of IEG Development Outcome Score by Intervention Type

Variable	Number	Mean	Standard
Intervention type			
BDS/TA	24	4.29	0.91
Line of Credit	12	4.17	0.83
Matching grant	7	4.00	1.15
Other	4	4.50	0.58
IDA classification			
IDA/blend	29	4.28	0.92
Non-IDA	18	4.17	0.86
Country income grouping			
High income, non-OECD	2	4.50	0.71
Low income	10	4.40	0.84
Lower middle income	18	4.00	0.69
Upper middle income	17	4.35	1.11
Total	47	4.23	0.89

SOURCE: World Bank lending project.
NOTE: IEG development outcome coding: 1 (highly unsatisfactory "HU") to 6 (highly satisfactory "HS"). BDS = business development service; IDA = International Development Association; OECD = Organisation for Economic Co-operation and Development; TA = technical assistance.

• Project characteristics that have significant association with outcomes are (i) overly complex design, (ii) flags for the way in which the project was managed, and (iii) flags for slow disbursement. The flag for weak M&E had a negative relation to IEG rating, but its coefficient is not significant.

The role of slow disbursement in the project is positive, which is quite surprising. It seems to indicate that taking time in disbursement can be associated with better outcomes. This merits further exploration, as other explanatory variables may be important and omitted.

Model 2

In model 2, an additional two variables are controlled for: length of project in years and log of size of project in millions of dollars to see if the results change. The length of project is constructed by difference in years between the project approved and project completion. The mean of length is a little over four years and the average size of loans is $178 million.

Controlling for these two variables does not change the main findings from model 1, although both length and loan size are negatively associated with the IEG rating.

Notes

[1] The outcome was also coded as a binary variable, grouping the projects with modestly unsatisfactory (no project was rated highly unsatisfactory) and unsatisfactory as 0 (outcome not achieved) and the rest of projects as 1 (outcome achieved). A logit regression specification was used and results were not ideal.

[2] Only major ones have been examined so far, as there is a long list of variables pertaining to the projects' characteristics. Preliminary efforts find that some of them are highly correlated; further efforts will be made to examine them.

[3] The exact reasons for lower rating for projects in lower-middle-income countries are not clear and need to be further explored. In the descriptive statistics (Tables C.1–C.3), it also shown that SME projects in lower-middle-income countries have lower IEG outcome rating, with an average score of 4, whereas projects in the low-income countries earned an average score of 4.4, which is higher than that in lower-middle-income countries. Future efforts will be made to determine the reason by introducing additional macro country-level data.

References

Denizer, Cevdet, Daniel Kaufmann, and Aart Kraay. 2011. "Good Countries or Good Project?" World Bank Policy Research Working Paper Number 5646, Washington, DC.

Khwaja, Asim Ijaz. 2009. "Can Good Projects Succeed in Bad Communities?" *Journal of Public Economics* 93: 899–916.

Kilby, Chrisopher. 2000. "Supervision and Performance: The Case of World Bank Projects." *Journal of Development Economics* 62: 233–59.

Kraay, Aart. 2010. "How Large Is the Government Spending Multiplier? Evidence from World Bank Lending." World Bank Policy Research Department Working Paper No. 5500, Washington, DC.

Rajan, Raghuram, and Arvind Subramanian. 2008. "Aid and Growth: What Does the Cross-Country Evidence Really Show?" *Review of Economics and Statistics* 90 (4): 643–65.

Appendix D
Social Media Outreach

Online stakeholder outreach was a planned component of the evaluation from the onset, given the many important actors in the SME field with various contributions and perspectives. With this in mind, IEG developed an outreach plan for the evaluation, using a blend of social media channels, launched in March 2013. The goals of the outreach plan were to connect with beneficiaries and stakeholders worldwide, to solicit primarily qualitative data (and quantitative data where appropriate) that could be combined with other sources of data. Additionally, the outreach intended to make the evaluative process transparent and participatory, building a natural audience and discussion forum for the completed evaluation.

Methodology

IEG identified a list of questions, paralleling the core evaluative questions, as a basis to solicit public feedback. These questions did not aim to evaluate the World Bank Group work to promote SME development, but rather to identify key constraints to SME development, avenues for progress, positive experiences for further consideration and integration with other research findings, and country-specific knowledge. Some of the questions were posted as open-ended; others were shared as polls. The questions were posted sequentially, allowing one to two weeks' time for users to respond. In total, polls and open-ended questions generated more than 700 responses from stakeholders worldwide.

IEG developed an outreach plan and strategy based on research on stakeholders and existing online channels. The strategy identified questions and information to be shared through online channels, identifying the activities and channels that would work best given the subject matter and time frame.

To implement the outreach plan, IEG utilized Facebook and LinkedIn as primary sources of feedback, particularly tapping existing LinkedIn groups. IEG used Twitter and YouTube as mechanisms to drive traffic to the main channels on LinkedIn and Facebook. IEG also held targeted advertisement campaigns to solicit feedback from individuals with particular interests on Facebook. The advertisements targeted people with interests in international development, small business development, private sector development, and similar interests.

IEG analyzed relevant existing LinkedIn groups that it could tap into to solicit appropriate feedback. The existing groups were chosen by their focus areas, percentages of members identified as SME professionals and experts, number of members, and, in some cases, geographical location to accommodate some of the country case studies the evaluation team looked into. The team tapped into the knowledge of groups that had more than 1,000 members and whose statistics showed that the groups were comprised of more than 50 percent relevant experts—bankers, SME owners, finance specialists, and so forth. The list of most actively used LinkedIn Groups included: Small Business Online Community (~33,000 members[1]); Kenyan Business Network (~4,000 members); Sri Lanka Professionals (~3,300); Nicaragua Business Network (~3,500); SME Professionals (~2,100 members), SME Bankers (~2,200 members), SME Banking (~1,700 members), SME Finance in Emerging Markets (~2,200 members, locked group), and SME Risk Management (~1,400). IEG also set up its own group on LinkedIn to tap into its networks and followers. See Figure D.1 for an example of one of the groups IEG used in its outreach.

To achieve its outreach goals, the team actively utilized IEG's existing Twitter account to cross-post updates and questions. This channel mainly served to direct traffic to IEG's LinkedIn group and Facebook pages when a new question was posted. For greater outreach, IEG used most popular hashtags[2] on Twitter that are relevant to private sector, including #PSDMatters, #private sector, #PSD, #SMEs, and #smallbusiness. IEG also tagged its posts to relevant individuals and organizations using their Twitter IDs/handles, including IFC's @IFC_org.

FIGURE D.1 Example of an Existing LinkedIn Network Used for the Outreach

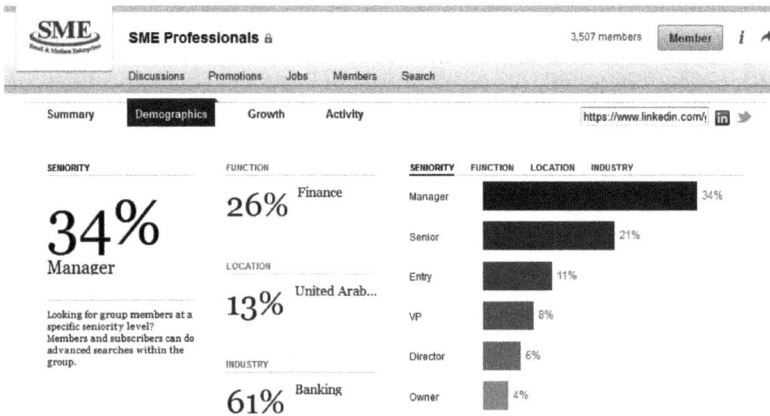

SOURCE: IEG.

Main Messages from the Outreach

Most of the qualitative comments were received from the members of selected LinkedIn groups. As mentioned, IEG only tapped into LinkedIn groups of certain size and thematic focus. Responses to the poll questions mainly came from IEG's existing and new Facebook followers.

DEFINITIONS OF SME

Responses from users both on Facebook and LinkedIn on the question of how SME should be defined were very diverse and a number highlighted that there is no single definition for it. This feedback coincided with the evaluation's research findings on this issue. One of the users on LinkedIn said:

> Within Asia-Pacific Economic Cooperation, there is no region-wide accepted definition of SMEs. Definitions vary across members and are based on several different criteria, including number of employees and maximum levels of capital, assets, or sales, which may again vary according to industry/sector. APEC economies adopt either single or multiple criteria to define SMEs.
> —Economic and Policy Researcher from Singapore.

OBSTACLES TO SME DEVELOPMENT QUESTIONS

Comments and polls on the topic of constraints to SMEs identified that stakeholders worldwide feel that main obstacles include (i) lack of internal capacity, including to keep adequate financial and accounting information; (ii) impact of external constraints beyond SMEs control, such as high tax, crime and theft, political instability, lack of electricity, and so forth; (iii) lack of tailored financial products and services in the financial system to flexibly deal with smaller SMEs; and (iv) a perception of SMEs as risky investments by banks, which further elevates the cost of bank financing. Table D.1 shows the codified percentages of responses for main obstacles mentioned in respondents' comments on LinkedIn. One of the LinkedIn users stated:

> [The] Sector-specific lending program approach is more appropriate to finance small size SMEs: The biggest challenge for SME bankers is to provide financing to small size SMEs having no financial records and collaterals while coping with high risks and costs associated with servicing them. To achieve this, banks should shift from traditional to sector specific program lending approach by providing packages of financing programs tailored to SMEs financing needs. . . .
> —SME Banking Consultant and Trainer, Pakistan, on SME Banking LinkedIn Group

TABLE D.1 LinkedIn Responses on Obstacles to SME Development

Response Categories	Number of Responses	Percent
Limited A2F and constraints to A2F (interest rate, collateral, credit info, and so forth)	11	48
SME management (entry, administration, exit)	8	35
SME environment (infra, corruption, political instability, crime)	7	30
Lack of targeted financial product and services	5	22
Limited access to markets (buyers) and suppliers	5	22
Tax rate	4	17
No. of responses	23	100

SOURCE: IEG.
NOTE: A2F = access to finance.

Broader groups of stakeholders identified nonfinancial obstacles to SME development more often than financial ones (Table D.2). Leading constraints included crime, theft, instability, lack of electric power, corruption, and so forth.

DRIVERS FOR SME DEVELOPMENT

Finally, IEG asked stakeholders about main factors for SME development in their respective countries. The question received more than 200 responses on Facebook (Table D.3) reflecting people's perceptions and opinions. Sixty-five percent of respondents indicated that having broad policies that level the playing field is important for SME development in their countries. Only 30 percent of respondents believe that targeted policies that channel finance, technical assistance, and business support help SMEs.